Gordon Cubie was born and brought up in the west of Glasgow, where he attended Jordanhill College School. He is a lifelong Rangers fan, and made his first visit to Ibrox in 1970.

He has worked in the Scotch whisky industry since 1978, and lives in Bearsden with his wife and two daughters.

His first novel, *Unprovable*, was published in 2014.

By the same author

Fiction:

Unprovable

Scouting For Vengeance

ONLY HERE TO SEE THE RANGERS

Forty-Five Years of Follow-Following

GORDON CUBIE

Copyright © 2015 Gordon Cubie

All rights reserved. No part of this publication may be reproduced, stored in any retrieval system, or transmitted, in any form or by any means, without the prior permission of the writer.

Except where direct quotations are made, all views, opinions and expressions are those of the writer and do not, in any way, reflect the views or opinions of Rangers Football Club or any of its employees.

Short extracts of this book have previously appeared in:

"Manchester Brace Yourself… Rangers Are Coming"   Brent MacFarlane
(Burgess Publishing, 2011)

"It's A Glasgow Rangers Story"   Duncan Whitelaw
(Upfront Publishing)

Whilst every attempt has been made to check the accuracy of all facts, dates, scores and scorers contained within this book, the writer apologises for any unintentional errors herein.

Cover photograph by Norma Cubie.

To My Father

PROLOGUE

Writing this book has been a labour of love. Looking back at various books, match programmes, videos and DVDs has brought back many great memories of championships being won, of cup finals and semi-finals, of big European nights, and seeing some of the most famous names in football strutting their stuff on our own Ibrox pitch.

Obviously, I have gone through my many recollections, looking back with "blue tinted spectacles", and I make no apologies whatsoever for writing in the first person, referring to "us" and "we" when I talk about The Rangers, as I feel that I have been part of the Rangers family for decades.

I am just an ordinary fan, who puts on a scarf and goes to the matches. I don't belong to a supporters' club, I don't go to every single game – home and away – as many fans do, nor do I follow my team to all corners of Europe or even the World. Such is the passion for our Club that I can remember John Greig describing, in a documentary how the team was once flying to New Zealand to embark on a tour of matches. The flight was delayed for several hours for some reason or other, but when the team finally stepped into the airport at the other side of the World, they were met by fans who had stood waiting for hours to greet them. The players realised just how much the Club means to some people – wherever the team goes, fans will follow follow. Distance, time or money is no object for some people when it comes to seeing your team, but I'm afraid that I can't claim to have that level of obsession.

I am amazed by stories from around the globe of fans heading for a bar at some ungodly hour to watch a game being shown live on television. What dedication that must take, but I dare say, if it was me over there, I would be doing exactly the same thing.

There is another humorous way of looking at it. A Rangers fan that I used to know years ago was asked if he could do a few hours overtime one evening as the company where we worked had some function on. He had to refuse as there was a game on that night, and his boss scolded him with "Sometimes you think more about Rangers than you do about your work." The man replied straight away, "Sometimes I think more about Celtic than I do about my work!"

I was once asked, at some work team-building event, what the most important thing in my life was. They didn't mean health or family, they were looking for some tangible item. I had no doubt – it was my Ibrox season ticket. I could hold it in my hand, or put it in my pocket - but it could open up an amazing world for me. The wins, the defeats, the ups and the downs, the cheers or the tears – all were made possible by that season ticket. Nothing else could do that.

There is never a day that goes by that I don't think about The Rangers. What is the latest news? Who have we signed? Who's been injured? What's the score? I used to look at newspapers and I would want to see Rangers getting more coverage than any other team. Now, of course, it's all on the internet, and I can look on a PC or phone anytime. It has been a lifelong obsession, and I can't imagine what my life would be like without it. That, of course, was a definite possibility a couple of years ago. The unthinkable was in real danger of happening, but we stuck together as our enemies were circling, until "reinforcements" arrived, and saved the day.

As we are taking the first tentative steps into our new era, with a new Board and a new Manager, it has been great to look back at happier times. Well, there were more of them happy than unhappy! As Bob Hope used to say, "Thanks for the memories!"

ONE
Dad's Story

A bit of background first before we get on to my story. Why Ibrox? That may sound like a rather daft question – but what was the big attraction?

My father, who I shall now refer to as 'Dad', was born in 1920, in Temple, north of Anniesland Cross, the youngest of four. His father worked at the nearby Barr & Stroud factory, on the site which is now the Morrison's supermarket. In his young days, my dad was very sporty and, like most other boys, he played football in the street as there were hardly any cars about. He also played for his school and his Boys' Brigade Company, the 130th Glasgow in Broomhill.

He played in most positions at football – anything to get a game. He had trials for, and represented, the Glasgow schools team, even saving two penalties in one match, and one imagines that he would have played with, and against, similarly aged boys who would go on to become professional footballers a few years later.

Glasgow had many football teams who attracted big crowds, who contributed players to international squads and who were all fairly easy to get to with the buses and trams of the day. As well as Rangers, there were Queen's Park, Partick Thistle, Third Lanark and Clyde as well as many well-known Junior Clubs. There was Celtic as well but they held little appeal for fans of a Presbyterian upbringing.

He started going to Ibrox in the 1930s, but I do not know why he chose to follow Rangers instead of the nearer, and easier to get to, Firhill. Perhaps he knew one of the players, or perhaps it was because they were so successful. He might even have been encouraged by a friend, or it could even have been due to the perceived link between the Boys' Brigade and Rangers. For whatever reason, he was drawn to Ibrox as a young fan, and he went to games with his brother, Robert, and his friend, Eddie MacDonald.

My dad's Uncle Adam lived in Dennistoun and it was traditional for the family, who by then lived in Knightswood having moved to a larger home after the Prime Minister, Stanley Baldwin, had declared open the new Baldwin Avenue, to travel east on New Year's Day to visit and 'first foot' their relatives. My father and Robert took advantage of this visit to attend the New Year derby match when it was held at Parkhead. Uncle Adam was not at all impressed by this when the boys arrived at his home.

"Football is just a game for ruffians!" he exclaimed.

"Oh really?" replied my father. "We were standing beside a minister!"

Church elder, Uncle Adam, never commented again.

At that time, Rangers attracted huge crowds and it is quite likely that Dad was at the Glasgow derby game at Ibrox in January 1939 when the world club record attendance of 118,567 was set for a league match.

When war broke out, football stopped for a while because it wasn't deemed safe for huge crowds to gather in case there was an air-raid, but it was soon back again (albeit in a limited capacity) to boost the nation's morale. My father attended a big game at Hampden where the spectators were packed in like sardines. They were, he often recalled, so tightly together that folk couldn't even get their hands into their pockets to get a cigarette.

Before the game started, Glasgow's Chief Constable addressed the fans by Tannoy. "In the event of an air raid ..." he began. "Run like hell!!" came a voice from the crowd. The whole place dissolved in howls of laughter and the rest of the Chief Constable's message went completely unheeded.

Dad had decided that his career lay in telephone engineering, and he started work for the Post Office which controlled the telephone network before it became British Telecommunications (BT). He attended evening classes at the Glasgow Technical College and, on his way home one evening in March 1941, he got caught up in the Clydeside blitz and a bomb landed and exploded right in front of his house.

He was soon called up into the Royal Signals and reported to Catterick Camp in North Yorkshire for training. He served in various countries, but after the war was won, he had to help with the efforts to re-connect the phone lines across Europe. For troop morale, games of football were organised, and my dad represented the army team in exhibition matches which often involved professional players who were either in the services or who had offered to take part in these popular games.

Word of his abilities must have spread because, when he was eventually de-mobbed, he was approached by Airdrieonians FC wanting to sign him. His father insisted that he complete his training and get "a proper job" so Airdrie were knocked back. Who knows what might have happened if ... His attention was now drifting from football to golf anyway.

His telephone engineering work took him down to the Post Office's national training centre at Stone in Staffordshire, often for weeks on end, and it wasn't always possible to come home at weekends so the Scots often went to see Stoke City or Wolverhampton Wanderers on the Saturday afternoon. One time, Dad was down there when Scotland were playing England at Hampden. The English Sunday papers were raving about the performance of Stanley Matthews since he was a local lad, but my grandmother posted Dad a copy of the Scottish papers and they gave a much different version. *The only time that Stanley Matthews got past Sammy Cox was on his way into the dressing room at half-time!*

After my parents got married in the late fifties, they often met in town for high tea and then joined hundreds, or even thousands, of fans at George Square from where fleets of shuttle buses would run over to Ibrox for mid-week European games. My mother was from Selkirk and had actually favoured Hibernian since they had a player from Selkirk that she knew. When she moved to Glasgow, she was soon put right!

One of their neighbours across the road worked for The John Lawrence Group (which owned Rangers) and free match tickets were often available at the last minute, so there was then a quick dash by tram or bus down to Partick and a ferry over the Clyde to Govan. They didn't have a car and the Clyde Tunnel didn't exist then.

My Dad was Captain of the 130th Glasgow Boys' Brigade, and I understand that discipline was very strict in his time. On one occasion, there was a big game – possibly a European tie - due to be played on a Wednesday evening that had to be delayed 24 hours because of the foggy weather. The Thursday night was the dress rehearsal for their Annual Inspection and Display – the biggest night of their year. Dad had a ticket for the game but he couldn't go, and he told the Boys that he expected them all to be at the rehearsal on the Thursday. One Boy, who was the leader of the pipe band, didn't turn up for the rehearsal, and it was obvious that he was at Ibrox. Things were very different back then, and on the night of the Inspection, the boy turned up expecting to take part as usual. My Dad told him that he had two choices – either to go and sit in the audience or to go home. The Boy went home and the Inspection started. When the Company and Pipe Band marched in, the Boy's parents were obviously puzzled at his non-appearance.

When they discovered that he'd been sent home, they left the hall in disgust and anger, but when they got the full story out of him, they phoned my Dad to apologise and said that they agreed with his decision. The Boy grew into an adult and became a respected Church of Scotland minister – and, as far as I know, he still goes to Ibrox.

I was born in 1960 and, when I was a wee boy, I used to hear my Dad talking about meeting his friend, Davie Dow, to go to Ibrox or Hampden, and I used to wonder what these places were like. For some reason, I was aware of the name of "Wee" Willie Henderson and, possibly, Jim Baxter but I had no idea what they actually looked like or what they could do. There was very little football coverage on TV in those days. The FA Cup Final was shown live as was the annual Scotland v England Home International. The European Cup Final, the World Cup and European

Championships were also shown but there was not the same 7-day wall-to-wall coverage that we get nowadays.

I must have looked at some of the pictures and match reports in the Sunday papers but other reading material was very scarce. "Shoot!" magazine and others like it gave 99% English coverage with an extremely rare look at anything north of the border. There were a few reasonable football annuals that came out for Christmas, and the Saturday lunchtime papers, like The Citizen, sometimes had a free colour poster which soon made its way onto my bedroom wall. The other way to find out about players was from football cards. These were collected at school and swapped at playtime as everyone wanted to be the first to get the complete set. Why were Drew Busby and Derek Whiteford always impossible to get?

I soon learned the words of "Follow, Follow", and I had a pretty basic idea of what went on at a game. I gradually got to know the names of most of the first team players and I started to nag my Dad to take me to a game. He kept putting me off until a game of golf changed his mind.

TWO
My First Visits to Ibrox

All our childhood holidays – Easter, summer and long weekends – were at our caravan at Carnoustie where Dad played a full round of golf every morning and often "a few holes" in the evening. It was on one such spring evening in 1970 that he arrived on the first tee where two other players were about to tee off, and they invited him to join them. They were George "Corky" Young and Davie White, who was at that time out of football having not yet become the manager of Dundee FC after his brief and unsuccessful stint at Ibrox. I'm not sure if he already lived in that area or was, perhaps, just visiting. Davie gave Dad a copy of the Dundee FC version of the "Wee Blue Book" and we saw from the fixture list that Dundee were due to pay Rangers at Dens Park on the 21st of March. So, it was decided that my brother and I, aged seven and nine, would be taken to Ibrox that afternoon to watch the corresponding Reserve fixture.

Strangely, I can't remember all that much about the game, but I'm sure I must have been impressed with Ibrox. We sat in the old wooden seats of the Main Stand and Rangers Reserves won, which was better than the First Team did that afternoon as they lost 2-1. Our only experience of football having come from the occasional game on television, my brother asked if we could "invade the pitch" at the end.

Our second visit, a month later was far more memorable. Dad was an elder at Broomhill Church, and one home that he visited in his district was that of Dr Alastair Ogilvie (Campbell Ogilvies's father). Alastair was a regular at Ibrox and went to every game with his friend, "Gentleman" George Brown, who had played for Rangers from 1929-42, and who was now a Director of the Club. He was also a member at Broomhill Church. As a G.P., Alastair was the unofficial reserve team doctor, and he invited Dad, my brother and me to go to another Reserve Game, this time against Kilmarnock, but to sit with them in The Directors' Box.

We got to walk in the front door and up the marble staircase. We could see how opulent and ornate the interior was, with the marble, the wood panelling, the Rangers crest on the carpets and the fine china. It was almost like a mansion or a castle. Before the match, we got a tour of the Blue Room and Trophy Room and we were thrilled to bits. We took our seats for the match and were given Rangers official rugs to put over our knees to keep warm. At half time, we went down to the Directors' lounge for tea, sausage rolls and cakes where we met Willie Thornton and Bob

McPhail who spoke to us and told us stories about his playing days. We were mesmerised, of course. Here was a Club legend who took time to speak to a 9 and 7 year old. He joked with us that his lack of hair was caused by all the years of heading the ball into the goal. I have visited the Trophy Room a few times since and, when I look at Mr McPhail's collection of medals on display, I always remember that very special day.

I must admit that I always thought that, after a couple of Reserve games, I'd been taken to my first 'proper' game in autumn 1970, and then to the League Cup semi-final – but on researching all the dates of games, I now realise that my first big games at Ibrox were not until autumn 1971, so I must have seen the team at Hampden before I saw them at Ibrox. I must have always had that wrong in my head. I don't know why there was such a big gap in my 'education' here.

I got taken to Hampden to see the League Cup semi-final against Cowdenbeath. The 14th of October 1970 was the birthday of one of my school-friends and, instead of a party, his dad (incidentally another minister!) took a car load of us to Hampden for the big match. I can remember being completely overawed as we climbed up the stairs and got our first sight of the floodlit turf. We'd never seen anything like it. The pitch looked massive and the lights made it look like something from a different world. We stood in the Rangers end, among the 35,000 who watched Rangers win 2-0 with a penalty by Willie Johnston and a goal from Colin Stein. My first ever live Rangers goal was a penalty and not some brilliant move from open play that I had hoped to see, and it wasn't even scored by someone in a "proper" Rangers shirt, as we were wearing our light blue and white alternative shirts that night

And so, Rangers got to the League Cup final – their first under our new manager, Willie Waddell. I can remember hearing on the radio that we would be without John Greig as he was injured, and I know that I was worried about this. We listened to the commentary on the radio as Derek Johnstone scored the winner and wrote himself into the history books. The 'Topical Times Football Annual' that Christmas had some great pictures from the game and post-match celebrations, and these pages were carefully pulled out and stuck onto my bedroom wall.

Mum and Dad decided to relocate our caravan and, in September 1970, it was permanently located at a site between Cove and Coulport on Loch Long. Only an hour from home, we spent lots of weekends there and, on the way home, we always stopped in Helensburgh for ice-cream cones. One time, sitting in the back of the car, on the pavement side, I casually glanced into a shop while waiting for my mum to return with the cones. I thought I recognised the man arranging stuff in the gift shop window. "That looks like Bobby Brown," I commented. Dad turned round, looked, and said, "It *is* Bobby Brown!" Unknown to me, his wife ran a small gift shop right beside the café where we'd stopped. How odd to see our goal-keeper from the 'Iron Curtain' post-war team, and Scotland's former manager, pottering about arranging gifts in a Helensburgh shop window!

The dreadful start of 1971 is etched deeply in my mind. It was, of course, the most tragic day in our Club's long history and it is a day that will never be forgotten. As a family, we were due to visit our next door neighbours on the evening of 2nd January. It was a very bleak, foggy afternoon, and an eerie winter sky hung over Glasgow. We had been out looking to buy something to take as a visiting present, and we were in the car driving along Maryhill Road listening to the full time radio reports as the news started to filter through about what became the disaster. As everyone knows, this was in the days before instant media coverage, live TV or mobile phones, and the updates were sporadic. We spent the evening at our neighbour's house where we were supposed to be celebrating the New Year but we were all huddled around the radio and television as the news got worse and worse. We didn't know anyone personally, but I could visualise the slope, the old stairways and the barriers which we were later to see as a twisted mangled mess. This was my Club and I just couldn't imagine the sheer scale of the trauma and devastation involved. I'm not ashamed to say that I went to my bed in tears that night.

I can remember seeing the players that I recognised on television as they all attended the hastily arranged memorial service. It was shown live and we saw all the grief stricken faces. Many of our players were just young men but they had to grow up very quickly as they attended all the victims' funerals, often on a daily basis, and visited the injured fans in the city's hospitals. These were grim tasks indeed for anyone to have undertaken but our players did so, and it is to their eternal credit.

From then on, it became the habit to tell supporters in the programme and over the Tannoy, to "Please take your time while leaving the Stadium" at every game.

As I said, I didn't get taken to a first team game at Ibrox until 9th October 1971, two days after my birthday so it might have been as a special treat. Dad took my brother and me to the Main Stand to watch us beat East Fife 3-0, so the first Ibrox goal that I saw was a penalty from Sandy Jardine. I thought that my next game was against Kilmarnock, three weeks later, but I know for certain that I was in hospital at the time so I can't have been at Ibrox. I did have the match programme but my dad might have brought that in for me to look at.

THREE
The Early 1970s

On 23rd October 1971, my brother and I were taken to our first ever cup final – but Rangers weren't even in it. It was the League Cup Final between Partick Thistle and Celtic. Our next door neighbour, Bill Johnston, was a fanatical Thistle fan and he got tickets for us to go with him and his son, Alex. I think that this may just have been a cunning ploy to help fill the seats at the Thistle end because they didn't exactly have the same number of supporters as Celtic did – even on such a special day. Alex's cousin Stuart, had won a schools competition to go to the Celtic dressing room after the game "to see them celebrating with the cup".

As we all know, it was one of the most bizarre matches ever seen, and it seemed that every time Thistle went forward, they scored. We were drenched with beer or champagne from the overjoyed fans sitting behind us – at least I think that's what it was! My dad was at Ibrox that afternoon (we were playing Motherwell) when the half time score was read out. Partick Thistle 4 - Celtic 0. The Rangers fans simply couldn't believe it, but when it was confirmed, it's said that half of them left Ibrox to head for Hampden to take the mickey out of the Celtic fans when they left the stadium!

We met up with Stuart afterwards and he said that he had been taken to the Celtic dressing room as planned – but, instead of celebrations, he heard Jock Stein coming out with tirade after tirade of every swear word imaginable!

Our house was along the road from The Esquire House, Anniesland, which was owned by the Chairman of Partick Thistle and, every Saturday, the players used to meet there to have lunch, watch the beginning of Grandstand on BBC Television, and get ready to go to their match. The Saturday after their League Cup win, we all went along to congratulate them on giving Celtic a 'doing'.

My visits to Ibrox were rather limited for the next year or so after that but I remember the first time I got to see Rangers live on TV - the European Cup Winners Cup semi-final against Bayern Munich. The crowd was given as 80,000 but it was said that there were probably another 20,000 squeezed in for one of the most famous night's in the old stadium's history. I didn't actually appreciate the enormity of there being two major European matches in Glasgow that night as there was another game in the East End as well. The fates were smiling on us that night as goals from Sandy Jardine and Derek Parlane meant that we won 2-0 against a formidable Bayern side and reached the final whereas Celtic lost on penalties. *Dixie Deans, Superstar. How many miles was it over the bar?*

I also remember sitting in our front room listening to the radio for the final since the game was not being shown live on television as Scotland had a game on that night. How crazy was it for another game to be on the same night as a European final? We cheered loudly as Colin Stein and Willie Johnston put us 3-0 ahead but we bit our nails as Moscow Dynamo clawed their way back into the game with two late goals. The next day, our Gym Teacher, who was a strict rugby man, had nothing good to say about the behaviour of "the Rangers hooligans" after the game. I didn't even know then what he was talking about. Someone in my class wore his Rangers scarf to school under his jersey, but was soon told to remove it. I bought a special souvenir Daily Record book that came out shortly afterwards to commemorate the event with lots of pictures from the semi and the final.

To my eternal shame, I must admit that I declined the suggestion that we go over to Ibrox on the Thursday night to welcome the team back with the cup. I had already arranged for someone from school to come for his dinner that night and we were going to the Odeon cinema at the end of the road to see my first ever James Bond film, 'Diamonds Are Forever'. I have obviously seen the film dozens of times since then and can't believe that I turned down the chance of a once in a lifetime happening at Ibrox. What on earth was I thinking of?

After that summer, I moved up to secondary school. There was now a group of four of us from our road who started going to every home game at Ibrox, taken by one of the dads. We met up with some others from school at our usual standing place in the Copland Road end. It cost us 50p to get in the Boys' Gate, and 5p for a match programme – a small issue, printed in light blue and white, with a few bits of red (the Club crest on the front). The front cover was usually a picture of a goal from the previous game, and there was a "lucky number" on the corner which gave you a chance to win £50 in the prize draw. A man with a long white coat used to walk round the track at half time carrying a blackboard placard with the winning number chalked on it so everyone could see it. Inside there was the "face in the crowd" picture where you won a prize if your photo was shown, and there was a full Scottish fixture list for that day. Each match had a number and these then corresponded with numbers that were displayed trackside along the front of each end of the ground, like a long cricket score-board. A man used to come out, again at half time, and put the match scores beside these numbers so the only way you knew which score was which was to buy the programme.

A pie cost 10p and there was man who wandered up and down the terracing selling chewing gum and macaroon bars from a tray like the old-style cinema usherettes. I can't remember how much these cost but I would guess they were only a few pence each. Were we spoiled or what? These were the early 70's days of Glam Rock, long hair and huge sideburns. The fashionable Rangers fan of the time would be wearing baggy, or flared, denims to the games, along with "bovver" boots, a scarf round his neck (tied like a necktie with the front hanging down the middle) and another tied round his wrist. Some fans wore knitted "tammie" hats or, even, a crash helmet – painted red, white and blue – very useful protection from flying cans and bottles! After Barcelona, a badge of honour was a sombrero hat, and many hats or scarves were covered with badges – metal or sewn on, and the obligatory 'carry-out' was taken in. And some people have the nerve to say that the 70's was the decade that fashion forgot!

We parked outside a factory or works somewhere in Govan and walked towards Ibrox, approaching from the eastern end. As we got nearer the Stadium, the throng grew larger. Thousands of fans all heading in one direction, all similarly dressed, some singing, some shouting, all eager to get in to stand at their favourite place to roar on their team. The crowd at that time would have been nearly all male, and the 1% of women who went to games would be sitting in the main stand – never in the standing crowd. Most folk smoked and, as the game progressed, there was a thick cloud of smoke hanging above everyone's heads.

The singing was loud, and there were no restrictions on what was sung. Some of the songs were to the tunes of current chart hits such as 'Hey Jude', 'Wandrin' Star', 'Those Were The Days' and 'Amazing Grace' as well as the more traditional favourites. At that age, I have to admit, that I didn't really know why were all singing about a sash or Derry's walls, and I did struggle to pick up some of the words – but I joined in as well as I could. Some of the songs poked fun at some of the opposition players. Aberdeen's and then Hibernian's diminutive, rotund striker, Joe Harper was usually compared to a barrel, while Celtic striker, Paul Wilson's darkened skin caused him to be likened to someone of Asian origin. There was no political correctness in those days.

Sometimes, there would be an outburst of "colourful language" directed at some incident, an opponent or the referee, and the dad who was with us that day would have to ask the culprit to mind his language "in front of the boys". That always seemed to do the trick.

Some weeks, I couldn't actually see the pitch that well because of all the men standing in front of me. At one game against Airdrie, I made that comment at half time only to be told that the game was so poor that I hadn't really missed anything – but I did manage to see our two second half goals.

At the end of the game, when the crowd had dispersed, the area down at the front of the terracing was covered in empty bottles and cans; enough to fill several re-cycling skips these days. There was the clink, clink of empty bottles that were helped on their way – a nudge from a foot - to roll them down the steps to the front. Did the ball boys really rummage through them to look for any empties that they could take to the shop to get money back?

When we got outside, there were already copies of the Evening Times and Evening Citizen being sold to exiting fans. Hot off the presses, and rushed out to the games, they even had the half time scores and details printed in them. Some fans headed for the bus, the subway or the pub but we made for the car to turn the radio on to hear all the other results and reports, and we all tried to guess the scores from the intonation of the voice of the man who was reading out the classified results.

I can't really remember a huge presence of away fans at Ibrox. Apart from Celtic games (which I wasn't allowed to go to), they didn't exactly pack out the west terracing for normal league games. Hibernian seemed to be the only team that brought fans who actually made some noise.

For my 12th birthday, I got a portable cassette recorder and, when visiting my relatives down in Selkirk, I discovered that my cousin had two LPs of Rangers tunes and songs (some were even by the players) so I taped them both. I realise that this illegal taping would have deprived the club of a small amount of royalty revenue but I couldn't afford to buy them for myself and, besides, everybody did it. Needless to say the tape was played again and again. At last I could clearly make out the words to these songs and I found out just what I should have been singing.

My cousin played the mouth organ and taught himself to play these tunes, and when it got to Hallowe'en, he set off round the neighbours' houses guising with his 'party piece'. The story was that he had gone into a house and cheerfully belted out "The Sash My Father Wore" just as he had learned it but not knowing that he was in the house of an ardent Celtic fan! Fortunately, he saw the funny side of it.

Season 1972-73 would have a dramatic finish but the results in the first half of the season gave no indication of what was to happen after Christmas. We beat most teams but lost to Celtic, Hearts and Ayr United, as well as drawing with Morton and Dundee.

We were to play Hibernian in the League Cup semi-final at Hampden on 22nd November, and Dad said he would take my brother and me. The Saturday before, we had beaten them 2-1 at Easter Road so we were pretty confident. We got ready and I came down the stairs to see someone standing right outside our glass front door peering in. My surprise lasted less than a second as I recognised Dad's golf pal, Davie Dow, who it transpired was coming to the game as well. We all went over to Hampden and first had to queue up at a wee window to buy our tickets. We sat in the main stand and watched Hibs score the only goal of the game to knock us out. In the last few minutes, Willie Mathieson (who I can't ever remember scoring!) cracked a 30 yard shot off the Hibs crossbar but that was as close as we got.

Just before Christmas, I got the chance to go and see a magician appearing at a Sunday School Party but I declined because we were at home to Aberdeen that day. At a cold Ibrox, the game was really poor and finished 0-0 - but I was told that the magician was really great. A wrong decision there?

Partly since we had no European football that season due to the UEFA ban after the Spanish police had over-reacted in Barcelona, and partly due to it being our centenary season, a special challenge match, over two legs, was arranged with the current European champions, Ajax Amsterdam, "to decide who was the best club in Europe". UEFA didn't endorse the match but it went ahead and was regarded as the first ever European Super Cup. The first leg took place at Ibrox on 16th January 1973 in front of 58,000 fans. We had tickets for the new Centenary Stand, created when benches were installed in the north enclosure.

The match programme for that game was a much bigger edition with far more pages. There were lots of player pictures and profiles, as well as articles about the history of each club.

Their team was genuinely full of skilful superstars, including Johan Cruyff, Ruud Krol, Johnny Rep, Arie Haan and Arnold Muhren. The Rangers team was: McCloy, Jardine, Mathieson, Greig, Johnstone, Smith, Conn, Forsyth, Parlane, MacDonald and Young – with two substitutes, McLean and Fyfe. Alex MacDonald scored, but Ajax won 3-1. Ajax also won the second leg a week later, 3-2, despite goals from Alex MacDonald and Quinton Young. There was no embarrassment whatsoever in losing to such magnificent opposition, and the Dutch players spoke very favourably afterwards about "this brave, young Scottish team".

Our family were up at Carnoustie for the Easter holiday (at a house belonging to someone Dad knew) and we saw that Dundee were due to play Hibernian on the Wednesday night in a cup match, so Dad, my brother and I decided to go down to Dens Park to watch the game. Both were fairly good teams at the time and we thought we'd see a decent game. We arrived in good time but the queues were massive and we were still waiting to get in when the game had started and the first goal had been scored. We admitted defeat and went back up the road. Coincidentally, the two teams were due to meet again in the league on the following Saturday, so we all went down to Dundee again – only to be told by a policeman when we got there that the game had been postponed due to a waterlogged pitch!

That season, 1972-73, was exciting and dramatic as, after drawing that game with Aberdeen, we embarked on a long run of victories, including beating Celtic in the New Year game, and were neck and neck with them. One unusual game was in April when we were at home to Dundee United. It was 0-0 until about the hour mark when John Greig scored. Then United went up the park and equalised. Within a minute, Greig scored again, and it finished 2-1 with all three goals scored within a couple of minutes. On the second last week of the season, we were away at Aberdeen, and we all gathered at one of the boys' houses to listen to the game on the radio. Alfie Conn scored a late equaliser as the game finished 2-2. We were now a point behind Celtic with just one game to go. The following Saturday, we would be at home to East Fife.

We all went over to our usual barrier and stood and watched Rangers defeat East Fife 2-0 but the news came through that Celtic had won their away game, and so won the league by a single point. So near and yet so far, as they say. Early that evening, I was at Anniesland Cross buying chips when a coachload of their supporters stopped at the traffic lights. They were 'full of it', singing and shouting. They couldn't tell what I was muttering under my breath!

The following week, we got our revenge - and how. It was the Centenary Scottish Cup Final and my two favourite players both scored goals. The match has now passed into legendary status among Rangers fans as the only time a member of The Royal Family attended a Scottish Final. Princess Alexandra arrived, dressed in blue and white outfit. A good omen, surely? A massive crowd of over 123,000 watched Celtic take the lead, but Derek Parlane – our hero against Bayern Munich the previous year, and celebrating his 20th birthday – scored a header from an Alex MacDonald cross before half time.

The second half began with Alfie Conn out-stripping the Celtic defence and putting us ahead. Then John Greig dived to make 'the save of the season' to stop a Dixie Deans goal. Nowadays, he would be shown a straight red card for such an action. They scored to level it at 2-2. With not long to go, we won a free kick. Tommy McLean, who could deliver a ball onto a sixpence, crossed it and Derek Johnstone, once again, out-jumped the Celtic defence to head the ball goalward. It hit one goalpost and then rolled tantalisingly along the line to hit the other post. Hampden held its collective breath until Tom Forsyth playing in his first cup final stuck out his right boot to nudge the ball over the line. The Rangers end erupted! Big Tam burst with joy and the other players could hardly catch him to celebrate. You could see how much the goal meant to John Greig as he gave Tam a huge 'bear-hug'.

The game finished and Rangers won the cup – their first trophy under manager Jock Wallace. John Greig climbed the stairs to the Royal Box, wiped his hands, bowed to the Princess in a dignified fashion, and accepted the cup. Cue exuberant celebrations in the Rangers end. As the late STV commentator, Arthur Montford, would say, "What a match!"

We were allowed to stay up to watch the highlights on Sportscene that night and, on the Sunday, I bought three newspapers and cut out all the match reports and pictures to stick them into a scrap-book.

Rangers' centenary that year produced some great colour posters in some of the Evening Citizen newspapers as well as the book "Growing With Glory" by Ian Peebles. I got my copy (which cost just 90p!) and read enthusiastically all about the founding of the Club, the legendary players from the past, as well as some of the most famous matches in our illustrious history. The team that won every league match in 1899, the 1928 Scottish Cup Final, the friendly against Moscow Dynamo, the first 'Treble', the superb team of the early sixties, the 1966 Scottish Cup replay – they were all there. I must admit that I didn't know how Rangers were founded. I had never heard of Moses McNeil, Flesher's Haugh or William Wilton, nor did I know that we used to wear something akin to a blue rugby shirt, and I think I just presumed that Rangers had always played at Ibrox and must have been run by a board of rich directors. Prior to the book, there wasn't really anywhere to find out that kind of important information, and it definitely opened up a whole amazing world to me. I even found out that we used to play in Glasgow's west end, at Burnbank Gardens, before moving to Ibrox. That was an area I was familiar with as friends of my parents lived there and we usually visited them on Hogmanay. I couldn't really imagine where a football stadium could have been in that residential area.

Expectation was high when season 1973-74 started but it was short-lived. Only one goal in our opening four league games, and none in our first three home games meant that we were always chasing the title which we eventually lost to Celtic, finishing 5 points behind.

Celtic beat us in the League Cup semi-final, 3-1, and Dundee knocked us out of the Scottish Cup with a 3-0 win at Ibrox, after we had thumped Queen's Park 8-0 in the third round. After our one year ban, we were back into Europe but we were knocked out in the second round by Borussia Moenchengladbach. I remember we had to ask the German teacher at school what the correct pronunciation of "Borussia" was. Was it "Russia" or "Rooshia"?

The start of 1974 was a time of shortages, strikes, power cuts and the three day week when the Government restricted businesses to be open for just three days each week to conserve electricity. Every night, television closed down at 10:30pm. To prevent the floodlights going off during a match, Rangers obtained a large generator so that power could always be maintained. Despite that, I can't actually remember it ever having to be used.

One of the few highlights of that season was a home league game against Clyde in March. Our first goal that day, by Derek Johnstone, was the 6,000th we'd ever scored in the league and our second goal was the 10,000th we'd ever scored in all competitions. Appropriately, our legendary captain, John Greig was the scorer. The final score was 4-0.

It was a season when we struggled to beat the likes of Ayr United, Partick Thistle, Morton and Falkirk. We lost at home to East Fife, Arbroath and Dundee, and yet there were good wins against St Johnstone, Dundee United and Hibernian. Crowds were down and the unthinkable was looming. Celtic won their ninth title in a row. Pressure was mounting on manager Jock Wallace as fans were becoming desperate for league success. Something had to be done about this!

I had a personal highlight during the summer. I had to spend five days in the new Gartnavel General Hospital and was thoroughly miserable. One of the nurses said she was from Rhu, and I perked up. "That's where Derek Parlane comes from!" I said. Imagine my surprise when she said that she knew him. She had a word and I was sent a copy of a team sheet signed "Best Wishes to Gordon from Derek Parlane". How fantastic was that?

For my 14th birthday, which was on a Saturday, I got a Rangers blue Adidas tracksuit which was bought from a sports shop on Dumbarton Road, somewhere near Partick station, and I can recall wearing it to Ibrox that afternoon. In those days, there was nowhere near the amount of team merchandise that is available today. I got a blue round-necked football top but my mum had to sew on a badge to make it look 'real'. The same team shirt was used for years but there really wasn't anywhere for fans to buy replica kits for themselves. A boy at school appeared at "Games" with a genuine looking top with the RFC embroidered on to it. I was so jealous. Perhaps these tops were available somewhere. Perhaps my parents just got me a top on the cheap. I guess I'll never know.

When I went to games with my dad, we went through the Clyde Tunnel and past the old David Elder Infirmary. Then, we turned into Shieldhall Road, and it always caused great excitement as we got nearer and could see the top of the stadium with the Union Flag flying to signify that there was a game on. As we walked towards the ground, we could see if there was a television outside broadcast unit parked behind the west terracing. That would mean that our game was going to be shown that weekend, and we could see if it would be on BBC Scotland or Scottish Television on 'Sportscene' or 'Scotsport'. In those days, only one game's highlights were shown on each programme – if the game was 0-0 or abandoned, there was nothing else except, perhaps, some English highlights. It wasn't until the late 80s that all Premier League matches were covered, and 'Match of the Day' was not shown north of the border back then.

Barcelona were kind enough to invite us back to the Nou Camp in August 1974 for a four club invitation tournament, IX Trofeo Juan Gamper. On Saturday 20th, we beat Athletico Bilbao 1-0, but we lost 4-1 on the Sunday to Barcelona.

The Texaco Cup was a competition for clubs from Scotland, England, Northern Ireland and the Republic of Ireland who had not qualified for any European competitions. The Irish and Northern Irish teams withdrew after 1972 due to political pressure and then held their own event. The competition was sponsored by the American petrol company Texaco, and Rangers took part in 1974-75 along with Hearts, Aberdeen and Ayr United, as well as English teams including Birmingham City, Manchester City, Newcastle United, Norwich City, Sheffield United, Southampton, Sunderland, West Bromwich Albion and West Ham United. It looked like a good idea, and a chance for us to pit our wits against some good teams that we usually did well against in various pre-season friendlies and testimonials – but we did terribly and were knocked out by Southampton. We lost the home leg 3-1 and the away leg 2-0 so that was the end of that.

Season 1974-75 would be the last season of the old Scottish Divisions 1 and 2. The next season would see the introduction of the all-new Premier League featuring only the top ten teams from Division 1, who would then play each other four times – twice at home and twice away. Rangers had won the first ever Scottish Division 1 – could they win the last?

FOUR
The Championship and Trebles

The opening league fixture would be away at Ayr United. The day before our Barcelona triumph, my dad's brother and sister moved from Glasgow to a new house in Alloway, outside Ayr. This would be where they chose to live when they retired. For the last few of their working years, they still commuted up to Glasgow every day. I invited myself to travel down with them on the Friday, to stay overnight and then to go to Somerset Park on the Saturday.

My uncle, who probably hadn't been to a game since he was in his twenties, took me to the game with the intention of sitting in the stand. When we got to the ground, the stand was already full so we went to the enclosure instead. It was jam packed and, by the time the game kicked off, we were about 7-8 feet apart. It took a Sandy Jardine penalty kick to earn us a point. Not a very auspicious start.

That same weekend, my dad was down at Lytham St Annes. He had qualified for the Post Office British Seniors' Golf Finals which were to be held there. At that time, the Post Office had a huge recreation organisation and there were city, regional and national finals for golf, football, bowls etc. Dad had already amassed a fair few golf trophies over the years at Glasgow and Scottish level but this was his first time at the British Championships for the over 50's. He teed off in the morning and thought that his score wasn't that great but, as the day progressed, the wind got stronger and the weather got worse. The other players' scores all suffered and Dad won it. He got a huge trophy to keep for a year, a miniature replica and was given a large box which he presumed was to carry the trophy. When he opened it, he discovered that he'd also been given a full coffee set as well.

After that opening league game, we went on a run – winning ten of the next eleven games. In fact, we only lost three league games that season. We beat Celtic home and away and, by the spring, things were looking good to say the least. Hibernian were our nearest challengers and when it came time to visit Easter Road on Saturday 29th March, a draw would see us as champions with four games still to play.

Legendary Barcelona goal-scorer Colin Stein, who had been sold to Coventry City, was brought back to add the necessary impetus to our title run-in, and he set about the Hibs defence. Easter Road was absolutely packed (38,585) with Rangers fans who had waited eleven long years for a championship win. Fans climbed onto the floodlights to try and get a better view. The whole ground seemed to be a sea of red, white and blue.

I wasn't there though. We were down at Selkirk and I was watching a Border Cup tie between Hawick Royal Albert and Gala Fairydean. Yes, really! Well, I say watching – everyone was glued to the radio commentary from Easter Road.

John Greig was injured and Captain for the day, Sandy Jardine, even missed a penalty. Hibs took the lead, but the wonderful midfielder Bobby McKean sent a perfect cross into the box. Colin Stein rose and bulleted an unstoppable header into the goal. Easter Road erupted! Rangers held on for the draw they needed and it was wonderful when Sandy Jardine allowed himself to be substituted with five minutes to go, to allow John Greig onto the pitch to savour the moment. That was a fantastic gesture from Jardine, and from 'hard-as-nails' manager Jock Wallace. He showed that day that he had a big heart, indeed.

The last game of the season would be at home to Airdrieonians and it was announced that there would be a title party and the league trophy would be presented. Ibrox was going to be the place to be that afternoon. For reasons I can't remember (possibly a 'vital' golf game), there was no adult to take me. Aged thirteen, I wasn't allowed to go over on my own and I was completely devastated at the thought of missing the celebration. Then, Mr McIver, who taught at the same school as my mum said he was taking his son and nephew and I was invited to go with them.

He picked me up just after lunch and drove me to his home near St George's Cross. We ditched the car, and then travelled by a packed underground over to Ibrox. 65,000 (a crowd only matched by the Celtic game) were there and we headed for the enclosure. On the way in, as well as match programmes, we were given blue song-sheets, and before the match there was raucous community singing led from the centre circle by some blue-nosed entertainer. Instead of running on from the tunnel, John Greig entered Ibrox on a horse-drawn carriage like some ancient gladiator entering the Circus Maximus. He did a lap of honour as the crowd roared and sang. To be honest, he looked rather embarrassed but nobody cared. Airdrie spoiled the party by having the cheek to win 1-0, but it really didn't matter.

Packed like sardines on the subway back, Mr McIver told me to enjoy the day as "it might be years until you see them winning another". How wrong he was!

Season 1975-76 meant the start of the new Premier League and the first game to launch this new venture saw Rangers at home to Celtic. A crowd of 69,594 saw goals from Derek Johnstone and Quinton Young as we started our league defence with a 2-1 win. There seemed to be an 'unwritten rule' in those days that Rangers always started the league with a draw, and were notoriously slow starters – but not that year. The next week, we beat Hearts at Tynecastle and then beat St Johnstone at Ibrox.

Rangers only lost five domestic games that season – the last of which was against Aberdeen at the beginning of December. They then went on a 26 game unbeaten run and clinched the league at Tannadice. Derek Johnstone scored after just 22 seconds and the title was won by six points.

I didn't see so many games that season as, most Saturday afternoons, I was selected to play for the Boy's Brigade. On Saturday 25th October, we were playing in a Battalion Cup match at Bellahouston Park. I don't remember the score but I remember one of our officers arriving on foot from Hampden. It was the day of the League Cup Final which had a one o'clock kick off to try to prevent crowd trouble. He told us that a diving header from Alex MacDonald had won the cup for Rangers.

On the 5th of February, 1976, I was playing basketball at school (a 'non-contact sport') when I went down awkwardly in a tangle. It turned out I'd broken my leg so I was taken by ambulance to the Western Infirmary. I was in hospital until April. The 'new' Western opened a week later and my parents asked the staff if I could get a room on my own so that I could study in peace for my 'O Grades'. That was agreed and, on moving day, I was supposed to be taken in the lift to an underground corridor and then to the ward in the new building. That plan back-fired as the struts on my bed holding my leg in traction meant that it couldn't fit in the lift. Instead, I was wheeled outside and across the car park to my new "residence".

On Saturday afternoons, I had to listen to the games' commentaries on the radio. Dr and Mrs Ogilvie (Campbell's parents) heard of my plight and gave my dad a spare portable television to bring into the hospital. That was great. One of the games I remember seeing was our Scottish Cup semi-final against Motherwell at Hampden. We were 2-0 down and looked out of it until a fight back with two goals from Derek Johnstone and an Alex Miller penalty saw us through to the final. A team that didn't give up!

On the day I finally got out of hospital, the family all went along to Esquire House for a celebratory dinner. My dad and brother went ahead to get a table as I slowly hobbled along on crutches with my mum. As we were entering the restaurant front door, out came Bertie Auld who was, at that time, the manager of Partick Thistle. Seeing my crutches, he held open the door and joked, "Alright there son? I could give you a game for Thistle on Saturday!" Rising to the challenge, I quickly replied, "I'd still be better than most of them!"

Still on crutches and, despite my begging, I wasn't allowed to go to the cup final. 1976 was the last year that the Scottish Cup Final wasn't shown live on television. With the league and league cup already won, there was a chance of a 'Treble'. We had already beaten Hearts three times in the league and the Cup Final was surely a formality. The referee started the game a minute early and, by three o'clock, we were already a goal up. Tommy McLean floated a cross and Derek Johnstone headed us into the lead. He scored again and one from Alex MacDonald saw us win 3-1. The 'Treble' was complete. We were domestically invincible!

A few years later, during a visit to London, my brother and I were browsing around a record shop in Baker Street when I found an album with Jock Wallace on the front cover. What was this? An LP (remember them?) of BBC Scotland's radio commentary of the Cup Final by the legendary David Francey. Needless to say, it was purchased immediately.

We thought we were invincible with all the domestic trophies in our cabinet, and when Season 1976-77 began, we expected more of the same. Quite a few new, younger players began to make appearances in the first team. Alongside our established, Treble-winning stars, we began to see Ally Dawson, Martin Henderson, Ian McDougall, Chris Robinson and Alex O'Hara on the team-sheets.

To say that things didn't go according to plan would be an understatement. We were knocked out of the European Cup 2-1 on aggregate by the 'giants' of FC Zurich, after only managing a 1-1 draw in the first leg at Ibrox, with a Derek Parlane goal. In the Premier League, we only managed to win 18 out of 36 games. There were 10 draws and 8 defeats. Hardly an auspicious defence of our title.

In the League Cup, we progressed from our qualifying section, conceding only 1 goal, away to Hibernian. The quarter finals saw us drawn against Clydebank. What a tussle that tuned out to be. In the first leg at Ibrox, we drew 3-3 with goals from Derek Johnstone, Alex MacDonald and Johnny Hamilton, and in the second leg at Kilbowie Park, we drew again, 1-1 thanks to a goal from John Greig. Still with no penalty kick deciders, we had to replay at Ibrox, and that finished 0-0 so a second replay was required. This would be at the neutral venue of Firhill. We stood in the north enclosure and finally saw us win 2-1.

What had made Clydebank so difficult to beat? That's an easy answer. They were inspired by a young number 11 called Davie Cooper. He'd been an ever-present for them and their top scorer in 1975-76 with 22 goals, as Clydebank were promoted to the Premier League. As the cup tie progressed, we all realised that he was a special player, and it was known that we was a huge Rangers fan, so it was no surprise when he put pen to paper. He was sold to Rangers for £100,000 in June 1977.

In a very disappointing semi-final, we lost 5-1 to Aberdeen, who were starting to assemble a side that would prove very difficult to beat over the next few years.

In the Scottish Cup, we knocked out Falkirk, Elgin City and Motherwell – all at Ibrox and with the loss of only one goal. We beat Hearts 2-0 in the semi-final to set up a final against Celtic.

This was to be the first ever Scottish Cup Final to be shown live on television. It was shown on both BBC Scotland and STV, and they both went over-board in trying to make it a big all-day event like the English FA Cup Final. BBC Scotland "entertained" us with Cup Final *Top of the Pops* where players could select their favourite pop videos which would then be shown. John Greig didn't let us down when he selected a current hit by ABBA.

The presenter then asked him, "Why have you chosen that one John?"

Back came the reply, "Because 'We ABBA People!'" Well done John!

The match itself was a farce. In the first half, the ball clearly hit Derek Johnstone, who was standing on the goal-line, on the thigh, as he lifted his arms out of the way. The referee awarded a penalty despite all the protests. Who says all these decisions go against Celtic? They scored, the only goal of the match, and that was that. A poor end to a very depressing season. Derek Johnstone still protests his innocence to this day.

During the following close season, Jock Wallace spent quite a bit of money in the transfer market. As well as Davie Cooper, he acquired Gordon Smith from Kilmarnock for £65,000 and Bobby Russell from Shettleston Juniors for free.

Despite these signings, the team made a poor start to the league campaign. The opening two matches were lost to Aberdeen and Hibernian. The Sunday Mail newspaper ran a big article entitled "What's Wrong with Rangers?" and that seemed to act as a catalyst. The players found their form the following week and beat Partick Thistle 4-0 at Firhill.

Celtic visited Ibrox the following Saturday and were 2-0 up at half-time. If Jock Wallace could have bottled whatever it was he said the the players during the interval, he could have made a fortune. Rangers recovered, Celtic were out-classed and two goals from Gordon Smith and one from Derek Johnstone saw us win 3-2. Knowing Big Jock's reputation as a hard task master, we could imagine him reading the riot act to the players, and yelling at them until the paint was peeling off the dressing-room walls, but subsequent stories from the players explained that he merely indicated that Celtic were there for the beating. No yelling. No grabbing slackers by the throat. No threats required.

We didn't lose another league game until a 4-0 defeat at Pittodrie on Christmas Eve, and then we went on another unbeaten run, including a 3-1 defeat of Celtic in the traditional New Year's game at Ibrox, until Aberdeen came to Ibrox in March and won 3-0. That same month, we lost 2-0 at Parkhead and then drew three of the next four games, against Hibernian, St Mirren and Ayr United, but we held on to win the title.

That winter, my school held a "Football Brains Trust" evening to raise money to buy strips for the Primary School team. There would be a "panel of experts" and questions would be invited from the hall, or could be submitted in advance. The school hall was packed. The chairman was Roy Small, a pundit from Radio Scotland who usually commented on Scotland games, and he had a connection with the school. The 'experts' were Jock Stein and Glasgow Herald and Scotsport reporter, Ian Archer, but I can't remember who else was there. I think there was a player from somewhere, and possibly another journalist. The opening question to the panel was "Do you think that Scotland can qualify for the World Cup?" The panel all gave their views on this and such matters as "Should part-time teams be allowed in the Premier League?" and so on. Whatever you might think of the panellists, they did give up their own free time to be there and they did seem to know what they were talking about. There were good questions and some lively debate and everyone had a good evening.

Back at Rangers, there had been another dismal showing in Europe, in the Cup Winner's Cup. We scraped past Young Boys of Berne in the first round by the odd goal in five but got knocked out by FC Twente from Holland. Wallace's European record certainly left a lot to desired.

The League Cup was a bit more straight-forward. St Johnstone, Aberdeen and Dunfermline Athletic were all defeated, and that included a 6-1 demolition of Aberdeen at Ibrox. We were then drawn to meet Forfar Athletic at Hampden in the semi-final. That should be a mere formality, shouldn't it?

The match should have taken place on Monday 28th November 1977 but was postponed until the end of February. Unbelievably, Forfar took the lead with a "sensational" (Arthur Montford) goal after Tommy McLean lost the ball when we were on the attack. Their player ran half the length of the pitch as our defenders chased after him. He looked as if he had gone too far, when he slotted the ball under Stewart Kennedy. We got a goal back but Forfar scored again, and they were winning with a few minutes left on the clock. Fortunately we equalised to send the match into extra time, where we ended up winning 5-2 to get us through to the final. And in that Final, it would be Celtic.

Years later, I got to know one of the Forfar players from that night, Gordon Cowie, through work. He said the players' heads were 'buzzing' in that last few minutes, beginning to think that they might actually win – but in extra time, their legs all just gave out. They had no strength left to summon up.

In the final, our two 'new boys', Davie Cooper and Gordon Smith scored and we won 2-1 after extra time, so two parts of the Treble were in the Ibrox Trophy Room.

In the Scottish Cup, we knocked out Berwick Rangers, Stirling Albion, Kilmarnock and Dundee United to set up a final against Aberdeen.

The spring of 1978 had seen a new development in our football attending. One of Dad's Post Office golfing pals was a member of the Queen's Park club, and invited him to become a steward in the North Stand at Hampden. This was long before the days of Rock Steady or G4S and all that was required was for Dad to be at Hampden before the gates opened. He put on a bright luminous vest, checked fans' tickets when they came in, and showed them to their seats. There was a five man team at each stairway and they had to do the stair at the very end, against the wall nearest the Rangers end. Two of them were based down at turnstile level to direct fans to the correct stairway, and the others were at the top of the stair to guide them to the correct seat. Once the game started and the fans stopped arriving, they could remove the vest, find a spare seat and watch the rest of the game. They got paid £10 for their trouble. So that meant that he was required at all cup finals, semi-finals and international matches. In other words, it was free to see all the big games and he even got paid for going. If it was a game that he wasn't particularly interested in, he could just leave once his work was done.

Before the end of the season, there was to be a massive game – the last 65,000 crowd to be seen at Ibrox. A testimonial match for our heroic captain, John Greig – the first benefit match for any Rangers players since Davie Meiklejohn in the 1920s. Ibrox was packed, and we were in the Main Stand, to see Rangers take on the Scotland national team, who were soon to be heading to Argentina for the 1978 World Cup. Andy Cameron 'entertained' the crowd before kick-off but it was announced that some of the Scotland players had been held up on the way, so the Rangers players in the Scotland squad would have to play for them instead of Rangers. Cameron said that Lou Macari of Manchester United had been delayed because he was "outside selling ice-cream!" Fortunately word came through that the delayed players had arrived and

Rangers would, consequently, be at full strength. Cue a big roar from the crowd.

Scotland were on a good run of form up to that game and manager Ally McLeod had them fired up. Even though it was a friendly, Rangers took them apart. Top Scotland star, Nottingham Forest's John Robertson, was marked right out the the game by a new Rangers teenage starlet, Derek Strickland. The final score was 5-0 and John Greig was on the scoresheet twice. Was this the start of the downfall of that Scotland team? They weren't as invincible as Ally McLeod had us believe. As for Strickland, we expected great things – but he was hardly heard of ever again.

Our Partick Thistle supporing neighbour, Bill Johnston, worked as a sales manager for Scottish Brewers who sold McEwan's Export, Harp Lager and Tartan Special beer. In the late 70's, Tartan Special were the official sponsors of the Scottish Cup, so he got tickets for the 1978 Cup Final for the centre of the North Stand for his son, my brother and me. My first Rangers Cup Final at last – and we were going for the Treble. The three of us went and sat on our own but Dad could see us from his stairway at the end and could keep an eye on us.

Rangers, of course, won the match (which is best remembered for Peter McCloy swinging on our cross-bar at the end when he'd completely misjudged an Aberdeen high ball which went over him and into the goal!) 2-1 with goals from Alex MacDonald and Derek Johnstone, but Bobby Russell was outstanding. To think he had only been playing Junior football the previous year just didn't make any sense.

Shirley Temple-permed Derek Johnstone was our top scorer that season. Mainly with his head, from crosses supplied by Tommy McLean and Davie Cooper, he banged in 38 goals in all competitions. He was also in the Scotland squad and scored in the Home Internationals against Wales and Northern Ireland. We all expected him to lead the line for Scotland in Argentina – but he wasn't even picked for one game. What was going on? Scotland were appalling in their first two matches and they had a top goal-scorer sitting on the bench. Was Ally McLeod daft? The story later emerged that the two had spoken before the tournament and Johnstone apparently expressed doubts as to his international abilities – so McLeod never picked him again.

The domestic season ended in a most surprising way. Jock Wallace resigned after winning two Trebles in three seasons – and he was to be replaced by John Greig. What was going on? Wallace took the reason to his grave but it was rumoured that there had been a disagreement with General Manager, Willie Waddell. It was never confirmed but, it was generally thought that Wallace believed that he deserved a bonus for his success, and he wanted to strengthen the squad for the next season but Waddell, controlling the purse strings, refused to release the money as it was ear-marked for stadium development.

At the end of May, I left school and got a job with Whyte & Mackay Distillers. I intended it to be a summer job until I went to University – but I ended up working there for 21 years! Having been at a school with only two Celtic fans, I now worked in an office full of adults and there were plenty of supporters of both sides. I could easily tell from some of the names which team they'd support, and there was a lot of good natured football banter especially on Mondays depending on the results at the weekend.

The World Cup in Argentina promised much but delivered little. Disastrous results against Peru and Iran, coupled with Willie Johnston's 'misdemeanours' meant that Scotland were a laughing stock. Some reputation was saved by a brilliant performance, beating Holland 3-2 in the last game, with Archie Gemmill's wonder goal, and nearly qualifying for the next round, but the team trudged home to lick their wounds.

FIVE
The John Greig Years

Season 1978-79 began as John Greig set about retaining the Treble, and he came within a whisker of doing so. He replaced himself in the team with Ally Dawson who had been on the first team fringes, and the team continued pretty much as per usual.

The biggest difference was that Ibrox started to be rebuilt. Following the disaster in 1971, Willie Waddell decided that the comfort and safety of supporters had to be taken seriously. After touring around Europe looking at various stadium designs, it was agreed that Ibrox would be rebuilt in the style of Borussia Dortmund's Westfalion stadium. The work would be done in stages with the first end to be the east terracing – the Rangers end. Bulldozers and diggers moved in and the roof, terraces, barriers, and the mound of earth were removed. The total cost of this re-development was estimated at £6 million and the money to pay for it came from the Rangers Pools which was the most successful club-based scheme in Britain, and which had generated substantial funds over the fourteen years it had been running.

Once the Copland Road stand was completed, the same process was repeated at the other end of the ground, and each of these new stands could hold 7,500 fans. Phase 3 would be the demolition of the Centenary Stand which was replaced by the 10,300 seater Govan Stand.

Games continued to be played at Ibrox, using just 3 sides of the ground. The exception to this was for matches against Celtic which needed a bigger capacity so these were played at Hampden. That meant that Dad was required for stewarding duties and it was now decided that I could go to these as well by supplementing the stewarding team. At last – my first games against Celtic, but I was told that, under no circumstances, was I to take my scarf – even though I would be in among nothing but Rangers fans. So, I tied it around my waist and hid it under my jacket!

The league season had started depressingly. Three draws and three defeats in our opening six games – in fact we didn't win a game until the end of September when we beat Motherwell 4-1 at Ibrox. This was followed by another two draws. We were dropping points all over the place – but amazing things were happening in the European Cup.

Our opponents in the first round in September were Juventus – a team including many players who were Italian internationalists, and who would go on to win the 1982 World Cup. In the team was the inappropriately named Gentile who proved to be anything but gentle as he tackled Gordon Smith as if he was trying to break his legs. We held them to a 1-0 defeat in Italy, and Ibrox was packed for one of the most famous European nights in its history. Goals from Alex MacDonald and Gordon Smith gave us a 2-0 win and a 2-1 aggregate score.

We were up against it in the next round, too. We were drawn against PSV Eindhoven, the champions of Holland (who had been runners-up in the 1974 and 1978 World Cup Finals). We got a rather disappointing 0-0 draw in the first leg at Ibrox and that appeared to be that. After all, PSV had never lost a home European tie. We listened to the radio commentary as PSV scored "before the ball had even warmed up". But a goal from Alex MacDonald drew us level. They scored again before we got a free kick in a dangerous position outside their box. Kenny Watson blasted a shot and Derek Johnstone got a glancing header to it to send it past their keeper. 2-2 meant we would go through on away goals. With time running out, Tommy McLean saw a run from Bobby Russell and played a superb pass to him. He ran on and guided the ball under the keeper and into the net. 3-2. PSV were defeated and we were into the quarter final. Yet again, Bobby Russell had turned in a masterful display, beating the Dutch at their own game. The whole team played with purpose, awareness, and plenty of skill. People were beginning to wander if John Greig was a tactical genius whose management style was more suited to the European game rather than the Scottish one. We learned that he had really done his homework on our European opponents, and had given each player definite instructions about how to get the better of their direct opposite number.

We began to dream of European success but that would have to wait until the spring. We were still stumbling along in the league. We drew 1-1 with Celtic at Hampden. Dad and I decided to nip away a few minutes early to avoid the crowd (and since his car was parked very close by, because we'd been there so early). We went down the stairs to be met with two Police officers chasing a Celtic fan towards us. He'd run in the open doors and was heading for the stairs that we were going down. Where on earth did he think he was going? The whole place was full of Rangers fans. I reacted fastest and pushed him with both hands right back into the grasp of the Police who led him away. Job done!

We were back at Hampden the following month to beat Celtic 3-2 in the League Cup semi final to set up a final against Aberdeen in March. Many people believe that was the game that seemed to kick-start the real animosity between Rangers and Aberdeen which simmered under the surface for years to come. Aberdeen were putting together a right tough team, and we always noticed that their striker, Drew Jarvie, seemed to be able to commit a bad foul and then be 50 yards away by the time the referee stopped the play. He was a master at it. Another big thug in their team was Doug Rougvie and he knocked Derek Johnstone to the ground in the final and was sent off, pleading innocence. That seemed to enrage the Aberdeen players, management and fans.

In the last minute, a corner was met by Colin Jackson, who had a terrible, swolen black eye, and couldn't even see the ball properly. He headed it past the flailing arms of Bobby Clark in the Aberdeen goal and we won the match 2-1. Alex Ferguson, the Aberdeen mamager, was livid.

We lost the European Cup quarter final 2-1 on aggregate to Cologne of Germany. The dream was great while it lasted.

It took us nine matches to win the Scottish Cup that year. We had replays with Kilmarnock and Partick Thistle (in the semi-final) to get to the final against Hibernian. For some reason, probably a golf match, Dad couldn't go, so I was to go over to Hampden myself to steward. Fortunately, there was a bus which passed the end of our road and went over to Mount Florida, so I travelled over on my own, with my packed lunch, and my scarf hidden once again under my jacket.

Just past Eglinton Toll, a fellow passenger turned round to ask me the time. Seeing that he had his Rangers scarf on, I answered, "A couple of hours until we thrash Hibs." Then I told him the correct time. How wrong I was. It had to be one of the most boring 0-0 cup finals ever. There was nothing to talk about afterwards. The replay proved to be just as bad. Again, it was 0-0. Penalty deciders were still a thing of the future.

The second replay was to be on the Monday night, and it would be 'Pay at the Gate' so we weren't required as stewards. There must have been some petrol shortage or strike or such like, and Dad decided that we would go over by bus, leaving the car. We went round to the bus top at the top of Crow Road to wait for a 44 over to Battlefield. After a few moments, a car pulled into the side of the road and offered us a lift, which we gladly accepted.

On the way over, my dad sat in the front seat and chatted away to the driver about the previous games, that evening's replay and so on. We parked near the ground and decided to head for the north enclosure. The driver said he'd join us, so we all went in. During the game, we chatted away about this and that. The performance wasn't really that much better. It was 2-2 after 90 minutes so another extra half hour was required. Fortunately for us – but unfortunately for him – Hibernian's Arthur Duncan put the ball into his own goal, so we finally won the cup 3-2, after 330 minutes.

There was more cheerful chat on the way back and the driver dropped us off at Anniesland. Feeling a bit ignored, I said to my Dad, "So, who was that guy then? You forgot to introduce us."

"I've no idea," he replied. "I've never met him before!"

"What? I thought you knew him from work!"

"Nope! He was a complete stranger."

I was utterly astonished. "So, he just stopped and offered us a lift?"

"Yes. He saw your scarf and knew we were going to the game."

I just couldn't believe it. I'd presumed the driver was someone my dad knew, and he'd recognised him and stopped the car, but he was just a friendly stranger who was quite glad of our company and chat at the game. I never saw him again so I've still no idea who he was.

Despite all our dropped points, we ran Celtic close in the league. It all boiled down to the run-in. We beat them 1-0 at Hampden, and then beat Aberdeen 2-0 at Ibrox. There was a two week gap (for the Cup Final and first replay) before we went to Parkhead, needing a draw. At 2-2, with Celtic down to ten men, we were within touching distance, but lost two silly late goals. Two days later, we beat Partick Thistle 1-0 and then we had the second Cup replay against Hibernian. Three days later, we played them again in the league but lost 2-1 at Easter Road. John Greig had come close to retaining the Treble, and had engineered a good run in Europe. Unfortunately, that was the best we got and it was mostly downhill from there.

It seemed that, with money being spent of the rebuilding of Ibrox and, with the reduced capacity, and therefore less gate money coming in, there wasn't much left to spend on players but, over the years, we still managed to sign Colin MacAdam, Ian Redford, Sandy Clark, Gregor Stevens, Jim Stewart and Ally McCoist. The successful team of the late 70's was by now splitting up. In the next few years, Alex MacDonald and Sandy Jardine would go to Hearts, Colin Jackson would retire, Tom Forsyth would succumb to injury, and Derek Parlane was to be sold.

Argentina had won the World Cup the previous summer, beating Holland in the final. The game was late in starting when the Argentinians complained about the plaster cast that one of the van der Kerkhof brothers had on his wrist as it might cause injury. Sitting impatiently waiting for the game to get started, my dad suggested that the Argentinians should all be told to remove their "far more dangerous" crucifixes that most of them were wearing round their necks!

The following June, the new World champions were due to visit Hampden for a friendly match against Scotland. Dad and I went over and got our first glimpse of the new "wonder kid", 18 year old Diego Maradona who was beginning to break into the team. Almost 62,000 fans turned up to see the game, and watched as Maradona dribbled easily past the Scottish defenders time and time again. He scored one of the goals as Argentina won 3-1, and were given a standing ovation at the end of the game.

At the start of the 1979-80 season, we heard that John Greig was going to build his team around a fantastic, new young player of our own called John MacDonald. At that time, there was a pre-season tournament to get everyone 'warmed up' for the start of the new season. Sponsored by a brewer, it was the Drybrough Cup, and it involved the top four teams from the Premier League and the First Division. The quarter finals were on one Saturday, and normally, the four Premier teams progressed to the semi-finals which were held on the following Wednesday night, with the final at Hampden on the next Saturday.

Reports came out that MacDonald was 'one to watch' and we beat Hibernian away in the semi-final and would meet Celtic in the final. It must have been "pay at the gate' as we weren't on stewarding duty. I'd been out with friends for a few refreshments the night before, and had been very late getting to bed. On the way over to Hampden, my eyes kept shutting, and my dad threatened to turn the car round and go home. I convinced him that I'd be alright so we went into Hampden.

John MacDonald scored, and then Sandy Jardine scored one of the best goals ever as he ran from his right back position past several Celtic players before playing a quick one-two, getting the ball back and then unleashing an unstoppable shot into the net. What a goal! That would be goal of the season. Little did we know what was to follow. Displaying fantastic skill, Davie Cooper scored the goal that would be voted as the greatest ever Rangers goal. He flicked the ball over and round all the mesmerised Celtic defenders, who turned this way and that, and the goalkeeper to slot it into the net. It was unbelievable. But, where were the cameras to record such an amazing feat? Nowhere to be seen. The game wasn't televised. Only later did a short clip of cine film, taken from behind the goal, show what we had all seen – a superb display of skill, confidence and a degree of arrogance. Celtic were beaten 3-1 and even Sandy Jardine's spectacular goal paled into insignificance after the artistry from Davie Cooper.

After the length of time it took to settle the 1979 Scottish Cup Final, it was rather ironic that we would meet Hibernian twice at the start of the new season – once in the Drybrough Cup semi-final and then in the opening game of the league – and beat them both times, and at Easter Road. On 11th August, we went across to Edinburgh and triumphed 3-1 with goals from Alex MacDonald, Davie Cooper and Bobby Russell. After their demoralising Cup Final defeat and the sale of one of their best players, midfielder Des Bremner to Aston Villa, Hibernian were in the doldrums. They only won two of their opening eighteen matches, were rooted at the bottom of the Premier League, and were genuine contenders for relegation. We beat them fairly easily 2-0 at Ibrox in October. The team which had always given us a good game had split up and gone their separate ways.

The previous year, the whole country languished in what was known as the "winter of discontent", and now Hibs were enduring a very bleak season of their own. Their chairman Tom Hart and manager, Eddie Turnbull had to look to the transfer market for a miracle. Hart got a tip-off from a reporter with the Edinburgh Evening News that George Best, the former Manchester United star, and 1968 European Footballer of the Year, was available for £50,000 from Fulham. Hart signed him on a "Pay per play" agreement – a very lucrative £2,000 per game – when the rest of the team were only earning around £120 per week.

At the age of thirty-three, he was nowhere near the peak of his playing powers, but he was still a huge personality, and the transfer caught everyone's imagination. After a couple of weeks' training, he scored on his debut against St Mirren, but Hibs still lost 2-1. The following week, against Partick Thistle, the crowd was up by 15,000, and Hibs won their first game in fourteen weeks. He might have been overweight, but there was no disputing his ability. He still had the control, the passes, and a competitive streak. There was even a joke at the time that he had only signed for a Hibernian when the Scottish licensing hours were extended!

He saved his best performance for our visit to Easter Road on 22nd December, and he gave the Hibs fans an early Christmas present with a virtuoso display. The pitch was like an ice rink, but he controlled the game. We took the lead from a Tommy McLean free-kick after 37 minutes, and our defence were keen to shackle Best, but his close control meant that he could shield the ball away from our defenders' challenges. He then made a 40-yard pass to Ally McLeod who crossed for Tony Higgins to score. Best also had a hand in the winner when he took a quick throw in to Higgins whose cross was headed in by Colin Campbell. He also tried a couple of shots and a free-kick, and was a constant threat to our defence. During the match, the Rangers fans had taunted Best by throwing cans of lager towards him when he went to take a corner kick. He defused the situation by picking up one of the cans and pretending to take a sip from it. He got a huge cheer from the travelling support.

When the full-time whistle sounded, the Hibernian fans were ecstatic. They might have been bottom of the league, but they had defeated Rangers. George Best had breathed new life into their team, and had lit up Easter Road with a great individual performance. Although we lost, what a treat it was to see George Best, Davie Cooper, and Sandy Jardine on the same pitch.

John Greig commented that the second goal might not have been scored on a better surface and said that he felt that we were beaten more by the conditions than by the overall skill of Hibs. He thought that it was a disgrace that the game had even been played under such hard, frosty conditions and he was relieved that none of our players had suffered serious injury.

Best scored against Celtic in a 1-1 draw and also scored a great solo goal against Dundee, but his presence could not save Hibernian from relegation. In February 1980, he went on a massive drinking session with the French rugby team who were in Edinburgh to play Scotland, and Hibs sacked him, only to bring him back a week later. When Hibernian came to Glasgow to play us in March, we beat them 1-0 thanks to a Derek Johnstone goal, and Best only lasted until half-time.

By now, it was a great help for me having a Rangers supporting boss. He allowed me to take slightly extended lunch hours when tickets for a big match went on sale at Ibrox so that a colleague and I could nip over to get them – as long as we also got his tickets as well. The Scottish Football League's offices were also very handy in West Regent Street and we sometimes got tickets there, too.

I went to Ibrox nearly every week since I was working and could afford it. I usually got a number 19 bus from Anniesland (it came out of the bus garage at Knightswood and was pretty empty when it got to my stop) to Govan Road, and went to the west enclosure. I thought nothing of walking home afterwards, along to the pedestrian Clyde Tunnel and up through Jordanhill. I could be home 45 minutes after the end of the game – and not standing ages waiting for a bus.

I'd made the mistake of travelling home by bus after the first league game of the season against Celtic on 18th August. This was the first Celtic game that I was allowed to go to on my own. I met and sat beside my boss in the main stand, and saw us go two goals up, from John MacDonald and Bobby Russell. Very disappointingly, they equalised and it finished 2-2. I walked over to Bellahouston Park to get a 59 bus since it started from there and would be empty, which would take me to Kelvindale. I waited ages, and when the bus came, it seemed to stop everywhere. When we were passing the King's Theatre in Bath Street, there was a Celtic fan on the pavement who was setting fire to a Union Jack! "They must have won then" said a woman passenger in the seat in front of me – but I quickly told her the score. That was a very slow way to get home after a match so, from then on, it was quicker to walk.

I passed my driving test in September 1979 but I had to wait a while until I could afford to buy a car – with plans to start going to away games ….

On a family trip to London in October, we all decided to go and visit the Wembley Stadium tour. We saw inside the dressing rooms before walking up the tunnel. A recording of the crowd roar was played and it got louder and louder until we emerged onto the track. We got to climb up the famous steps and pose for photos with a replica cup, and then we got to sit in the Royal Box.

Season 1979-80 saw Rangers finish embarrassingly fifth in the league, mainly due to their appalling away form. Aberdeen were now a force to be reckoned with and were champions that season – the first team from outwith Glasgow to win it since Kilmarnock back in 1965. We dropped daft points to the likes of Partick Thistle, Kilmarnock, St Mirren and Dundee as well as losing too regularly to Aberdeen and Celtic. Aberdeen also knocked us out of the League Cup in the third round over two legs, winning both of them.

In the Cup Winners Cup, we had a straightforward tie against Lillestrom from Norway before we met Fortuna Dusseldorf, whom we beat 2-1 on aggregate. Then we were drawn against Valencia from Spain – a team which boasted Argentinian World Cup winner Mario Kempes and Germany's Karlheinz Rummenige. We managed to draw 1-1 in the first leg before they ripped us apart at Ibrox. Kempes turned on a magnificent display that night and scored two of their three goals, and they eventually went on to win the cup.

Our only hope of silverware that season was the Scottish Cup. We got past Clyde, Dundee United, Hearts and Aberdeen - three very difficult draws but we won them all. Was this a good omen? We faced Celtic in the final, and I was on duty in the North Stand as usual. After 90 minutes, the score was 0-0 but they scored in extra time with help from a massive deflection from a George McCluskey shot, so we won nothing that season and hadn't even qualified for Europe.

The 1980 Scottish Cup final was remembered for all the wrong reasons. A tall fence had been built around the perimeter of the track at Hampden to prevent pitch invasions. It didn't work. Just after they were presented with the cup, some Celtic fans climbed over the fence and began to celebrate on the pitch, taunting the Rangers fans who reacted, predictably, by climbing over their fence to chase them off the pitch. A series of pitched battles soon broke out as fans from both sides invaded the pitch. The huge television audience saw scenes which resembled Culloden, and commentator Archie MacPherson had to state the obvious. "Make no mistake. These fans hate each other!"

I'd left just as the presentation took place and heard on the car radio what was going on. When I got home, I saw the television pictures and even saw someone I knew helping a blood covered friend in the Rangers goal. The Police had all moved outside to await the fans spilling out after the final whistle and were nowhere to be seen inside the ground. After several minutes, we saw mounted Police charge at the fans to try to separate them with batons swinging. Eventually, a degree of calm was restored as fans left the pitch area but with many still nursing serious looking wounds. There were bottles and cans all over the grass.

A Government inquiry blamed excessive drink for the trouble and new legislation was brought in which made it against the law to take drink into football grounds or to try to get in whilst under the influence.

In June 1980, Howard Davis the American boxer arrived in Glasgow to face World Lightweight Champion, Glaswegian Jim Watt, at Ibrox. A boxing ring was constructed in the corner in front of the Main and Copland Road Stands and, despite the weather, after fifteen rain-soaked rounds, Jim Watt retained his title. He then proved that he should have stuck with boxing as he, rather tunelessly, led the crowd in a rendition of "Flower of Scotland"!

The two ends of Ibrox had now been re-built and huge, square, all-seated stands replaced the semi-circular terracings at the ends. Both were opened with glamourous pre-season games against Arsenal and Spurs (we won both matches) with Willie Waddell cutting a huge ribbon to declare each stand open. Then work began on demolishing the Centenary Stand to complete the fourth side of a modern, safe new Ibrox.

That summer saw us sign Jim Bett from Lokeren in Belgium and Colin McAdam ("Beastie") from Partick Thistle. The clubs couldn't agree a fee so he became the first transfer to be decided by an independent tribunal. It was decided that we were to pay £165,000 for his services. With his brother playing in defence for Celtic, they were the first brothers in living memory to play against each other in an Old Firm match. Colin got the first laugh as we beat them in the first two games. We won at Parkhead for the first time in years. With the score at 1-1, we won a throw in mid-way into the Celtic half. Celtic player Davie Provan stood right in front of Willie Johnston as he prepared to take the throw so 'Bud' simply tapped the ball on Provan's head before throwing it towards Alex Miller. He took the ball perfectly and curled a shot right into the goal.

We then went on a fifteen match unbeaten run before dropping lots of points in November and December. That ended our title challenge.

After 1975, when Texaco withdrew their sponsorship from The Texaco Cup, the competition was reformatted as The Anglo-Scottish Cup. Over the years, the English teams were drawn more and more from the third and fourth divisions, and the public interest dwindled. Celtic took part in 1978-79, and we entered it in 1980-81, having no European games that season, along with the likes of Airdrieonians, Falkirk, Hearts, Kilmarnock, Morton and Partick Thistle, as well as Blackburn Rovers, Bolton Wanderers, Burnley, Fulham, Hull City, and the team who were to become our nemesis, Chesterfield.

First of all, we eliminated Partick Thistle, winning 3-1 at home at the end of July, but losing 3-2 away at the beginning of August. We went through with an aggregate score of 5-3, and were drawn to face minnows Chesterfield in the second round in October. In one of the most embarrassing results in our history, we drew 1-1 at Ibrox in the first leg – but lost 3-0 in the return. It was no consolation whatsoever that Chesterfield went on to beat Notts County 2-1 in the final. Being the last ever final, they got the hold on to the trophy and it's still on display at their stadium.

The following Saturday we were at home to Celtic and they really rubbed it in. They were soon silenced as two goals from Colin McAdam and one from John McDonald gave us a 3-0 win. It was strange watching it against a backdrop of a building site on the far side of the ground.

We were knocked out of the League Cup by Aberdeen under rather controversial circumstances as they got two very contentious penalty kicks, and finished third in the league, twelve points behind Celtic – but we did win the Scottish Cup.

After thumping Airdrie 5-0, we were drawn away at St Johnstone who were inspired by their new star, Alistair McCoist. We were on the way out, losing 3-2, until Ian Redford equalised in stoppage time to great sighs of relief. We won the replay at Ibrox 3-1, and then beat Hibernian and Morton to reach the final against Dundee United.

The final was instantly forgettable until the last minute when Rangers were awarded a penalty, and handed a chance to win the cup. Unfortunately, Ian Redford missed it so there would be a replay the following Wednesday. John Greig made a couple of team changes and these worked wonders. Davie Cooper 'played a blinder', scored our first goal, laid on the second for John MacDonald and crossed a free kick for Bobby Russell to score a third. United scored one and my dad said, "That's them going to get back into it now." Wrong! John MacDonald scored another and we won 4-1.

As we drove home, there was thunder and lightning and bright flashes lit up the sky. We went along Victoria Road as the huge flashes seemed to be right above us. We watched the highlights on television when we got home. They were too busy showing a replay of something that they almost missed John McDonald's second goal. That would have gone down well!

The Govan Stand was completed and Ibrox now had a capacity of 44,000 with the two enclosures under the Main Stand being the only standing areas. The new stand was first used for the league game against Celtic on 19th September 1981. I went with a colleague from work and his mate and we sat down near the front, in row D. Unfortunately, Celtic spoiled the party and won 2-0.

The estimated building cost of £6 million had risen to £10 million which obviously made a significant dent in the Club's finances. With poor performances on the pitch, attendances fell off and this was partly blamed on the stadium since some fans thought that the new ground lacked atmosphere due to the spaces between the stands.

The season continued with no real improvement. We were third in the league, twelve points adrift of Celtic. The financing of the Ibrox improvements was really biting as there was hardly anything available to strengthen the team. Scotland played Northern Ireland in a World Cup qualifier at Hampden, and we awoke to the news that, after the match, we had signed big Ulsterman John McClelland from Mansfield Town. He would later become the Club captain. Early indications were that he was an able defender and could take a really long throw-in. The one highlight that season in the league was an exciting 3-3 draw at Parkhead in November.

Dukla Prague beat us 3-0 away, and we won the home game 2-1, but it wasn't enough. We did mange to battle our way through to the League Cup Final against Dundee United. They took the lead in the first half, and Derek Johnstone picked up a nasty head injury and left the pitch for quite a few minutes. We were fortunate to make it to half time just one goal behind. As time seemed to be running out, Davie Cooper curled in a superb free kick to equalise and then, with just moments to go, United headed the ball out of their area straight to Ian Redford who looped a shot right over Hamish McAlpine into the goal, before sprinting away in celebration.

That was the date of my parents' Silver Wedding party, but I stayed to see the cup presented, and the customary lap of honour before hurrying home to get changed for the 'do'. My aunt, who lived in Battlefield, near Hampden, was very late because she was held up in the traffic – not even aware that there was a game on!

On the Sunday night, I was out at Blanefield with some friends having a refreshment or two in The Beech Tree Inn when in walked Ian Redford, our cup winning hero who had atoned for his Scottish Cup penalty miss earlier that year. He looked over as I gave him a happy 'thumbs up'.

In October 1981, work began to demolish the old North Stand at Hampden, which reduced the capacity, and the terracing which had been covered with black ash was all concreted over. Our end, which was covered, didn't get any rain, and when Rangers scored and everyone celebrated, the clouds of black dust got up everyone's nose – literally. Not to put too fine a point on it, you could blow your nose and your handkerchief would be black!

On the 15th of November, just 25,000 fans turned up to pay tribute to our long-serving central defender, Colin Jackson, in his testimonial match. We drew 1-1 with Everton, but went on to win 3-1 on penalties.

With the building work all completed, Ibrox was now a modern, comfortable, state of the art stadium – but, more importantly, it was a safe stadium. European champions Liverpool, with a team full of household names, came up to Ibrox on a very cold night just before Christmas to officially open the completed stadium, and beat us 2-0.

We made fairly routine progress to the Scottish Cup Final, where we would meet Aberdeen. One thing that was in our favour was that we just didn't lose cup finals to provincial teams, and when we went a goal up through John MacDonald that looked like continuing. Alex McLeish equalised (almost a repeat of Ian Redford's League Cup Final goal) to take it into extra time where we just collapsed. Aberdeen won 4-1, having beaten us 4-0 at Pittodrie the week before as well.

That summer, having become a Boys' Brigade officer, I attended the Company's annual summer camp which, that year, was held near Bunessan on the Isle of Mull. During our fortnight, it was arranged that a team made up of Officers and Boys would play a football match against the local village team. This wasn't just an ordinary team – they were led and coached by Peter Bonetti, the ex-Chelsea and England goalkeeper who had played in the 1970 World Cup Quarter-Final. Still as fit as a fiddle in his forties, he played outfield while his son played in goals. It took two of us to mark him, and at the end of the game which finished in a draw, he shook my hand and told me I'd played very well against him. High praise indeed!

With a bit more money available at last, John Greig made some big-money signings in the summer and during the season but, yet again, the season ended trophyless. Dave MacKinnon came from Partick Thistle, Craig Paterson came from Hibernian, Robert Prytz from Malmo and Sandy Clark arrived from West Ham United.

We had a somewhat unusual game at Ibrox on the 11th of August. We played against a Chinese International XI who were on tour. Not since John Greig's testimonial match had we gone up against a national team. The stadium announcer had his work cut out reading out all the players' names, and he really struggled with the pronunciations of the substitutions. We won 3-1 thanks to goals from Ian Redford, John McDonald and Craig Paterson.

In October, we got to the League Cup Final against Celtic, and I stood in the Rangers end to see them go 2-0 up by half-time. One goal looked off-side and the other looked like a foul! At the start of the second half, Jim Bett scored a super free kick and, thinking that we'd fight back, the crowd tried their best to roar them on. Gordon Smith had even been brought back on loan from Brighton & Hove Albion to boost the team but we just couldn't get back into it.

We lost both home games in the league against Celtic. 2-1 at New Year and, in the last league game of the season, we went 2-0 up by half-time, but they got two penalty kicks and finished 4-2 winners. We ended up fourth, eighteen points behind champions Dundee United. A week later, we lost the Scottish Cup Final 1-0 to Aberdeen, who had just won the European Cup Winners' Cup. Despite or relatively poor form, we'd been in every Scottish Cup Final since 1976.

In the UEFA Cup, we were drawn against Borussia Dortmund and drew the away leg 0-0. I got a ticket for the return leg, but Campbell Ogilvie stepped in and gave us two tickets for the centre of the main stand. What to do with my ticket? I told Dad to go to Ibrox and I'd meet him there. I got the bus from Anniesland and climbed upstairs where it was full of 'Bears'. "Anyone need a ticket?" I asked, and loads of hands shot up. I sold it easily for what I'd paid for it, and then met Dad at the game. We won 2-0 but got knocked out in the next round after a trouncing in Cologne.

There was even a joke doing the rounds at the time that there was a serious fault with Rangers' new stands ...they were built facing the pitch!

In the spring of 1983, Ibrox welcomed a special visitor. Bob Sutherland was a Rangers player from 1959 to 1964 whose career was ended by a knee injury. He began playing bowls a few years later and, in February 1983, he achieved great success by winning the World Indoor Bowls Championship at Coatbridge. He was welcomed back to Ibrox to resounding applause befitting a World champion.

As well as all the new seats at Ibrox, there was also modern office space under the stands and that brought in revenue for the Club, and there was now an official Club shop – at the corner of Copland Road and Mafeking Street – where fans could buy jerseys, books, scarves, hats, sweets and posters.

With undersoil heating installed, it meant that our games could always go ahead despite the ravages of the Scottish winter weather. There were some weeks when we went to games and were absolutely frozen to the bone up in the stand while the players ran around a spring-like pitch. One year, we were allowed to re-arrange our fixtures, swapping away games to Ibrox, so we could keep playing every Saturday while the rest of the country shivered. That kept momentum going and prevented a fixture back-log once the weather improved.

A new type of season ticket was to be available – a Rover Ticket. This allowed the holder to go to any turnstile in any of the three new stands, tear out a page from the ticket book and then choose any seat there. For routine games, there were always plenty of available seats, but for big games (Celtic), you tore out a page from the ticket book to exchange it for a ticket for a specific seat. We usually went and sat about four or five rows from the front of the Govan rear Stand.

It also gave us admission to all the Reserve Games, so our routine was now set. One week we saw the first XI in action and the next week we saw the Reserves. Radio commentary always featured Rangers or Celtic – whoever was playing away from home – so we could listen to the 'main' game while watching the Reserves. To be honest, considering the way the 'big' team was playing at that time, it was often better to watch a Reserve team that featured the very young Derek Ferguson, Ian Durrant, Robert Fleck, and the likes of John Spencer and Gary McSwegan.

In those days, the radio commentary was limited. They only did the last five minutes of the first half and the whole of the second half of a routine league game, but the whole of a cup final. David Francey would always start his commentary by saying, "Let me just run through the teams." It became a standing joke in our house that Dad and I would instantly mime someone running about as if Francey was actually down on the pitch running through the teams.

Finding out midweek scores in those days was quite difficult. There just wasn't the level of coverage that we get nowadays. We had to listen to Radio 2 just before the ten o'clock news, when they did a very quick round up of any scores from either side of the border, and that was it. No analysis, no reports, no phone-ins – just the score. You had to wait until the next morning's paper to find out what had actually happened.

One of the people we often met outside Ibrox before we went in was a colleague of my dad. His name was Hugh Gray, and he used to go to games and provide commentary for blind and visually impaired fans. Campbell Ogilvie gave them Main Stand tickets together so that Hugh could sit with a blind person on either side of him as well as two in front, and he gave them a full 90 minutes of commentary and explanations, added to by the roars from the crowd. Hugh did this for many years, and was originally helped by Alistair Alexander who would go on to become a well-known match commentator on BBC Scotland.

We were sitting watching the Reserves one week in the spring – the day of the Grand National at Aintree – and some of the youngsters who weren't in the team that day were sitting in front of us. All through the match, a boyish, curly haired Ian Durrant kept getting up and going out. He was more interested in checking the racing results than watching the football.

The 3rd of March was to be the date of Tom Forsyth's testimonial match. "Jaws", the iron-man defender "whose boots were made at Yarrow's shipyard!" had to end his career as a succession of injuries took its toll. On the day, the match programme paid tribute to his great career – particularly the 1973 Cup Final winner and the tackle against Mick Channon – but the saddest article was the one about "the battle Big Tam just couldn't win". It was a heart-breaking end to a great career – but what was even more disappointing was that only 10,000 turned up at the game. We played Swansea City and beat them 6-3 with a young Derek Ferguson making his first team debut, aged just sixteen. Surely, a bigger team could have come to help attract a crowd that he deserved.

Down at York for the Easter weekend, we decided to go and take in the York City vs Grimsby Town match in the English Fourth Division. We couldn't believe the level of policing. It was wall-to-wall Police dogs and horses, escorting fans into the ground. We'd been at cup finals and Old Firm games but had never seen anything like this – for a Fourth Division game!

Now having a car of my own, I started going to a few away games – at Falkirk and Kilmarnock, as well as Partick Thistle. They were usually 'pay at the gate' or by tickets which were all reasonably priced and very easily available, right up until the last minute, since these terraced grounds could easily host 10,000 visiting fans. When we went to Firhill, the ground lay-out meant that fans could walk round the inside of the ground and go to whichever end Rangers were shooting towards, and then move round to the other end for the second half – with no hint of any crowd trouble. At Falkirk for a cup game in 1983, someone had a very stupid idea. There would be a collection for charity by having some people walking round the pitch holding up a big blanket and inviting fans to throw coins into it. Coins were flying everywhere. Whilst having good intentions, it was surely the daftest way to raise money!

I was back at Ibrox that summer – but not for football. On Saturday 27th August, the Boys' Brigade commemorated its founding 100 years ago in Glasgow with a Centenary Salute. My dad and uncle, who had both attended the Golden Jubilee celebration at Queen's Park in 1933, and I went to the event. Officers and Boys from all over the world attended and a special casket containing a message from 1933 was opened and read out. On the Sunday, all of Glasgow Battalion attended a Centenary Service and Parade/March past. Fortunately, the sun shone all weekend, and it also stayed dry for the torch-lit procession on the Saturday night from the Arena Show at the Kelvin Hall, along Kelvin Way and into Kelvingrove Park for a firework display – the very place where Rangers founders met and discussed the forming of our Club in 1872.

By now, the north stand at Hampden had been removed, so our stewarding team relocated across to the main stand, to the stairway closest to the centre – but at the 'wrong' end. Imagine having to be polite, courteous and helpful to Celtic fans when they had a game there. Before the 1983-84 season, we both got to the final of the Glasgow Cup (an historic tournament organised for the senior Glasgow teams – usually to raise money for charity) which would be held at Hampden. We showed everyone to their places, and then I went up and found a seat in the back row. At half time, for fans' entertainment, there was short a display of women's football and they came up and sat in my section of the stand once they'd all changed. Sandy Clark scored the only goal of the game – and only two people at that end jumped up and cheered – me and one the ladies! As the game fizzled out, the fans at that end all left, so it was empty which meant that I could wander down to the front to get a close, unobstructed view of the cup presentation.

Season 1983-84 would see big changes at Ibrox, but the league started with only one point from four games. In the European Cup Winners' Cup, we achieved our record European score when we beat Valetta of Malta 16-0 on aggregate. Dave McPherson scored four goals in the away leg, having never managed that before – "even when playing for the BB". We beat FC Porto 2-1 in the first leg of the second round but got knocked out over there in the return leg.

We won six games in the League Cup but, after only getting ten points from twenty seven in the league, the stress got to John Greig and he resigned as manager on 28th October. The search was on for a replacement, and Alex Ferguson, from Aberdeen, and Jim McLean, from Dundee United, were both interviewed before turning the job down.

We had another chance to prove ourselves against international opposition on Hallowe'en when we took on New Zealand in a pre-arranged friendly at Ibrox. Although managerless, we won comfortably 5-0 with two goals from Robert Fleck, and singles from recent signingAlly McCoist, David Mitchell and Robert Prytz.

SIX
Big Jock's Back In Charge

Jock Wallace was persuaded to return to the Club from Motherwell and he would start on 10th November. The night before, care-taker manager, Tommy McLean took the team to Clydebank for a League Cup tie. Dad and I decided to go. We parked the car and made our way to the ground, not awfully sure of which way to go in. We found a turnstile and went in – only to find ourselves walking along the grass to the stand, as all our players ran past us on their way from the dressing room to the pitch. Were we in the wrong place? Nobody stopped us or challenged us so we stood and watched the players go past. We went to the main stand of Clydebank's famous all-seated stadium but found that the rows of seats were so close together, we had no leg-room at all, and decided that we couldn't sit there. We transferred to the bench seats where we had plenty of room. We watched Rangers win 3-0 with the fans shouting to Davie Cooper that he'd be running up 'Murder Hill' at Gullane by next week once Big Jock took over again.

'Big Jock' was famous for his arduous training methods, being an ex-army fitness expert, and he soon boosted the team's fitness and morale. His job was simple: bring back success. He added Nicky Walker from Motherwell, Stuart Munro from Alloa Athletic and brick-layer Bobby Williamson from Clydebank who soon lost a couple of stones when he started full-time training.

There was another match against an international side in November when we played Australia, again at Ibrox. We won that one 2-1 thanks to two Davie Cooper goals.

One cold January evening, Dad and I went over to watch a reserve game. I can't remember who we were playing, but what we do remember was our young winger Billy Mackay going down with a very bad injury, possibly a leg-break, in front of the Copland Road Stand. We saw Dr Alastair Ogilvie go down from the stand to offer assistance. We were told that it was a bad one and his career was finished so we went along to his testimonial match between Rangers and a New Zealand XI. We weren't too happy when he later recovered enough to sign for Hearts and had the cheek to come back and play against us!

As the Scottish winter weather gripped the country outside, in January 1984, a new event gripped the nation's football fans inside. A new indoor six-a-side tournament was launched for senior clubs, sponsored by Tennent Caledonian Breweries, known as The Tennents' Sixes. It was held at Coasters Arena in Falkirk and, each night, the highlights were shown on BBC Scotland. Unlike normal 5-a-sides, the pitch was the same size as an ice hockey rink, with high see-through walls around it which meant that play was pretty continuous. Substitutions could be made at any time, and each squad consisted of twelve players. Teams were split into two groups and, having played each other once, the top two teams in each section made up the semi-finals. Matches were fast and a lot of goals were scored. There was no offside rule but a new concept was that teams had to keep a minimum of two players in their opponents half at all times – failure to do so meant that a penalty kick was conceded. Any player shown a yellow card had to spend two minutes in the Sin Bin.

A tournament like this was just made for a player with the abilities of Davie Cooper. He dribbled past opponents, scored goals and led Rangers to victory in the very first competition. Despite being behind to Dundee in the final, Cooper inspired us to a 6-4 win. We won it again in 1989, when it was held closer to home at the S.E.C.C in Glasgow, beating Motherwell 2-1 in the final. Tennents eventually withdrew their sponsorship in 1993 and that was the last year of the event.

After losing Wallace's first match in charge, 3-0 away at Aberdeen, the team went on a twenty two game unbeaten run. We continued to progress through the League Cup to meet Celtic in the final. It would be the first League Cup Final to be shown live on television and it was to be moved to the Sunday afternoon, and played in March instead of the usual October or November.

Before that, we played Dundee in the Scottish Cup quarter final. I went up to Dens Park with three colleagues from work. We got a bit lost on the way, but we still arrived in time to see us draw 2-2 which meant a replay at Ibrox the following week. Ally McCoist took pelters from the crowd as he missed chance after chance in an ill-tempered match. Referee Alan Ferguson sent off Ian Redford and Robert Prytz – ruling them out of the cup final the following weekend. He made some unbelievably baffling decisions against us, and the players were provoked into losing their tempers. In the days long before internet forums and radio phone-ins, I wrote a letter to the football page of the Scottish Daily Express. It was printed on the following Friday:

Dear Sir,
I do not condone anyone being sent off but Ian Redford and Robert Prytz were both severely provoked by the actions of the referee. Time after time, his decisions were infuriating and always seemed to favour Dundee. The headline in The Sunday Express was 'Ferguson the Dundee Hero'. Did they mean Iain the player, or Alan the referee?

A fellow-minded supporter looked up our phone number in the directory and called me to agree with my comments.

My brother and I went to the final and stood in the Rangers end to watch Ally McCoist score a penalty just before half time and then a goal in the second half after a massive Peter McCloy kick-out. Celtic got one back and then Ally gave away a last minute penalty. 2-2 so extra time was needed. There were two lads beside us who were over from Northern Ireland and who were worried about missing the last ferry back. They agonised over the decision but decided to stay. We got another penalty which was saved but Ally scored the rebound and we won the cup. Jock Wallace had brought back success after just a couple of months in the job.

As we were at the match, we weren't aware of Big Jock's unforgettable comment on his way in. "I fancy us very strongly today. We've got the battle fever on!" And, afterwards – "When I looked at their end, there were big gaps, but there were no gaps at our end." How could he fail to rally the troops with quotes like that?

On the back of the cup win, Rangers brought out their first video, "Follow Follow" which told the Club's story from its founding up to the present date. There were some great clips that I'd never seen before as well as interviews with Willie Waddell, Willie Thornton, George Young, Jock Shaw, Jim Baxter and Jock Wallace.

In April, we beat Celtic 1-0 at Ibrox with an over-head kick from Bobby Williamson. We couldn't wait for the new season to start. With Big Jock back in charge, surely league success was coming our way.

It wasn't. We finished fourth in the league, twenty one points behind champions Aberdeen.

We'd signed Cammy Fraser and Iain Ferguson from Dundee, and Ted McMinn from Queen of the South, and we managed to hold on to the League Cup, beating Dundee United 1-0 in a pretty dull final, but Dundee again ended our Scottish Cup hopes in the fourth round. In the third round, we'd been drawn away at Morton and had to play on a pitch that resembled an ice rink. We were lucky to draw 3-3 without any serious injuries, and we won the replay 3-1.

The highlight of the season was in round two of the UEFA Cup, where we were drawn against the star-studded Inter Milan. We lost the first leg 3-0 at the San Siro, but Jock Wallace boldly announced that, for the second leg, we would attack and "go for the jugular". My brother and I sat in the back row of the upper Govan Stand. Ibrox was full and making a lot of noise. The place erupted when we scored in the first minute. Could the impossible actually happen? We kept attacking and scored three goals. Unfortunately, Inter scored one goal and beat us 4-3 on aggregate.

Our old friends, Moscow Dynamo, visited Ibrox on 13th February for a friendly match. We won 1-0 with a Craig Paterson goal.

On 29th of May 1985, a tragic event happened, across the North Sea in Brussels, that would have major ramifications for Rangers especially, as well as the whole of Scottish football. The European Cup Final was taking place between Liverpool and Juventus. As usual, we were going to watch the match which was to be shown live on BBC1. We turned on just as 'Wogan' was finishing, and he handed over live to a smiling Jimmy Hill in the football studio. As soon as the chatty link was finished, Hill's face became gravely serious as he announced that there was trouble over at the Heysel Stadium.

It was reported that, about an hour before kick-off, Liverpool fans had breached a fence which separated them from the Juventus fans who tried to move away. They pressed against a concrete wall and fans already there got crushed and the wall collapsed. Thirty nine fans died and 600 were injured, but the game still went ahead – to prevent further violence - and Juventus won 1-0.

Some Liverpool fans were arrested, found guilty of manslaughter and jailed, and UEFA made the decision to impose an indefinite ban on all English clubs from European competitions. It was described as the darkest hour in the history of UEFA competitions. Having visited the stadium myself a few years later, I would have to say that it was totally inadequate for hosting a major European final. Despite being at the tram terminus and beside a wide road at the Atomium which was ideal for car and coach parking, the stadium itself looked basic, old fashioned and far too small for a match of that importance.

The top English players could no longer compete on the European stage. How were they to get round this? We would find out in a year's time.

In 1985-86, we only managed to achieve 35 points from 36 league games. We were knocked out of the League Cup by Hibernian, the Scottish Cup by Hearts, who were going for the league and cup double under Alex MacDonald and Sandy Jardine, and we lost the first round of the UEFA Cup to the unknown Spanish side CA Osasuna.

Amazingly, the two Old Firm games at Ibrox saw us score seven goals. There was a television strike at the time of the first game so the country couldn't watch the highlights of our 3-0 win. We tore them apart that day and could easily have scored more. I met a work colleague after the game who exclaimed that "we were brilliant". I replied that we didn't even need to be, since Celtic were just rotten!

We played them again in March. Dad and I got tickets for the last two seats at the Rangers end of the front row of the Govan Stand. It was a wet, blustery afternoon and suddenly, during the first half, the fire escape door beside us just flew open with a clatter. What a fright we got! We were losing 2-0 before we got one back by Cammy Fraser. Just after half time, they scored again to make it 3-1. Ever the pessimist, Dad suggested that we should just go! Thank goodness we didn't. We got our act together as the Celtic defence started to make mistakes. We scored one, two, three to take the lead 4-3. It was utter mayhem! Unfortunately, they equalised and it finished 4-4. What a match!

SEVEN
The Souness Revolution

On Sunday 6th April, we lost a friendly 2-0 at home to Tottenham Hotspur, and the Club's owner (Lawrence Marlborough over in the USA) had seen enough. Chief Executive, David Holmes, sacked Jock Wallace, and made the most amazing appointment ever seen in Scottish football. Our family watched the Scottish News and gasped in amazement as it was announced that Graeme Souness was to become our new player-manager.

He still had contractual obligations at Sampdoria before he could be released to Ibrox and the fans and media eagerly awaited his arrival. Television reporters spoke to fans outside our next game at Clydebank to gauge their reaction. "He will bring lots of European experience" and "I'm more excited by Souness the player rather than by Souness the manager."

One abiding memory of Souness's earlier playing career was in a Scotland match against Iceland. He clattered Sigi Johnsson with a ferocious tackle that would be a straight red card these days. Johnsson had actually been a John Greig signing target a few years earlier. This type of behaviour made it easy for non-Rangers supporters at work to label him as "Dirty Souness".

Souness appointed Walter Smith as his assistant and their first task was immediate. Rangers needed to win their final game at home to Motherwell to ensure UEFA Cup qualification for the next season. We won 2-0 but our attentions were focussed elsewhere as well.

Hearts, managed by our former heroes Alex MacDonald and Sandy Jardine, were away at Dundee needing only a single point to win the league. Celtic in second place needed to win at St Mirren, hope that Hearts would lose, and turn around a goal difference of six. Radios were tuned for all the latest updates. There was no doubt who we would prefer to see as champions. Celtic started banging in the goals against a feeble St Mirren – but it was still level at Dundee.

Then came the news – "Kidd has scored" – and Ibrox erupted with loud, ecstatic cheers. But, wait a minute … it wasn't Walter Kidd the Hearts captain; it was Albert Kidd of Dundee! What? Hearts were losing, and then Albert Kidd scored another. Celtic won 5-0 and stole the league title from a devastated Hearts side. Fans sat on the Dens Park terraces and wept as their team had come so close but had blown in on the last day. Now they had to psyche themselves up to face Aberdeen in the following week's Scottish Cup Final.

Meanwhile at Ibrox, there was another important matter. On the Friday night before the Cup Final, we would play Celtic in the Glasgow Cup Final. It was announced that both would field their strongest sides so it was a sell-out. It was the Friday one week before the Boys' Brigade's Annual Inspection and Display – and, as I've mentioned, I was an officer in the Company. "I'll miss the start of the night but I'll be along later." My brother and I headed for Ibrox and we saw Rangers play with a new vigour. We took the lead twice but Celtic equalised both times. It finished 2-2 so extra time was required. To rally the players, Graeme Souness walked onto the pitch looking like a model for designer Italian clothes. We roared with approval. Ally McCoist scored his third goal and we won 3-2. Souness had 'laid down a marker' for the next season – and I was very late for the BB!

My gran from Selkirk was in hospital in Edinburgh and my mum asked me if I would drive her through to visit her on the Saturday afternoon as I wouldn't be watching the cup final. Dad went and stewarded without me. We headed east along the M8 and it seemed as if half of Lothian was travelling in the opposite direction. Tens of thousands of Hearts fans were heading for Hampden in the hope of getting something out of their season. Edinburgh itself was almost deserted, and we heard on the radio on the way back through that Aberdeen had won 3-0. Hearts must still have been suffering post traumatic stress disorder after losing the league the week before.

Dad was a member of Lenzie Golf Club – they'd appealed for new members after the war and there was a direct bus from Glasgow right to the Club House – and he played against John Greig, who was also a member there, a couple of times. One of Dad's regular group was Billy Williamson and his brother Joe. Billy played for Rangers between 1941 and 1951, under Bill Struth. He scored in the first ever League Cup Final in 1947 and in both the 1948 and 1949 Scottish Cup Finals. I met him on many occasions and he was one of those people who always had a cheery smile on his face.

During that summer, Souness got to work. He was given money to spend and he spent it on big names from England. In the past, all the top English teams had Scots players in their line-ups. The successful Leeds United team, Liverpool, Nottingham Forest, Manchester United and Chelsea all attracted players to go down and sign since the money was so much better, but in 1986, English football was in the doldrums. With no European football, it was easy for Souness to tempt the big names to Ibrox. Before that, Rangers had always had a strict wages policy. It back-fired big time in the 60s when Jim Baxter thought he should be earning a lot more than the other players. "It was like paying Frank Sinatra the same as The Alexander Brothers!" He left Ibrox and signed for lowly Sunderland because they offered him a lot more money than he could earn at Ibrox. For years, the Rangers players who had met up on international duty with their team-mates from south of the border were told all about the money available down there. Souness smashed the wages policy and signed English internationalists Chris Woods and Terry Butcher who would both be heading to Mexico that summer to play in the World Cup – as would Souness himself.

That summer, BBC Scotland screened a major documentary series about the history of Scottish Football called "Only A Game" and the episodes featured the managers, the players, the teams and the games. When one of these included a clip, recorded some time before, showing Graeme Souness being interviewed and saying that, one day, he would like to manage Rangers, everyone's ears pricked up, and we began to wonder if he already knew at that point that he was coming to Rangers or did word of that interview reach David Holmes, prompting him to talk to Souness. We never knew.

After the World Cup, the players all arrived for pre-season training and we saw them on the News as Souness put them all through their paces in the grounds of Jordanhill College. He was super fit and he led from the front. The team looked lean, fit and ready for action.

There was a pre-season match at Ibrox against Bayern Munich. Although we lost 3-1, it showed the level we were aspiring to. A fan, interviewed on television afterwards, said "Terry Butcher? Worth every penny!"

Our opening league game was to be at Hibernian, and the fans flocked through to Easter Road. Dad and I were at Ibrox to watch the Reserves as usual and there was a widespread groan when everyone heard the radio announcing "Graeme Souness has been sent off". Our hearts just sank. The game was played on a very hot afternoon and all the players were overly hyped up. There was a melee in the centre circle and Souness lashed out at Hibernian's George McCluskey (ex-Celtic) and the referee, seeing himself as the centre of attention and itching to be a big man, couldn't get the red card out of his pocket quickly enough. The SFA leapt in as well and every player except Hibernian goalie Alan Rough was given a yellow card against their disciplinary records. The media and other fans had a field day. What a start! Had it all back-fired? We later learned that David Holmes had gone home and spent the Saturday evening wondering exactly that.

We got the chance to get up and running with a midweek game at Ibrox against Falkirk, but we struggled to win that 1-0 with an Ally McCoist penalty.

Our next game was on the following Saturday and we were at home to Dundee United. At last, things began to 'click' as we raced into a two goal lead with a double from Ally McCoist. However, it didn't last the full 90 minutes. Dundee United fought back and equalised, and then, with almost the last kick of the game, scored the winner – and it was our ex-player Ian Redford (whose Ibrox career had been notable for games against Dundee United) who scored their winner. I remember trudging out of Ibrox saying to my dad that, after three games, all we had to show was a 1-0 penalty win against Falkirk. I was not impressed.

We beat Stenhousemuir 4-1 in the League Cup and then we won away at Hamilton the next week. On the Wednesday night, we just managed to scrape past East Fife in the League Cup on penalties after a 0-0 draw, and then Celtic were due at Ibrox. The game was the first ever Scottish league game to be shown live on television and it was moved to the Sunday afternoon. As Ibrox filled up, the Celtic fans were in full voice with "What a waste of money! What a waste of money!"

When the game kicked off, it immediately became aware that there was a difference with the Rangers play. They controlled the game and pushed Celtic back time and time again. Their end was a lot quieter, and you could see that there was a vast improvement in the way we were going about our business. In the second half, a sublime flick from Davie Cooper, turning Celtic defender Roy Aitken inside out, laid the ball on for an on-rushing Ian Durrant. He steadied himself and then slotted the ball into the net. Ibrox absolutely erupted (well, three sides of it did), and television commentator, Archie MacPherson, enthused, "If ever a team deserved to take the lead, it's Rangers!" We had the ball in the net again but it was ruled offside – by a whisker. Celtic were well and truly beaten and the Rangers resurgence had started.

Season ticket sales went up from 7,000 in 1986 to over 30,000 in the next few years and the Club's commercial income shot up almost ten times in just three years. Modern seating, computerised ticketing and CCTV made Ibrox a stadium that the fans were proud of, and the team on the pitch wasn't doing too badly either.

Moving into September, we beat Dundee 3-1 in the League Cup at Ibrox, and we won our next two league games, against Motherwell and Clydebank, and then lost 1-0 away at Dundee. Our next game was at home to Aberdeen – far too often our nemesis in big games. Ibrox was beginning to see the crowds coming back and the only seats my brother and I could get for this game were in the very back row of the Broomloan Road stand, such was the demand.

Souness inspired the team that day and scored our first goal in the second half with a long-range shot that Aberdeen goalie, Jim Leighton tried to claim hadn't crossed the line, looking in vain to the linesman. Meanwhile Souness ran towards the Copland Road Stand with a determined fist in the air. Ally McCoist added a second, just beating the offside trap and Leighton charged out of his goal to remonstrate with the linesman. Graceful in defeat? Not a bit of it.

In the UEFA Cup, that we had just got into at the end of the previous season, we were drawn against Finnish unknowns Ilves Tampere. A colleague, whose brother lived in Finland, told me, "If you don't beat them easily, there's something wrong." We did. 4-0 in the first leg at Ibrox with a Robert Fleck hat-trick, one of which was unselfishly laid on by Davie Cooper after he'd dribbled his way past most of the Finns. Television commentator, Arthur Montford, was ecstatic in his description of it.

An away draw at Tynecastle followed, with more trickery from Davie Cooper, and then there were wins against St Mirren, Hibernian and Falkirk. My brother and I went to Love Street accompanied by one of the international sales managers from work, my good friend, Dick Edwards (I used to send him our match programmes and he sent me up those from his team, Portsmouth. His future son-in-law played for Exeter City.) and one of our customers from The Netherlands who was a big football fan. On the September holiday Monday, my brother and I went to Love Street to try and buy the tickets, but we couldn't find a ticket office. Someone directed us to the St Mirren shop instead, telling us to go to the other side of the railway, "past the hole in the wall." We looked everywhere for a passage under the railway only to find that the Hole in the Wall was actually the name of a pub. We found the shop and got the tickets. We were quite surprised to find that what we thought would be the "home" part of the stand was full of away fans on the night. We struggled a bit but won 1-0 thanks again to Davie Cooper.

For the next day, I'd arranged a visit to Ibrox for Dick and our guest. I'd contacted Campbell Ogilvie and he'd set it up with Willie Thornton as our guide. He escorted us around Ibrox to the Blue Room, Trophy Room and tunnel area, and when we went back inside, we met Chris Woods who, although he had the day off since they'd played the night before, was there for a sponsor's event. He came over for a chat and I couldn't believe how tall he was. That was nothing as Terry Butcher also joined us and he was even taller. Dick was in his element chatting away to these top England stars, and our customer, Eric was equally impressed. I handed in bottles of 12 Years Old whisky for Campbell, Willie and Graeme Souness to thank them all.

We won our next two games and then drew two – away to Celtic and Dundee. Motherwell were up next and it was time for me to do some more corporate hospitality. Our agent from Taiwan sent his nephew, Stephen Chen, over to Scotland to learn all about Scotch whisky. He was about my age and I had the 'job' of looking after him on a Saturday. Where better to take him than a game at Ibrox. After lunch in town, I picked up my dad and we all went over to Ibrox, telling Stephen how exciting this would be, how big the crowd would be, and he'd probably see plenty of goals.

It didn't work out that way. Motherwell won 1-0 and Stephen must have been the only person in the Govan Rear Stand who stood up and cheered when they scored. How embarrassing!

Before that, we had the 'small' matter of a League Cup Final against Celtic, having beaten Dundee United 2-1 in the semi-final with Ted McMinn mesmerising their defence, and most of our own players as well, to be honest. Cup Final tickets went on sale at Ibrox during the school mid-term week and, for some inexplicable reason, there was no priority for season ticket holders. I went over to Ibrox with two colleagues at lunch-time expecting to get our tickets – but they were all sold out. Pensioners, those not at work, or holidaying school kids had bought them all up and we, who had been going to Ibrox for years, including through all the 'bad times' lost out to folk who had just 'jumped on the Souness band-wagon'! We were thoroughly disheartened at the thought of missing the match and the possibility of Souness's first trophy.

I was explaining my misery to one of our UK based salesmen that afternoon. Brian Cunningham, a Scouser Everton fan, wasn't just a salesman – he was the nearest thing to Arthur Daley I knew. He could wangle anything. "Leave it with me," he said after I'd explained that you couldn't get a ticket for love nor money. Five minutes later, he'd arranged four tickets! He'd contacted Alloa Breweries, sponsors of the Skol Cup, and sorted out some kind of deal. I was to go and meet someone from Skol in the Bellahouston Hotel after our UEFA Cup game against Boavista just before the final. I did and got four tickets for the north enclosure.

My brother and I went, with two senior boys from the Boys' Brigade, Keith Walton and Leslie Stewart, and we saw Ian Durrant and then Davie Cooper score the goals in an ill-tempered 2-1 win. Looking back, the game was fast and furious, but controlled by our midfield of Durrant, Cooper, Derek Ferguson and Ted McMinn. Celtic had Maurice Johnston sent off with three minutes to go, and then Tony Shepherd as well – before referee David Syme changed his mind! Syme thought that Shepherd had struck him on the back of the head but the players showed that, in fact, someone in the crowd had thrown an object at him. A fracas developed and Celtic's manager, Davie Hay even went on to the pitch to remonstrate with the referee. A senior Police officer had to have words with him. This was the first time that we heard Celtic come out with the word "aggrieved" in their post-match comments. In our post-match celebrations, Leslie was up on Keith's shoulders waving a huge Union Jack. First trophy to Graeme Souness – we were on the way back!

On 22nd November, Chris Woods let in a goal to Aberdeen at Pittodrie as we lost 1-0. We didn't know it at the time, but he wouldn't let in another domestic goal until the end of January. He was to break the record for the longest run of minutes without letting in a goal. Before that, Souness decided that our defence wasn't quite the finished article and needed a bit of strengthening up. He did that by signing another top English player – Graham Roberts. He made his debut in a 2-0 home win against Dundee United at Christmas, looking immediately as if he knew what he was doing, and he fitted straight into the team.

Celtic visited Ibrox for the traditional New Year game and there was a blizzard. Sleet and snow fell as Souness imposed his superiority on the Celtic midfield. He strutted about with pomp and purpose and Celtic just couldn't get the ball off him. He looked up and sprayed perfect passes out to Davie Cooper who looked altogether like a new player. Robert Fleck scored and then Celtic goalie, Pat Bonner, reached up to clutch a Cooper cross but, thanks to the snow, he dropped it right at Ally McCoist's feet. 2-0 and game over.

We were knocked out of the UEFA Cup by Borussia Monchengladbach on away goals, but in the league, we continued winning – against Motherwell, Clydebank, Hamilton Academical – and a draw with Aberdeen without conceding a goal. Next up was a simple Scottish Cup tie against Hamilton Accies at Ibrox. We had just beaten them and, by now, were imposing our presence in the league. The team had scored ten goals without reply in January. All was going well. The scoreboard flashed up the news that Chris Woods had beaten the record of 1,196 minutes without letting in a goal with the score at 0-0 and then, the unthinkable happened. Hamilton's Adrian Sprott scored the only goal of the match. The run was over and Rangers were out of the cup. Try as they might, Rangers just couldn't score. As we slowly trudged out of Ibrox at the end, Dad commented that it was like a funeral march all around us. The newspapers summed it up the next day when they called it a "humiliation". The awful joke going round was, "What do you call the new Japanese Rangers player?" "Cannae-whack-an-Accie!"

Fans were likening it to the day of infamy at Berwick ten years earlier, when the Wee Rangers had knocked the Big Rangers out of the cup in the third round. As in 1967, when we put five past Hearts the following week, we did the same in 1987. We then won six out of the next seven matches until losing 3-1 at Parkhead – Celtic's only win against us out of five games that season. We then beat Dundee, Clydebank and Hearts – and the championship was within touching distance.

If we won our second last game, away at Aberdeen (always a difficult venue for us), we would win the league. My brother and I got our tickets without difficulty, and we headed north. By the day of the game, the demand for tickets was immense. Lots of Aberdeen fans had sold 'home end' tickets to Rangers fans and there seemed to be as many fans outside the stadium as were inside. We sat in the beach end and watched as the teams locked horns. Once again, as we assumed at the time, Graeme Souness got caught up in the occasion and got sent off in the first half. At Pittodrie of all places, we would be up against it, but the team persevered. We won a free kick outside their box and Davie Cooper took it. Terry Butcher bulleted his header into the Aberdeen goal and the place erupted. Were there actually any Aberdeen fans there? All round the ground were Rangers fans celebrating.

Aberdeen caused a bit of tension by equalising but, before our game finished, word came through that Falkirk had beaten Celtic at Parkhead so our own score didn't actually matter – we were champions. The game finished 1-1 and, as soon as the final whistle sounded, the Rangers fans charged onto the pitch to hail their heroes. The fans waiting outside the ground were let in, too, and the whole place was a sea of red, white and blue. The championship had been won after a nine year absence. Souness had proved David Holmes correct. As the celebrations continued, we met Robert Ellis from my office who had a big chunk of Pittodrie turf in his hand!

Eventually, we moved outside and back towards the car. We saw a policeman stop a fan who was carrying a bit of a seat with him. "That belongs to Pittodrie Stadium!" he said sternly as he took it from him and sent him on his way. They couldn't get the Rangers fans onto the road and out of Aberdeen fast enough. The party continued all the way down the road. Horns tooted and flags waved, and when we were brought to a halt on the main road by the sheer volume of traffic, fans got out of their cars and started sharing out cans of beer. We had decided to stop in Forfar for a Chinese meal on the way down and we didn't get back home until Sportscene was about to start. I set the video recorder and headed out to the pub for a proper celebration, with my Rangers top on – just to rub it in to a guy who'd gone there with a Celtic top on the evening after they'd won a month before. Revenge was sweet!

The following Saturday, we were to be at home to St Mirren (a week before their Scottish Cup win) and 43,510 fans were there to party –

many in fancy dress. We even saw fans dressed as bears. There might have been a few Saints fans there, but they were in a very small minority. Robert Fleck scored a volley in the opening minutes, and Dad said his usual pessimistic remark, "That'll be the only goal of the game." Obviously we discounted this as we always did, but on this occasion, he was actually correct. Never mind, the League trophy was presented and paraded and Ibrox was in full song. Well, when I say full, there was one exception. The day before, I'd developed a bad throat infection and my voice dropped three or four octaves before drying up altogether. I didn't feel ill or anything, but I couldn't join in the community singing or shouting. Of all the times for that to happen …

Due to Souness's fairly instant success, the crowds came back to Ibrox and it was decided to do away with the Rover Season Tickets and allocate everyone who had, or was now buying, a season ticket, with a fixed seat. When the renewal letters came out, we were asked to select a section of the stadium where we wanted to sit, as well as an alternative second choice. Dad and I wanted to have seats in the Govan Stand as we considered that it had the best view but, since the rear was a bit dearer, we opted for the front. Thinking that the centre areas would be the most popular, we asked for seats in what was then the orange section – one away from the middle towards the Copland Road end (GF6). We got what we wanted and got two seats in the back row right in line with the penalty area, and under cover.

In the early summer, I got the chance to be on the pitch at Hampden when a group of us went to see Genesis perform live. The pitch was covered by a strong tarpaulin surface that was pegged down in big sheets. We stood where the centre circle was and the stage was in front of the main stand. At the end, I was able to bend down and pluck some blades of grass from between the tarpaulins. To this day, I still have some of these blades of grass from the centre circle at Hampden in an envelope at home. I realise that it's not like the patches of turf that were removed from Wembley in 1977, and which are still on many people's lawns, but it's my own souvenir.

Also that summer, I got my first chance to play on a "proper" pitch. Every June, Elgin City's Boroughbriggs stadium hosted the Malt Whisky 5-a-side Competition. The pitch was converted into two smaller pitches across the way, and the teams played in four groups, with the winners going into semi-finals and then a final. It was decided that Whyte & Mackay would enter a team to represent one of our distilleries, Dalmore. We had to leave Glasgow very early on the Saturday morning and we stopped in Pitlochry for juice, coffee and bacon rolls before driving on up to Elgin in time for the start. We got to change in their dressing rooms and there was a reasonable crowd of spectators. I played in goal, and on a warm summer day, we progressed with our matches, not letting in a single goal, and reaching the semi-final. It finished 0-0 so it was to be decided on penalties. I saved the first two, but we lost 3-2. We got changed and headed home, stopping in Aviemore for a "post-match feast" and a few refreshments.

The following year, we went up again, got to the semi-final and lost 1-0. I twisted my knee and it was quite sore. By the time we got back to Glasgow, having sat for a couple of hours, I could hardly stand when I got out of the car. The third year, I played outfield and we did terribly (not because of me, I hasten to add). That was the day of the Under-16 World Cup Final at Hampden, and we stayed in Elgin to watch Scotland lose the final to Saudi Arabia. It was very late by the time we got back to Glasgow.

Dad and I had taken a wander over to Hampden a couple of Saturdays earlier to see the tournament's opening and we saw the great Pele walking round the track before the game and signing autographs. Unfortunately, we were up in the main stand and couldn't go down to meet him. The boys who were getting his autograph all looked far too young to have seen him play, and we guessed that their dads had sent them forward.

EIGHT
Success With Souness

Souness continued to strengthen the squad with big names coming in, and others who were 'surplus to requirements' being sold. The front door at Ibrox was now being likened to a revolving door. Mark Falco, Avi Cohen and John McGregor arrived, and, as the season progressed, were joined by Richard Gough, Ray Wilkins, Trevor Francis, John Brown, Mark Walters and Jan Bartram. All this chopping and changing upset the rhythm of the team and we got off to a poor start – drawing one and losing three of our opening five games, including a 1-0 reverse at Parkhead when Souness was once again sent off.

We did win our first two League Cup rounds and, when September started, we seemed to get back on track winning all our league games, our League Cup quarter and semi-finals as well as making our first appearance in the European Cup for nine years. The first round draw could hardly have been more difficult when we were up against Dynamo Kiev, who were one of the favourites for the competition. We lost the first leg away 1-0 in front of 100,000 fans, but the second leg was one of the great Ibrox nights. The atmosphere was electric as a crowd of 44,500 came in to see something unusual. Knowing that the Ukrainians preferred to play up the wings, Souness got the ground staff to narrow the width of the Ibrox pitch to the absolute minimum – all within the rules despite the Kiev protests. The sheer noise that greeted the teams when they walked out lifted Rangers and frightened Dynamo. Rangers pressed forward looking for an early goal. Their goalkeeper made a hash of a throw out and the ball went straight to Ally McCoist who rolled it to Mark Falco who scored easily. The fans were ecstatic and when Ally scored a header in the second half, it was absolute bedlam. We held on to win 2-1 on aggregate and the rest of Europe no knew that Ibrox would not be an easy place to visit.

We dropped league points at Hearts and Dundee United in October before Celtic came to Ibrox. The night before, I was at a party at Dundee and drove back to Glasgow on the Saturday morning feeling rather 'the worse for wear'. After a very small lunch, I picked up Leslie Stewart and headed to the game. Dad was away somewhere for the weekend. The pre-match atmosphere was electric, some would say almost poisonous, and it wasn't long before all hell broke loose. Chris Woods collected an easy catch but the Celtic striker, Frank McAvennie, barged right into him when he was holding the ball. Woods retaliated and shoved McAvennie away. Graham Roberts and Terry Butcher rushed to Woods's assistance and Roberts flattened McAvennie. The referee charged in and separated the players before showing McAvennie a straight red card. He then gave a shocked Woods a straight red as well, and yellow cards to Roberts and Butcher. With no substitute goal-keeper, Woods removed his jersey and handed it to Roberts before jogging off the pitch.

Roberts took time to settle into his new role, Celtic scored twice and Terry Butcher was also shown a second yellow card for a bad tackle so he, too, was sent off. We managed to get to half time just two behind, with the Celtic fans in full voice, shouting, "We want seven!" We also realised that Woods and Butcher would be suspended for the following week's cup final against Aberdeen.

Souness reshuffled the team and brought Avi Cohen and John McGregor into the defence. Avi Cohen was immense in the second half. Instead of lunging into tackles, he held back, so that, instead of getting past him and in on goal, the Celtic forwards were held back and forced to re-think what they were trying to do. This knocked them off their stride. We still managed to push forward and, amazingly, Ally McCoist got a goal back. Richard Gough got pushed forward from defence and the game continued at a frenetic pace. Time was running out when Ian Durrant broke forward on the right wing. He sent a dangerous cross into the box and the Celtic players flapped about. Gough got his foot to the ball and scored. To say, once again, that Ibrox erupted would be an under-statement. Television highlights would show that the noise distorted the sound levels and Terry Butcher, sitting down in the dressing room, said he heard the loudest noise he'd ever known. Celtic were shell-shocked. We weren't finished. Graham Roberts got control of the ball and, to waste time to see out the game, famously started conducting the rapturous Rangers 'choir' as we 'raised the roof'.

The game finished 2-2 but, in the aftermath, McAvennie, Woods, Roberts and Butcher all found themselves up in court to answer charges of breach of the peace – as if the SFA suspensions weren't enough. It was seen as a test case to teach the fans a lesson. If the players could be charged for behaviour at a match, it was a severe warning for the fans of both sides. The Strathclyde Assistant Chief Constable gave evidence and said that the players' behaviour could have caused a pitch invasion. The Sheriff found Woods and Butcher guilty and fined them £500 and £250 respectively. McAvennie was astonishingly found not guilty while the case against Roberts was not proven.

On the Wednesday after the game, Rangers beat Gornik Zabrze 3-1 in the first leg of the European Cup second round, before preparing for the League Cup final. Some great scheduling by the Scottish League there – we could have had an away game with a lot of travelling days before a national cup final. As it was, we were already hampered by being without our regular goalkeeper and our captain.

On a personal note, I had been finding that my eyesight was not so good for distance vision, and I got my first ever pair of spectacles on that Friday. When I got to Hampden, I was standing in the Rangers end near the south corner, and I couldn't believe how clear everything now was. I was just worried that my spectacles might fly off when I was celebrating a goal.

The match turned out to be one of the best cup finals ever. Aberdeen scored first but we got an equaliser from a famous Davie Cooper free-kick. The Aberdeen defensive wall lined up and with my line of vision, I saw Cooper blast the ball right past the wall and into the goal. Jim Leighton was utterly helpless as the ball zoomed past him. Before half-time, Ian Durrant ran into their penalty area and slotted the ball under Leighton. 2-1. In the second half, Aberdeen kept pressing and scored twice to put them 3-2 ahead. With minutes to go, a long ball from captain for the day, Graham Roberts was knocked down by Ian Durrant to Robert Fleck who scored the equaliser. In the closing moments, both sides came close to scoring but it finished 3-3. No goals were scored in extra time and so it would be the first Scottish final to be decided on penalty kicks. We won the toss and the kicks would be taken at our end.

Cooper scored, McCoist scored, Fleck scored. Trevor Francis took the next one – with no run-up. What was he doing? He scored. Despite all the racket we made to try and put them off, Aberdeen kept scoring – until Peter Douglas's penalty clipped the top of the bar. Ian Durrant walked forward to line up to take the crucial kick. He ran up and scored. We all went crazy! He had to wait for the rest of the team to run from the half-way line to jump all over him to celebrate. What an incredible final. The SFL decided to award Aberdeen a consolation prize to reward them for their contribution to such a memorable match.

The next main thing that happened was that Terry Butcher broke his leg during a home league game against Aberdeen in November so that was the end of his season. We dropped a lot of silly points that, with him, we would have probably expected to get so we ended up losing the league, finishing third behind Celtic and Hearts, and we got knocked out of the Scottish Cup away at Dunfermline.

The time when English teams were banned from European football, coincided with a period of domestic success for Everton which they have not been able to recapture in the years since, so they were denied the opportunity of competing in the lucrative European Cup which the other clubs, known regularly as the "Top Four", were subsequently able to do with great regularity. The rewards for winning the English league at that time look like pocket money compared with the tens of millions that are available now. Everton were open to offers to boost their bank balance by playing invitation games wherever and whenever they were invited. In 1987, they were invited to participate in the Dubai Champions Cup, where they would play against the Scottish Champions, Rangers, in a match that was dubbed the unofficial British Championship. Held in a stadium that could seat 50,000, it attracted a crowd of just 8,000 – and the vocal majority of them were Rangers fans.

Everton led 2-0 through goals from Dave Watson and Kevin Sheedy before Ian Durrant scored twice in the last ten minutes to level it at 2-2. There was no extra time, so it went straight to penalties. Rangers won the shoot-out 8-7, and captain Graham Roberts was presented with the cup. Unofficial Champions of Britain – and a healthy pay-day as well. Not a bad day's work – but it was not to be repeated.

Over the Christmas period, our new signing from Aston Villa, Mark Walters played his first couple of matches away at Tynecastle and Parkhead. He was subjected to the most disgusting racial abuse that should have seen both clubs severely punished – but that didn't happen. Walters was black, and the Hearts fans threw bananas at him whenever he went to take a corner kick. Utterly revolting – but nothing compared to what happened at the New Year game at Parkhead. It was even reported (although this might be apocryphal) that every banana in every store for a square mile had been bought by Celtic fans, and he was showered with them when he was taking corners. Archie MacPherson described it as sickening. Walters must have wondered what he'd walked into.

In March, we lost 3-2 on aggregate to Steaua Bucharest so that was the end of our European Cup dream. Three rounds - and all in Eastern Europe. At that time, a lot of the away games were beamed back to Ibrox and we paid to sit and watch them being shown on a big screen (the side of a big van). Due to the time difference, they were on during the afternoons so a few of us took time off work to go and see them.

After doing so well in Souness's first season, the loss of Terry Butcher in the second season had been too much, but after his time out, he was fit and raring to go for the start of 1988-89, and what a start …

The revolving door was in action again. We welcomed Kevin Drinkell and Gary Stevens but said farewell to Avi Cohen, Trevor Francis, Graham Roberts and Jimmy Phillips.

The next player to receive a testimonial to reward his long service was Davie Cooper. We played Bordeaux at a packed Ibrox on the 9th of August, also by way of a pre-season warm-up game. We won 3-1 with goals from Terry Butcher, Kevin Drinkell and Ally McCoist.

Our opening league game was away at Hamilton Academical and Gary Stevens scored the first goal in a 2-0 win. Little did he realise how historically significant that goal would turn out to be. We beat Clyde in the League Cup, and drew our next game with Hibernian 0-0 before a 6-0 spree against Clydebank in the cup.

At the start of this season, a new publication hit the streets. A Rangers fanzine called 'Follow Follow' was launched with a picture of Mark Walters on the cover and the headline 'Blue Is The Only Colour That Matters'.

Walters was about to get into his stride and wreak his revenge on Celtic when they came to Ibrox on 27th August – a day that nobody who was there will ever forget. As the teams ran onto the pitch, John Brown and Ian Ferguson fired up the fans and encouraged us to make some real noise. 42,858 saw Celtic score an early goal after a rebound off our post, in the rain – but the sun was just about to come out.

Undeterred by this early set-back, Rangers began the fight-back with a goal from Ally McCoist after a John Brown shot was blocked. Just before half time, a throw in from Gary Stevens was headed out towards Ray Wilkins. He lined up, and wham! The ball hit the net for one of the greatest goals ever seen at Ibrox. In the second half, Celtic 'goalie' Ian Andrews proved to be as adept as Julie Andrews as a header from McCoist, a bullet header from Kevin Drinkell and a shot from Mark Walters made it 5-1. We were in absolute dreamland. This was like nothing we had ever seen. There was still plenty of time to go, and we urged the team to go on and score more to really rub it in, but Graeme Souness brought himself on and decided to 'showboat' and stop Celtic getting the ball instead of pushing for more goals. The players who were serious Rangers fans have regretted it ever since as we have never had a better opportunity to really embarrass them.

My abiding memory was the time I saw the biggest smile on my dad's face and the only time I ever remember him singing at a game. It was Celtic's centenary year and Ibrox was resonating to the sounds of "Happy Birthday to you" as we basked in the celebrations. It was one of the best days ever to be a Rangers fan. The cover of Follow Follow's second edition summed it up perfectly, "Gubbed!"

We then went on a good run with wins against Dundee in the League Cup, Motherwell in the league and Katowice at home in the UEFA Cup.

Then I was able to enjoy a real treat. Whyte & Mackay were involved in sponsorship of sporting events – boxing, sailing, golf and football. They sponsored Scotland's Word Cup qualifying matches and these were occasions when customers could be given match hospitality. On the 14th September, Scotland were due to play Norway in Oslo, and that was one of the countries that I dealt with. We had a sales manager who went on lots of international trips and, when he was away, I was his office contact. I kept him up to date with anything and dealt with any enquiries that came in. He decided that it would be a good idea to invite all our Norwegian customers (the cruise lines, ferries, airlines, bars etc.) to hospitality and then go to the game, so I got invited to go and 'help' him. We flew out to Oslo with the Scotland squads, management, press and other sponsors. We met up at Glasgow Airport and Bill Wilson, the SFA's Assistant Secretary gave us our tickets and boarding passes. When we arrived in Norway on the Monday, we were taken by coach to a great hotel in Holmenkollen which had an area for the players to train beside it.

On the Tuesday morning, we visited a few customers. We went to the office of SAS (Scandinavian Air Services) and our contact there had a fridge in his office so we were given an ice-cold beer. We had lunch near the Viking Museum and I got a taste of reindeer. We then went to see the Under-21 match at Drammen before heading into the city for our dinner. Walter Smith and Alex Smith were outside the hotel, and heading into town as well, so we offered them seats in our people-carrier taxi. Unfortunately, the taxi they'd booked arrived so they had to decline. We had a very good dinner before 'hitting' The Scotsman bar which was packed with travelling fans.

On the Wednesday, we met a few more customers and before the match, we hosted a buffet reception across the road from the stadium before going over to watch the match. We had to sit in with the Norway fans, which wasn't a problem, and we had a bottle of Scotch and lots of small metal tumblers to keep us refreshed. Paul McStay scored first but Norway equalised. I was sitting at the end of the row and the Norwegian fan beside me was kidding me on about the score. Then Roy Aitken got taken off, and Ian Durrant came on – which had me telling them that we could only improve now. We did and Maurice Johnston scored the winner.

After the match, the coaches took us back to the airport for the flight home. I even had to tell Roy Aitken that he was picking up the wrong brand of Scotch whisky in the Duty Free Shop! I'd bought ten match programmes and I went to ask Andy Roxburgh if it would be alright for the squad to sign them for the boys in The Boys' Brigade. This was no problem and he asked Tommy Craig to arrange this for me.

Back in my seat, we were sitting in the row in front of Rangers director, Freddie Fletcher, and Celtic Chairman, Jack McGinn. They had ordered a rather large bottle of champagne and shared it with us. We got chatting and Freddie Fletcher was moaning about Rangers always having to go to Eastern Europe to play European matches. We were back in Glasgow in no time, but the plane landed with a right bump. We saw in the newspaper the next morning that the plane had burst a tyre when it landed!

Rangers good run continued. We beat Hearts in the league and also in the League Cup semi-final. I missed that match because I was in Yugoslavia (before it split up) on a short holiday. I had to place a call home, by asking the receptionist for a line, and then phoning from a kiosk. There was a simple question for my mum, "What was the score and who do we play in the final?" The reply was "3-0 and Aberdeen."

We continued winning – against St Mirren, Dundee United and Dundee before going over to Katowice to beat them 4-2 to progress to the next round. On the 8th of October, we were up at Pittodrie, and we'd signed a 'former tormentor' Neale Cooper, from Aston Villa (who used to play for Aberdeen). He scored on his debut – but the match was to be remembered for something else. The Aberdeen midfielder and thug, Neil Simpson, fouled - or rather assaulted - our midfield genius Ian Durrant with one of the worst, and as a photographs later proved, deliberate fouls ever seen. Durrant had to be carried from the field while Simpson only received a yellow card for his thuggery. He was later rewarded by being appointed as an SFA Youth Coach!

Twenty-one year old Durrant was one of the brightest prospects in the country, but he would be out of the game for three years and would have to endure a host of operations to re-build his knee. The match was particularly bad-tempered, and we lost 2-1, but we would get our revenge two weeks later in the League Cup Final.

The players set out to win it for Durrant and duly did so. Ally McCoist scored twice and Ian Ferguson once as we won 3-2 in front of a crowd of 72,122.

In November, there was a significant development in the Rangers story. David Murray, a friend of Graeme Souness, who had accumulated a vast fortune from his Murray International Metals company, bought Rangers from Lawrence Marlborough. Over the next few years, he would prove to have very deep pockets as Rangers, with his personal backing, went on to dominate Scottish football.

We were knocked out of the UEFA Cup by Cologne, 3-1 on aggregate, but our league form continued. Old 'war horse' Andy Gray, a lifelong Rangers fan, was signed from West Bromwich Albion to boost our attack. We beat Celtic at Ibrox in the New Year game 4-1 again after giving them a goal of a start, and we won at Parkhead for the first time in eight years. Kevin Drinkell scored first, and then Ian Ferguson hit an unstoppable free kick that Pat Bonner couldn't hold. Ally McCoist claimed to have got a touch to it before it crossed the line, but it was awarded to Ferguson. Celtic scored and were also awarded a penalty after the ball hit a divot, bounced up and hit Richard Gough's hand with no Celtic player anywhere near him. Fortunately, Joe Miller blasted it over the bar!

Despite having to play a couple of replays, we had reached the Scottish Cup semi-final which was to be played at Parkhead against St Johnstone. A friend from Perth, Gordon Smith, came down to go to the match with me. I also gave a lift to two other friends, Gordon McKeeve and Ruaridh McIntyre. On the way in, we met another friend, Gordon Munro, and we had to suggest to Ruaridh that he would have to change his name to keep the coincidence going. It was a pretty poor 0-0 draw so there would need to be yet another replay, but when we got back to the car, we heard the news of what was to become the Hillsborough Disaster. A big crowd of us, with wives and girlfriends went out to Café India that evening, and all the conversation was about the awful tragedy that afternoon. As Rangers fans, we knew only too well what this meant for the club, the families and the people of Liverpool.

We beat St Johnstone 4-0 in the replay on the Tuesday night to set up a final clash with Celtic.

Hearts came to Ibrox on 29th April and a win would clinch the title. We went about our business in a professional manner and won 4-0 with doubles from Kevin Drinkell and Mel Sterland.

With the championship and League Cup in the Trophy Room, Celtic were desperate to stop us completing the Treble. For the final, we would be without the influential Ray Wilkins and Derek Ferguson in midfield, while Celtic were boosted by the announcement that they would be re-signing striker Maurice Johnston.

I had other things to worry about. I wasn't allocated a ticket for the final. We weren't getting asked to be stewards any more since that had become a far more organised and professional business, so where could I turn? On the Thursday before the match, my then girlfriend Norma and I went to The Overflow bar at Yorkhill. Someone we knew lived near there and said there was a guy who often went in there who might have tickets. It all sounded a bit vague but, sure enough, the guy was there and he did have some tickets. He sold me one, once I'd explained that I couldn't get one anywhere, so I was sorted.

The match was a farce, and was decided by two crazy decisions. Celtic were somehow allowed to take a throw-in that had been clearly given as ours. Roy Aitken threw the ball towards Joe Miller but international full-back Gary Stevens appeared to have it covered, but a slack pass-back let Miller nip in to score. It would obviously be disallowed ... but it wasn't!

As the match wore on, we got a corner and it was played into the Celtic area. Pat Bonner bumped into his own defender and the ball broke to Terry Butcher who hit it into the open net. We all celebrated, as did the players ... but the goal was disallowed for a foul on Bonner! Who was it that said that all the officials are biased and never give any decision to Celtic?

With time running out, Celtic got a free kick. To prevent us having any chance of getting the ball, Roy Aitken simply ran up and blasted it into the crowd. Time up and they stole the cup, denying us the Treble. Their fans celebrated by chanting about "Mo, Mo, Super Mo!" That was going to come back and haunt them big time!

During the close season, the revolving door kept going. We sold Davie Cooper to Motherwell, Mel Sterland to Leeds United, Jimmy Nicholl to Dunfermline and Davie Kirkwood to Hearts. In came Trevor Steven from Everton, but the biggest signing sensation was Maurice Johnston. Everyone thought he had signed for Celtic – he was paraded to the media in a Celtic top – but he hadn't actually put pen to paper. There was still some tax detail to be sorted out. Graeme Souness and our new owner, David Murray, spoke to Johnston and his agent, dealt with the tax, and signed him. Not only was Johnston a Celtic player with history against us, he was a high profile Roman Catholic. When appointed, Souness had said he would sign Catholics but we'd heard all that before. Willie Waddell had said this years ago, and we expected it to be an unknown South American or Italian – not a high profile, West of Scotland, Celtic fan! The media went haywire and Rangers fans were seen burning season tickets and scarves outside Ibrox. The Celtic fans went crazy, describing Johnston as a "turn-coat" or "Judas".

I was away at Boys' Brigade Summer Camp when he signed so I missed most of the furore. When I spoke to Norma on the phone, she told me that it was all over the front page of The Sun. I chose to disbelieve this, knowing The Sun's propensity for exaggeration or making up a story out of nothing. I said I'd wait until the more reliable newspapers said so. The next day, they did. Maurice Johnston was a Rangers player. Apparently, he turned up at the Rangers' training camp and was given a warm welcome from Ally McCoist and Ian Durrant – by getting a table for one, in the corner, at meal-times!

We got off to a bad start in the league, losing our opening two games. On day one, at home to St Mirren, their striker Kenny McDowall scored the only goal after clattering into Chris Woods and the foul not being given. We then lost at Hibernian, and our third game was away at Parkhead. Every time Johnston got the ball, he was booed incessantly.

He missed a few chances but Terry Butcher scored a great header before they equalised. After three games, we had one point.

Our next game was at home to Aberdeen. Johnston scored the winner and began to win over the Rangers fans, but we drew the next two games. We were winning in the League Cup and progressed to our third final in a row against Aberdeen, scoring 14 goals and conceding only 1 on the way.

In the first round of the European Cup, we drew German giants, Bayern Munich. I had to go down to London to an international trade fair, but got a flight back up in time to get to Ibrox. I sat behind the Broomloan Road goal and watched us lose 3-1. We drew the away leg 0-0 and were knocked out.

Back in the league, Johnston scored the winner against Hearts, as well as goals against Dundee United and Hibernian. On 4th November, Celtic came to Ibrox. Again, Johnston was booed by the Celtic fans but he had the last laugh. In the final minute, their defender Chris Morris made a mess of a clearance and the ball went straight to Johnston at the edge of the area. He hit a low shot straight into the net and Ibrox went wild. He ran off the pitch straight to the Rangers fans, and the other players joined in the celebration. He got a yellow card for his troubles – becoming the only person to get one for celebrating goals for both sides against each other.

Our League Cup run of success finally ended as Aberdeen won the final 2-1, but we started to find form in the league, only losing one game until the end of March. At the end of November, Ray Wilkins' contract was coming to an end and he chose to move back to London for family reasons. As he left a fogbound Ibrox pitch at the end of the game against Dunfermline, he had to fight back the tears as the whole stadium gave him a standing ovation. Midfielder Nigel Spackman, another English player, moved the opposite way, from Queen's Park Rangers, and he scored the winner in the New Year game at Parkhead, becoming an instant hero.

There were five wins and four draws before we out-played Celtic at Ibrox, winning comfortably 3-0, and Maurice Johnston scored one of the goals. We drew at Aberdeen and then beat Motherwell, and we could win the title the following week at Dundee United.

I got a ticket for Tannadice, but there was a Boys' Brigade sponsored walk that morning from Bowling to Partick along part of the Clyde Walkway. I set off and walked very quickly becoming one of the first to finish. Norma picked me up and we drove straight up to Dundee. We stopped on the way so that I could change into my Rangers top, and we got sandwiches for lunch. She dropped me near the ground and went shopping with a school-friend who lived in Dundee. I watched as Trevor Steven scored the only goal – a header that I was right in line with – and the league was won. Terry Butcher and the team all paraded about the pitch, and the trophy was presented the following week after our home win against Dunfermline.

The Scottish Cup continued to elude us as we were knocked out in the fourth round at Parkhead.

Many World Class, international superstars have graced the Ibrox turf over the years and fans have their own special memories of players such as Johan Cruyff, Ferenc Puskas, Franz Beckenbauer, Ronaldhino, Mario Kempes, Lionel Messi and Brian Laudrup - but none of these could get anywhere near the fame of the man who appeared at Ibrox in June 1990. These might have been great names in the footballing world but they couldn't compare with the legendary Frank Sinatra.

He might have been past his best, and the show might have been over-priced and a bit shambolic but it was one of the most memorable events ever to take place at our stadium. Considered by many to be the greatest singer and entertainer in the world, he was booked to come to Ibrox. Tickets were expensive (some at £60) and it was decided to use the Govan Stand with its capacity of 11,000 fans. For some reason, there were delays getting in, queues began to build up, and thousands were still outside when the show started. Refunds were given to disappointed fans, who had queued for hours, but that was little compensation.

At the age of seventy-four and after decades in show-business, 'Old Blue Eyes' was moved to tears. He performed on a specially built stage in the middle of the pitch but that was too far from the audience. He sang all the big hits and then decided to leave the stage and walk to the track in front of the seats, shaking hands with many of the fans. Apparently, back at his hotel afterwards, he said that in all his time in show-business, he had never been so moved by anything in his life before. Yes, Frank, playing at Ibrox can do that to a person!

He wrote to Graeme Souness to say he had been overwhelmed by reception from the people of Glasgow, and the warmth of the Ibrox crowd was a memory he would always cherish.

For the start of the new season, Souness brought in striker Mark Hateley, a player I knew a lot about as Dick Edwards told me all about his days at Portsmouth. For some reason, he wasn't an instant hit with a lot of the fans as they perceived that he was keeping goal-scoring hero Ally McCoist out of the team. In fact, it was Maurice Johnston who was keeping him out. McCoist spent a lot of time on the bench, and soon gained the nickname, "The Judge". Pieter Huistra also arrived from the Netherlands as did 'hard-man' Terry Hurlock from Millwall.

There were two wins and a draw before Celtic came to Ibrox. We absolutely out-played them but it finished 1-1. Terry Hurlock scored our goal with a hard, low shot. We progressed through the League Cup, as usual, but met Aberdeen in the semi-final. A Trevor Steven goal won the match.

In the first round of the European Cup, we met our old 'whipping boys' Valetta of Malta. We won 4-0 away and 8-0 at home. During the Ibrox game, we were awarded a penalty and to loud cheers, goalkeeper Chris Woods ran up the field to take it, since he had never scored before and the game was well won by then. He ran up ... and missed it. So much for that! In the next round, we lost 4-1 on aggregate to Red Star Belgrade.

We also signed Oleg Kuznetzov from Dynamo Kiev, but in his first match, away at St Johnstone, he injured his knee, and would be out for months.

We won the League Cup with a 2-1 win over Celtic after extra time with goals from Mark Walters and Richard Gough.

We then went right through to March only losing one game, with goals regularly coming from Johnston, Hateley and McCoist as well as Walters and Steven. Terry Butcher had been sold to Coventry City following a disagreement with Graeme Souness after he was dropped for a game against Dundee United – which we lost. Captain or not, there was only going to be one winner in that argument!

Celtic knocked us out of the Scottish Cup again in March, and in April, Graeme Souness announced that he would be leaving Ibrox to become manager at Liverpool. Owner David Murray decided that he should be told to leave immediately, which he did, and his assistant Walter Smith was appointed as manager. We wondered if we would still be able to attract the big names that Souness had been able to attract, especially as UEFA were introducing a new rule restricting to three the number of 'foreign' players in European competition. English players would all count as being 'foreign'.

One very happy occasion in April 1991 was the return to playing of Ian Durrant for a reserve game against Hibernian, and a crowd of 47,453 packed into Ibrox to see him make his comeback. Fans were still coming in when the game had started and they had to open up more stands to accommodate everyone.

NINE
Walter: The Cup, The Treble and The Champions League

With the league title still 'in the balance', we beat St Mirren and Dundee United both by 1-0 and could win the championship the following week at Motherwell. I headed off to Fir Park full of expectation – but Motherwell had other ideas. They beat us 3-0 and we even missed a penalty. There was only one game to go – at home to Aberdeen – who were now ahead of us on goal difference and only needed to draw to win the league. Over the years, our results against them had been very varied with them sometimes winning or drawing at Ibrox, and us sometimes winning or drawing at Pittodrie. It was too close to call. Saturday couldn't come fast enough and the fans were at fever pitch.

On the Wednesday before the game, Dad and his friend Bob Kyle went to Kirkintilloch Rob Roy's ground to watch our reserves. Standing beside them on the terracing were Walter Smith and his new assistant manager, Archie Knox, looking quite relaxed despite all the unbearable tension that was gripping the Club. Dad told him, "You had better win on Saturday." Walter calmly said they would do their best.

As the crowds approached Ibrox, nerves were at breaking point. The match started with Aberdeen playing well and they missed a succession of good chances. The Rangers team was ravaged by injury with players playing out of position to make up the numbers. Just before half time, Mark Walter swung over a fantastic cross, and Mark Hateley rose to bullet a header into the goal. We went absolutely wild. We'd got our noses in front but there was still a long way to go. In the second half, play swung from end to end and then Aberdeen goalkeeper, Michael Watt couldn't hold a Maurice Johnston shot. He spilled the ball and Hateley nipped in to score the second. Aberdeen were deflated and had no answer. With the team stretched, Walter Smith had rallied them to victory and his first objective – to make sure we won the league – was achieved, and we now had three in a row.

Norma and I got married that year – during the close-season of course – and we got a presentation at the Boys' Brigade Inspection from the boys and their parents. The minister commented that "With Rangers winning the league and Gordon getting married, he couldn't really be happier!"

Walter Smith set about re-structuring the team with an eye on the UEFA rule by selling Chris Woods and bringing in Andy Goram, as well as buying Scottish players David Robertson and Stuart McCall. Mark Walters and Trevor Steven also left but Smith proved that he didn't need Graeme Souness to attract the big names when he paid Sampdoria £2 million for Alexei Mikhailichenko. Maurice Johnston was sold to Everton as Smith obviously preferred a strike force of Mark Hateley and Ally McCoist – a decision that was to be proved more than right over the next few years.

We began with five wins from our opening six league games, including a 2-0 win over Celtic, and we progressed through to the League Cup semi-final without even conceding a goal. Clearly, Walter Smith knew what he was doing and had picked up the management 'reins' easily.

In the League Cup Semi-final against Hibernian, an error from Andy Goram allowed Hibs to score the only goal of the game. They went on to win the cup and Goram commented, "If I was still a Hibs player, I would have a League Cup winner's medal." Ally McCoist was quick to reply that "If you were still a Hibs player, we'd all have League Cup winner's medals!"

We got knocked out of the European Cup by Sparta Prague on away goals but our league form kept going. By Christmas, we'd won 22 and drawn 4 of our games, and lost just 5. We then lost only one more game and the league was won with a convincing 4-0 victory over St Mirren on Easter Saturday. That was now four in a row, and we were winning well. Thoughts began to wonder if we would go on to win nine, and equal or beat Celtic's run in the 60s and 70s.

Argyle House, a £4 million extension behind and under the Govan Stand, was opened in 1990, and this included executive boxes, office space and hospitality suites. Yet more developments were started in the early 1990s to increase the capacity of Ibrox to over 50,000. David Murray asked an architect to find out of there was a method of adding another level to the Main Stand. The famous red brick facade had become a listed building, meaning it had to be maintained, and Murray also needed the building to be kept open during the construction. The builders managed to remove the original roof and install a temporary cover while all the work was going on above. The Club Deck, as it was known, which cost approximately £20 million, was opened with a league match against Dundee United in December 1991. This redevelopment was partially financed by a grant of £2 million and a debenture issue that raised £8.5 million. Fans were offered debentures for between £1,000 and £1,650 each, and they guaranteed the right to buy season tickets for at least 30 years, as well as some other benefits.

Once the Club Deck was opened, Ibrox had a capacity of 44,500. A year later, a new pitch was installed and three extra rows were added around the stands. The new pitch was lowered meaning that a further 1,300 seats were added. Another two years later, the only remaining standing area of the ground, the enclosure under the Main Stand, was converted into seating to comply with the Taylor Report and UEFA regulations. The multi-coloured seats were all replaced in 1995 with blue seats, and by moving the seats closer together and removing the barriers between sections, an additional 1,200 seats were added bringing the capacity up to 47,998.

One thing that Walter Smith managed, that Graeme Souness hadn't, was to win the Scottish Cup. We beat Aberdeen, Motherwell and St Johnstone to reach the semi-final against Celtic. We hadn't actually scored a Scottish Cup goal against them since Tom Forsyth's winner in 1973, but on a pouring wet night at Hampden, Walter Smith's team 'came of age'. We were all under cover, but the Celtic fans were exposed to the elements as the rain battered down. After just three minutes, Joe Miller ran into David Robertson near the halfway line. A simple foul, and not in a dangerous place. No more than that. We were absolutely furious when incompetent referee Andrew Waddell pulled out a red card. We had to play almost the whole game with only ten men. Once again, who says we get all the refereeing decisions?

The players rolled up their sleeves and stuck to the task. Just before half-time, Stuart McCall won the ball in the Celtic half and laid on an almost perfect pass to Ally McCoist. He struck it perfectly on the run and the ball went in. There were jubilant celebrations in the Rangers end but we knew the game wasn't over. We put up a real 'backs to the wall' performance in the second half, and Celtic even hit the bar – but we held on to win a most memorable game. By the time, I'd walked to the car and got home, I was soaked - but I didn't really care.

In the final, we beat Airdrie, then managed by Alex MacDonald, 2-1 to win the cup for the first time in ten years, and our goals were scored by McCoist and Hateley. It wasn't a great final, and Airdrie nearly equalised at the end but it was a relief to win it.

Our league domination was continuing, as players came and went, and there was now a feeling at the start of each season that we expected to win the league instead of hoping to win it as we had done in the 70s and 80s. We might drop points to other teams such as Celtic, Aberdeen or Dundee United for example but, over the full course of a season's fixtures, we now could expect to gain more points than we lost. Ibrox was pretty full each week, and we were able to watch top international players representing us.

On a lighter note, there was also a notable change in the names of the players we were supporting. Having grown up watching players with 'traditional Scottish names' such as Willie, Alex, Derek, Jim, Davie or Ian, we were now watching players called Maurice, Nigel, Trevor and Richard, as well as Avi, Oleg and Alexei. Rangers were forcing other teams to become more cosmopolitan as well as they attempted to keep up with us.

One Wednesday night, Norma was out for a meal with some friends from work and the arrangement was that she was to call me and I'd go and pick her up. When she called me, she enthusiastically told me that Ally McCoist was in the restaurant, she'd spoken to him and told him I was a season ticket holder, and I just had to go and meet him. Did she really think I was that stupid? I knew I would appear at Sannino's in Bath Street, walk in expecting to see Ally, and all the girls would just have a right good laugh. It was so obvious!

I drove into town, parked the car and walked in to the restaurant expecting to be ridiculed. Norma met me at the entrance and took me round to "Ally's table". Unbelievably, there he actually was. He looked across and shouted, "Hi Norma! Hi Gordon! Come over and join us!" We shook hands and I told him that I'd thought this was a complete wind-up. Sitting with him were Ian Durrant and Stuart McCall. They should have been playing at Aberdeen that evening but it had been postponed so they'd decided to go out for something to eat. Ally couldn't have been more welcoming and he invited us to join them for dinner. The other two hardly seemed to notice us and just looked at their menus. Unfortunately, we'd already had our dinner, so he invited us to have a drink with them. This was rather flabbergasting but I declined, saying that we really couldn't impose on them. They wanted peace to enjoy their meal so we said our farewells and left them to it.

After the Hillsborough Disaster, the Government decided that the days of cramming fans in to stand on terracing, had to come to an end. Clubs could now ask for financial assistance to upgrade their ground even though Rangers had done this themselves, while the quality of the team and signings did suffer to some extent. Other clubs could now do up their grounds while still buying players, but they couldn't keep up with our quality. Walter Smith was, by now, building a real team spirit among the squad that would see them through tough matches – but this would be stretched during the following season.

Season 1992-93 would see another 'Treble' as well as a fantastic run in the new Champions' League. Realising that many top European teams could get a bad draw, be hit by injuries or have an 'off night', Rangers Secretary, Campbell Ogilvie, proposed an idea to UEFA that, instead of being a knock out tournament as it had always been, the Champion's Cup should become a league so that every club in it would get a set number of games and, if they lost a game, would not be instantly knocked out. They would be guaranteed revenue and UEFA could market the competition differently, attracting major sponsors. Qualifying clubs could sell a package of tickets for three home games, and the games could be shown live on television. UEFA accepted this proposal and the Champions' League was born. Only national champions could take part and there would still be an element of knock-out games but, when it got down to the last eight, the teams would be split into two leagues of four, playing each other home and away, getting points for winning or drawing, and the two league winners would meet in the final.

That wouldn't start until September so there was domestic business to take care of first. We started the league with wins over St Johnstone and Airdrieonians before drawing away to Hibernian. We then beat Dumbarton 5-0 in the League Cup. Andy Goram picked up an injury and was replaced by Ally Maxwell for the away game at Dundee. He didn't exactly cover himself in glory.

Norma and I had been given the chance to go to an apartment in Spain's Costa Del Sol and we flew out on the morning of the Dundee game. I checked the British newspapers the next day and saw that we were beaten 4-3, but we recovered to beat Stranraer in the League Cup during the week by another 5-0 margin.

Next up were Celtic at Ibrox. We had planned a day lying on sunbeds on the beach but I had to know what was happening back home. I lay in the sun, wearing my Rangers top, and listening on the radio to commentary on the BBC World Service. That was great until, at four o'clock, just as the second half was starting, they broadcast a world news bulletin that lasted fifteen minutes. I tried tuning up and down the dial in case the game was on somewhere else, but it wasn't. I had to wait for the commentary to resume at four-fifteen. We were a goal down but I was able to hear Ian Durrant blasting in our equaliser. In fact, most of Benalmadena beach also heard of this goal as, forgetting where I was, I let out a very loud cheer and everyone turned to see a crazy man wearing a Rangers top making a real racket.

We then had a tight game at Tannadice, but got through to the League Cup semi-final by winning 3-2. We were due to fly back to Glasgow on Saturday 29th August which had us at Ibrox playing Aberdeen – but we wouldn't land until after two-thirty. I actually called the airline to ask if there was any way of getting back sooner but that turned out to be futile, so we agreed that we would fly back to Glasgow, collect our cases, get a taxi back to our flat in Kelvindale where I would grab my scarf and season ticket, put on my top and get over to Ibrox as quickly as possible. My car, which had been sitting for two weeks took three goes to get started but I got over to Ibrox, listening to the commentary on the way, and found a parking space. I hurried to the ground - we were losing 1-0 – but the second half was just starting and all the turnstiles were closed. A steward directed me to the only one that was still open for late-comers and I got in to my seat, causing some amusement and consternation as my dad had told everyone beside us what I was planning to do. The second half progressed and three well taken goals from Durrant, McCoist and Mickhailichenko saw us win 3-1. Needless to say, I claimed all the credit for turning up and turning the game round.

Unknown to everyone, we had just embarked on an unbeaten run that would extend, in all competitions to 20th March. In the process, we would score four goals in each of our away games at Motherwell, Partick Thistle, Dundee United and our home games against Falkirk and Motherwell, as well as a 5-1 win away at St Johnstone. Ally McCoist seemed to score in every game.

In the first knock-out round of the new Champions' League we beat Danish side Lyngby both at home and away. We were unseeded and were drawn against German seeds, Stuttgart who had knocked out English champions, Leeds United. Or had they? Stuttgart had fielded an unregistered player against Leeds, so UEFA decided the teams would meet again in a one-off game at a neutral venue. Unseeded Leeds beat seeded Stuttgart and the draw would not be changed so, instead of playing a seeded team, we would play Leeds instead. Scottish champions against English champions for a place in the group stages of the new Champions' League. The English media decided that it would be no contest at all – Leeds would be far too superior for us. The tie soon became known as "The Battle of Britain".

Dad and I got our tickets and took our seats as the noise level, the excitement and the tension built up. To prevent trouble, there would be no Leeds fans at Ibrox and no Rangers fans at the return leg at Elland Road. As the teams came out, the noise became deafening. This was a good Leeds team with a lot of internationalists in it, including Eric Cantona. Ibrox was silenced when Gary McAllister scored within the first couple of minutes. Were the English media correct in their confident belief?

Ally McCoist got us back into it and then Leeds' goalkeeper John Lukic made a hash of a cross and punched it into his own goal. It finished 2-1 but the press were all still certain that Leeds would easily win the second leg.

Three days after that, we met Aberdeen in the League Cup final at Hampden. Their goalkeeper, Theo Snelders, made a mess of a pass-back, not being able to pick up the ball due to the new rule that had come in, and this allowed Stuart McCall to score. Aberdeen equalised but, in extra time, their full-back, Stephen Wright, headed into his own net and we won the cup 2-1 What an exhausting few days!

Dad came up to our flat to watch the European second leg, and our neighbour from across the landing came over with a few cans of beer to watch it with us. Despite the ban, there were some Rangers fans at Elland Road – where there's a will, there's a way. Without team colours, they had to keep quiet and sit on their hands. This must have been impossible because, in a reverse from the first leg, we scored right at the start. Mark Hateley hit an unstoppable shot past Lukic, and it was now 3-1 on aggregate. In the second half, a brilliant move involving Ian Durrant and Hateley saw a perfect cross hit into the Leeds area, on the break, and Ally McCoist dived to score our second goal. Although Leeds got one back, it was just a consolation. We won 4-2 on aggregate and the 'unfancied' Scottish champions out-played and knocked out the 'superior' English champions to become the first British team to qualify for the Champions League.

Joining us in Group A were Marseille, CSKA Moscow and Club Brugge. The first game would be at Ibrox against Marseille, a quality team of top international players. Dad and I got our tickets and took our seats for this new competition. The atmosphere was once again electric as both teams entered the field to loud music which had been chosen as the Champions' League Theme. It was a version of Handel's "Zadoc The Priest". A priest at Ibrox? Whatever next? On television, commentator Brian Moore introduced the match, "No home or away goals now, just league points remember" as we kicked off. For over an hour, we were completely out-played and were 2-0 down. I was actually beginning to wonder if this new league was a step too far for us and were we really not up to this level? Then Walter Smith threw on substitute Gary McSwegan. With his first touch of the ball, he sent a looping header over Fabien Barthez and into the net. Ibrox erupted and Rangers continued to press forward. A low header from Mark Hateley and it was 2-2. "Can Rangers now go on and win this?" asked Brian Moore. Unfortunately, time ran out but there was a feeling that, if we had just had another five minutes ... Still we had our first point.

Our second game was against CSKA Moscow but, because Moscow in December is a rather inhospitable place, the game was played in Bochum, Germany. We won 1-0 with a shot from Ian Ferguson. Marseille won their next game so it was beginning to look like it might be between us for that place in the final. The competition would now take a break and would resume in the spring.

We beat Celtic 1-0 in the New Year game at Ibrox thanks to a Trevor Steven header and, in January, we beat Dundee United 3-2 and Hibernian 4-3. We beat Aberdeen 1-0 away and then Falkirk 5-0 at Ibrox. We got through to the semi-final of the Scottish Cup by beating Motherwell, Ayr United and Arbroath without even conceding a goal. Games were coming thick and fast but the Rangers juggernaut kept rolling along, still unbeaten since August. Motherwell, Hearts and Hibernian were all beaten before the Champions League got going again.

A goal from Peter Huistra got us a 1-1 draw in Brugge and then they came to Ibrox. It was a very wet night but we got off to a good start with a goal from Ian Durrant. They equalised but then we witnessed one of the most bizarre goals ever seen at Ibrox. Scott Nisbet hit a cross from midway inside the Brugge half and the ball spun viciously, coming off the wet turf at an odd angle. As the Brugge goalkeeper, the experienced Danny van Linden, came out to meet the ball, it bounced in front of him, continued its unusual trajectory, spinning as it went, and bounced right over his head into the goal. It was a quite unbelievable goal, and we won 2-1, but there was a dampener to the night. A petulant Mark Hateley pushed a Brugge player and was shown a red card. There was nothing in it at all, but he got a two game suspension. Marseille, who we would play next, and who were frightened of Hateley's presence, couldn't believe their luck.

The following weekend, our long unbeaten run came to an end at Parkhead, when we lost 2-1. Scott Nisbet picked up an injury which, although it looked trivial at the time, was to end his career. His hip was damaged and doctors told him that if he ever tried to play again, he might never walk again. What a devastating blow to a good hard-working professional who had lived the dream. He will be forever remembered for the freak goal against Brugge.

Basically, if we beat Marseille in our second last group game, we would go into the final. If it was a draw, it would be down to the last game. Marseille scored early on but we battled back to equalise with an Ian Durrant shot. It would all go down to the last game. We were at home to CSKA Moscow and Marseille were away to Club Brugge. If they dropped a point and we won, we'd go through. Work colleagues and I began to think nervously of how we would get to the final in Munich. We wanted to think ahead but we didn't want to tempt fate.

Ibrox was unbearably tense as the game against CSKA began. We pressed and pressed, and got chance after chance, but try as we might, we just couldn't get the ball past their goalkeeper. Meanwhile the news came through that Marseille had beaten Club Brugge and were in the final. At the final whistle, the exhausted players were in tears. So near and yet so far. Unbeaten but knocked out. If only we'd had Hateley's presence in either one of the last two games.

Marseille beat a rather lacklustre AC Milan 1-0 in the final, and there was a definite feeling that we could have beaten them as well had we got the chance. It was then revealed that Marseille had been investigated for match-fixing in their French league, having bribed Valenciennes into throwing a league game enabling Marseille to wrap up their league and concentrate on the final against Milan. They were stripped of their title and relegated to the second division. UEFA banned them from European competition as well. It was also rumoured that their owner, Bernard Tapie, had paid CSKA's goalkeeper to let them boost their goal difference – Marseille won 7-0, while he went on to save everything that Rangers threw at him, as if his life depended on it. Tapie was found guilty of financial irregularities and was jailed, leaving us with the lingering doubt that we should have won the group and should have had the chance to take on Milan in the final.

To round of an incredible season of sixty-four games, we beat Aberdeen in the Scottish Cup Final 2-1 at Parkhead since Hampden was out of use at the time, clinching our fifth Treble. Goals in the first half from Neil Murray and Mark Hateley won the match but the abiding memory was of SFA Secretary and Rangers hater, Jim Farry, looking like he was sucking ten lemons as he stood and watched Richard Gough collect the cup.

It had been an utterly exhausting season. Walter Smith had put together the core of a very strong team that played well together, and battled for each other all the time. The defence was solid, the midfield was creative and the strikers were lethal. We had managed a huge unbeaten run domestically, and had gone 10 games unbeaten in European competition. We now had five titles in a row and our thoughts were becoming focused on achieving, and then beating, the holy grail of nine in a row. In fact, it was often said that, if Terry Butcher hadn't broken his leg in 1988, we would already have seven in a row.

TEN
Nine In A Row

The first part of the "modernisation" of Hampden was to make our covered end all-seated. That was done in 1991, and the Government then provided funds to begin work to make the whole stadium seated. The League Cup semi-final in 1992 had been the last match to be played in front of terraces. Hampden was re-opened in 1994, with a much-reduced capacity in time for the 1994 Scottish Cup semi-finals and final.

During the summer, we put out a firm statement of intent by smashing the Scottish transfer record by paying Dundee United £4 million for striker Duncan Ferguson. With Mark Hateley in the team, I personally couldn't see the point in paying all that for another tall striker, especially since it was Ally McCoist who was injured at the time, having broken his leg playing for Scotland, but it sent out a message that money was no object if we really wanted a player.

On the 3rd of August, we played Newcastle United at Ibrox, as a pre-season warm up and as a testimonial match for our record-breaking striker, Ally McCoist, who had been at the Club for ten seasons. We lost the match 2-1, and Mark Hateley scored our goal.

Season 1993-94 was a season when we really struggled with injuries. We started off with wins against Hearts and St Johnstone in the league, and Dumbarton in the League Cup. We then failed to win any of our next five league games – but we did keep winning in the League Cup, beating Dunfermline and Aberdeen. We then faced Celtic in the semi-final and since Hampden was being re-built, it had to be played at either Ibrox or Parkhead so a coin had to be tossed to decide. Live on radio, Celtic won the toss and cheered – before the League official told them that they had only won the right to call for the actual toss. They made that call and lost. The semi-final would be played at Ibrox but the stadium would be split 50/50. We would get the Main and Copland Road stands while they would get the Govan and Broomloan Road stands, so I had to move to another area. I got a seat up behind the goal in the Copland Road stand and watched Ian Durrant dispossess Celtic defender Mike Galloway before sending a perfect pass to Mark Hateley who was clear in the middle. He slotted the ball home and we won 1-0 despite Peter Huistra being sent off.

In the final against Hibernian at Parkhead, with the score at 1-1, Ally McCoist was sent on as a substitute near the end. He then scored a fantastic overhead kick which Hibernian goalkeeper Jim Leighton couldn't get near. The League Cup was our sixth domestic trophy in a row.

Our League form continued to be erratic. We lost or drew as many games as we won, and we were knocked out of the Champions League by Levski Sofia on away goals. Our form did pick up as we only lost one game in November and December, and we boosted the team by signing Gordon Durie from Tottenham Hotspur.

During the summer of 1993, Norma and I had met and become friends with a guy from Southampton called Keith. He was a massive Saints fan and still goes to most of their matches at home or away. We invited him to come up and visit us to see "a traditional Scottish New Year". He arrived on Hogmanay and we had a party that night for a few friends and neighbours. The next day, Rangers were at Parkhead but my dad and I took Keith over to Hampden which was still being used for Queen's Park games but not big matches. We sat in the stand and watched the game there – but listened on the radio to what was going on at Parkhead.

Rangers got off to a great start and I told Keith the score right away was 1-0. Then 2-0, and 3-0. Television commentator, Jock Brown said, "You could drive a bus through the Celtic defence!" This was incredible and I got more and more excited – until the grumpy faced guy sitting in front of us turned round and told me to stop going on about it. Meanwhile, Celtic fans were throwing Mars bars at their directors and we ran out comfortable 4-2 winners.

We were then unbeaten in the league until the end of April, but when we played Raith Rovers at Ibrox on 16th April, it was a bad afternoon. Duncan Ferguson head-butted Rovers' John McStay and was booked. When I say "head-butted", he only gave him a gentle tap but McStay went down as if he'd been shot by a sniper. Ferguson was charged with assault and served three months in prison. The SFA did nothing to help an international player when they could have dealt with the matter themselves. He didn't even get sent off, even though the referee was Celtic fan, Kenny Clark.

At Easter, Norma and I went to York for the week-end. On the Saturday night, our Ford Escort was stolen from the hotel car-park. We went through the rigmarole of describing it to the Police and we resigned ourselves to getting the train back home. We were just stepping on to the train on Easter Monday when my name was tannoyed saying I had to go to the Station Master's office. I ran up the stairs to be met by two policemen who told me that our car had been found – but it was badly damaged. I explained that we were just about to leave – but the Station Master said we could transfer our tickets so we let the train depart without us. The police were very helpful and they drove us out to a forest on the way to Scarborough where our car had been cleaned out and smashed up. We got the rescue service to tow it all the way back home and we finally got there very late. At work the next day, we told everyone what had happened. On the Friday, I was summoned to the Personnel Director's office. He said that he'd heard all about our misadventure, and he offered me the use of a spare company car over the weekend if we needed to do our shopping etc. I was obviously very grateful, and then he said that the only spare car was a BMW 5 Series. Wow! But there was a downside. It was dark green!

Nevertheless, I got the car for the weekend, and used it to go over to Hampden for the Scottish Cup semi-final against Kilmarnock on the Sunday afternoon. The match finished 0-0 so there would be a replay on the following Wednesday. This was still before the days of penalty deciders. On the way home, in a queue of traffic leaving Hampden, the car behind me banged into the back of the BMW! I put the brake on and went out to have a look. Fortunately, there wasn't a mark on the car. I was so relieved! The man behind me, who had caused the incident, wasn't the friendliest of drivers as, going by the make of car, he shouted and called me a "snobby bastard"!

We won the replay on the Wednesday 2-1 with two goals from Mark Hateley.

Despite only winning 22 of our games, (out of 44), we won title number six, and we seemed to be un-stoppable. Unfortunately, our end of season form was poor and we drew two and lost three of our last league fixtures. In the Scottish Cup final against Dundee United, Dave McPherson made a hash of a clearance; goalkeeper Ally Maxell didn't deal with it properly, allowing United's Craig Brewster to score a very easy goal to win the cup. Having won 7 competitions in a row, we had failed to win back-to-back trebles.

Across the city, Celtic were in turmoil with debts of £7 million. Following on from the New Year "Mars Bar" game, their board became figures of hatred among their fans who protested for their removal. Their bank decided to call in the debt, but Scottish Canadian businessman, Fergus McCann, arrived in Glasgow with minutes to spare, bought a 51% share of the club, under-wrote the debt and saved them from going bust. If ever there was a time when you wished that a flight had been delayed, or the air traffic controllers had been on strike, that was it!

Despite Rangers creeping closer to Nine in a Row, McCann didn't invest money on the team. Instead, he set about re-building Parkhead first and that prompted a lot of criticism from the Celtic fans. Parkhead was demolished and, for a season, Celtic arranged to play all their home games at Hampden.

Walter Smith was busy during the summer as usual. He signed defender Basile Boli from Marseille (Boli had scored the winning goal in the 1993-93 Champions' League Final against AC Milan), but the signing that really caught the imagination was that of Danish internationalist Brian Laudrup, a genuinely World Class player who would go on to be voted our greatest ever foreign player. Leaving the Club was misfit Duncan Ferguson who was loaned and then sold to Everton for £4.2 million so, at least, we made a small profit on the deal.

In a pre-season friendly, we played and beat Manchester United 1-0 at Ibrox, albeit through an own goal. In the match, their international star, Eric Cantona, was sent off for a wild tackle on Stephen Pressley.

Laudrup took time to settle into Scottish Football and, in the space of a week at the end of August, we were knocked out of the Champions' League by AEK Athens, lost to Celtic in the league at Ibrox, and were knocked out of the League Cup by Falkirk, again at Ibrox.

On the day of the Celtic game, we were flying back from Spain, and I attempted to hear the score on a small radio. We were flying over Wales at the time that the Classified Results were being read out – and they were all in Welsh! I could understand the names of the teams – but hadn't a clue what the numbers were. Different numbers were read out for our game so I knew that it wasn't a draw – but I didn't find out the actual result until we got home.

We were unbeaten in September, and in October, we won our home games but lost the away ones. We swapped central defender Dave McPherson to Hearts for Alan McLaren, and his debut would be away to Celtic. This was the game when Laudrup started to really show what he could do. With a solid defence and Laudrup firing on all cylinders, we coasted to a 3-1 win. Mark Hateley scored two and Laudrup took the ball round Pat Bonner in the Celtic goal before scoring our third.

We then went on an unbeaten run to the end of the year. STV had the contract for Sunday afternoon live games that season, and we watched Laudrup demolish Dundee United, scoring the first goal in a 3-0 away win, after turning their defence inside-out.

Goals were coming from all over the team and we continued our league run until a 2-0 defeat at Pittodrie on 12th February. Hearts knocked us out of the Scottish Cup in round four with a 4-2 win at Tynecastle, and we dropped league points in February against Hibernian, Falkirk and Hearts.

Football was overshadowed in March with the sudden death of Davie Cooper at the age of 39. I was at work when word came through that he had collapsed while filming a new STV series at Cumbernauld, coaching youngsters with ex-Celt Charlie Nicholas. Cooper had, by then, returned to his first club, Clydebank and was beginning to enjoy the twilight of a glittering career. He had come out of his shell and was developing into a popular media star. He was rushed to hospital and it was diagnosed that he'd had a brain haemorrhage. At work the next day, word came through that he had died.

Cooper was one of the greatest players for Clydebank, Rangers and Motherwell. The gates at the Copland Road end of Ibrox were soon covered in tributes from fans of all clubs. Norma and I went to see them after work one day, and we were both stunned by the sheer number of flowers, scarves, shirts and pictures that covered the ground and gates. At his funeral, Walter Smith paid tribute by saying that "God gave Davie Cooper a talent. He would not be disappointed with how it was used."

One of the most well-known players in the Word, Dutch internationalist Ruud Gullit said that Davie Cooper was one of the greatest players he had ever seen, and listed him in his greatest eleven in 'Four-Four-Two' magazine. Ray Wilkins described him as "a Brazilian in a Scots body". Motherwell renamed the North Stand at Fir Park in his honour.

Rangers won four games in April and clinched the league title with a sixteen point lead over second placed Motherwell. Without a doubt, Brian Laudrup had made a huge contribution to league championship number seven. We were inching closer …

On the 1st of May, Rangers played a Rangers Select (ex-players) in a benefit match for Scott Nisbet whose career had been ended prematurely by injury, and nearly 28,000 turned out to see us win 3-2 with goals from Alexei Mickhailichenko, Mark Hateley, and Ally McCoist.

At the end of June, our first daughter, Hilary, was born and after I'd registered the birth, I went over to the shop at Ibrox to buy her a couple of Rangers bibs. Red, white and blue and saying "I'm the best dribbler at Ibrox", they were just perfect for her.

Around this time, when Dad was on door duty as an elder at Broomhill Church, one Sunday morning, Ian McColl, our 'Iron Curtain' player from the 40s and 50s, the former manager of the Scotland national team and the manager of Sunderland who had lured Jim Baxter away from Ibrox in 1965, turned up with his wife. Dad recognised him straight away and welcomed him to the church. They both became attendees most Sundays, and got to know a few folk. We were on "nodding terms", and I always got a friendly "Good morning" from him whenever I met him going in.

During the summer, Walter Smith was relaxing on holiday when he met, and got chatting to, England internationalist Paul Gascoigne. After asking if he would fancy coming to play in Scotland, Smith paid Lazio a record Scottish fee of £4.3 million to sign him. His fame and popularity were such that a huge crowd gathered outside Ibrox to welcome him. Lots of fans bought tops with his name on the back as he became a signing sensation. We also bought Oleg Salenko from Valencia and Gordan Petric from Dundee United. Mark Hateley lost his place in the team to Gordon Durie, and he would leave for Queen's Park Rangers in November.

Our pre-season game at Ibrox that year was against Graeme Souness's old club Sampdoria, and we beat them 2-0 with goals from Gordon Durie and Ally McCoist.

Fans wondered how Paul Gascoigne would fare in the Scottish game as he had picked up a few long-term injuries during his career. It didn't take long for us to find out. In the first Old Firm game of the season, at Parkhead in September, he ran half the length of the pitch before slotting home a superb pass from Ally McCoist for our second goal. He ran over to join the Rangers fans who were celebrating ecstatically.

Celtic were starting to get their act together, determined to stop us reaching our eighth title, never mind our ninth. They'd appointed former player Tommy Burns as their manager and he fired up the team against us. That season, that 2-0 defeat was their only loss in the league – we drew the other three games against them – but they drew other games as well. We went on a run and had only lost one game by the end of the year.

In the Champions' League qualifier, we scraped past Anorthosis Famagusta of Cyprus 1-0 on aggregate thanks to a Gordon Durie goal at Ibrox, to get into the group section where we were drawn with Steaua Bucharest, Borussia Dortmund and Juventus – a very difficult section.

We didn't win a single game – drawing 3 and losing three including 4-1 and 4-0 defeats by Juventus – and we crashed out of the tournament. We reached the semi-final of the League Cup only to lose 2-1 to Aberdeen although we would do better in the Scottish Cup.

The highlight of the Christmas period was the 7-0 thrashing of Hibernian with Gordon Durie scoring four goals. The game is also remembered for Paul Gascoigne picking up the referee's dropped yellow card and jokingly waving it at him. To our astonishment, the referee then gave 'Gazza' a yellow card for his cheek! How pathetic!

There was a memorable televised game against Celtic at Ibrox in November. It finished 3-3 with goals from Laudrup, McCoist and an own goal by Tosh McKinlay, but left-back David Robertson had also scored a goal. He had run past the Celtic defence and scored. STV added the goal to their score at the top of the screen, commentator Gerry McNee described it several times as they showed the replay, and it was spoken of repeatedly. Unseen by them, the goal had wrongly been disallowed for offside even though Robertson had run past the defence. The linesman had got it completely wrong. It was some time until someone pointed out STV's error. Once again, it was one of these refereeing decisions that always go our way!

From 25th November away at Hibernian, we didn't concede a single goal in the league until 20th January when we lost 3-0 away to Hearts.

In the third round of the Scottish Cup, we were drawn against Highland League side Keith, and we beat them 10-1. The Keith players seemed more interested in swapping shirts at the end of the match as they tried to swap with Gascoigne and Laudrup particularly.

Clyde were beaten 4-1 away, and Inverness Thistle 3-0 away in the quarter-final and we were drawn against Celtic in the semi-final. The SFA in all their wisdom scheduled the game for Easter Sunday – a holiday when folk like to spend time with their families. Norma, Hilary and I had booked to spend the weekend down in York. In the morning, we visited Castle Howard where they'd filmed 'Brideshead Revisited' and took pictures of Hilary sitting among the daffodils. We headed back to York with the plan that I could find a pub showing the game while they went for a walk. There was a blackboard outside The Punchbowl saying that they were showing the game so I went in, ordered a pint, and went to stand among the fans through the back who were watching the TV. There were obviously a lot of fans in a similar position as me judging by the Glasgow accents all around. When Ally McCoist scored our first goal, half the pub cheered and half didn't. This was weird. We had fans of both teams sitting together watching the game. You certainly would not get that at home!

The atmosphere was interrupted by an English girl walking into the bar, looking up at the screen and then asking loudly, "Who's playing?" You wouldn't get that at home either.

Brian Laudrup scored a second and we were on our way to the final. They scored a 'consolation goal' right at the very end but that didn't matter.

With two more draws against Celtic and two defeats by Hearts, the league championship could be won by beating Aberdeen at Ibrox in our second last game. It didn't start well with Aberdeen scoring first. Then 'Gazza' got going. He went on a run with the ball and equalised before half time. As the game wore on, it was still 1-1 but we needed the victory. 'Gazza' then ran from the half-way line on a lung-bursting run past several Aberdeen players who were unable to stop him, and he scored a fantastic goal to put us 2-1 up. We then got a penalty, which he took to complete his hat-trick, and we'd won title number eight. That night, was he was voted Player of the Year. He'd scored 19 goals, many of them vital. Not bad for an "injury prone" wreck!

I travelled over to Hampden by bus for the Scottish Cup Final, and watched us play some fantastic football. Laudrup scored the first, and just after half-time, he added a second after a nightmare error by Hearts goalie, Giles Rousset when the let the ball squirm under him and into the goal. Laudrup then destroyed the Hearts defence and laid on three great goals for Gordon Durie. It would forever be known as 'The Laudrup Final' as, despite Durie's hat-trick, Laudrup was voted Man of the Match. No contest really.

There were some disconsolate Hearts fans in the bus heading back into the city, and they said to us, "Could you not have stopped at three?" I retorted, "Did you mean three goals – or at three o'clock?" They were utterly sick and fed-up at their humiliation.

Now the quest was on for league title number nine, and Walter Smith kept strengthening the team. He made one of his best signings when he paid £4 million for Jorg Albertz from Hamburg. Soon to gain the nickname, 'The Hammer' because of his ferocious shot, Albertz would become a great Ibrox favourite who would score a lot of very important goals, and who would soon develop a strange Glasgow-Germanic twang to his accent.

We had a great pre-season match that year as we beat Arsenal 3-0 at Ibrox on the 3rd of August in a testimonial for our captain, Richard Gough. Over 41,000 saw goals from Ally McCoist, Peter Van Vossen and Jorg Albertz.

The season opened with a Champions' League qualifier against the unknown Russian team, Alania Vladikavkaz. The first leg was at Ibrox and they took the lead. Derek McInnes equalised and there were goals from Ally McCoist and a bullet header from Gordan Petric, but nobody knew how we'd get on in the second leg, which was to be played a very long way from Glasgow. We needn't have worried as a hat-trick from Ally McCoist, two from Brian Laudrup, and one each from Peter Van Vossen and Charlie Miller gave us a 7-2 win and a huge aggregate of 10-3.

We won our opening six league games, before Celtic came to Ibrox. We were due back from Spain about five o'clock that afternoon so Dad used my season ticket to take a guest to the game, our minister, Reverend Bill Ferguson. Although he was a Falkirk fan, he thoroughly enjoyed the afternoon – despite some of the colourful comments that were being shouted at the opposition. We won 2-0 with goals from Richard Gough and Paul Gascoigne who had run the whole length of the pitch before getting on the end of a Jorg Albertz cross and bulleting in his header.

On another occasion that I can't remember, I couldn't go to a game and Dad invited a friend from Currie near Edinburgh, George Armstrong, who with his son was a Hearts season ticket holder, to go to Ibrox using my ticket. The fans around my seat made George very welcome and he thoroughly enjoyed his visit. To reciprocate, George took Dad to a Hearts v Rangers game at Tynecastle. Instead of enjoying it, he was utterly sickened by it. For 90 minutes, he had to endure the most anti-Rangers and anti-Glasgow venom and hatred from the Hearts supporters – in the main stand! To say he was disgusted was an under-statement. It was abundantly clear which team and stadium had the more hospitable fans – and Dad made sure he told plenty of people about it.

Before the Celtic game, we had lost our opening two group games in the Champions' League - away to Grasshoppers Zurich (their manager commented that our players seemed to treat the match as a holiday!) and at home to Auxerre. We lost our next two games to Ajax - this group was turning out to be a total nightmare. The Ajax manager said afterwards that he had noticed that every time we had the ball, we gave it straight to Laudrup or Gascoigne so the Dutch simply marked the two of them out of the game. We beat Grasshoppers 2-1 at Ibrox but lost the last match in France to Auxerre. What a European fiasco!

After beating Celtic, we stuttered in the league, winning just one of our next four games. Then we had a mid-week visit to Parkhead. Brian Laudrup scored an early goal but there was lots of drama still to come. We got a penalty – but 'Gazza' missed it, giving the Celtic fans some hope in a match they needed to win. Then Dutchman, Peter Van Vossen, with an empty goal in front of him, and just a couple of yards out, proceeded to miss the goal completely. It was a howler that would define his career and haunt him forever. To confound matters, Celtic got a late penalty. The whole stadium held its breath as Pierre van Hooijdonk stepped forward. He struck the ball ... and Andy Goram dived and saved it. Celtic were absolutely devastated.

In the League Cup, we had seen off Clydebank, Ayr United and Hibernian before beating Dunfermline 6-1 in the semi-final. We would meet Hearts in the final which was to be played at Parkhead.

I was at church on the morning of the final, collecting for 'BB Week' with the senior Boys and, as we came out, it started to snow. As I drove home to Bearsden, where we'd moved to a month earlier, it got heavier. The plan was that Norma would drop me at Anniesland Station and I would get a train to Bellgrove, near Parkhead. She and Hilary would go shopping or something. The snow got heavier. As we left our house, the transit van of the local milk delivery firm was struggling to get up the hill near our house, which takes us to the main road. Try as he might, he just couldn't get up the slope. We carefully got past him and, once we got onto the main roads, they were slushy but driveable. We got down to Anniesland and I got out the car, only to suddenly realise I'd left my match ticket in the house! We had to drive all the way back up to Bearsden to the house to retrieve the ticket. (What a twit!) Then it was back down to Anniesland, onto the train, and I was beginning to look at my watch as kick-off approached. When I got out of Bellgrove Station, it was very snowy and slushy underfoot. There were still a lot of fans walking to the game, delayed by the weather, and it was announced that the game would start late. I got in to my seat just as it kicked off. That was nice of them to delay it for me!

Ally scored two – but Hearts fought back to equalise. 'Gazza' scored one and then another even though Hearts manager, Jim Jeffries was moaning about the ball going out of play just before the third goal. Hearts got a late goal but we hung on to win 4-3. Then, out came the stories that Gascoigne had gone to the Parkhead lounge bar before the second half and helped himself to a strong drink – it certainly helped – and, afterwards, he had led the team singing all the Rangers songs in the Celtic dressing-room.

Meanwhile, in the league, we regained our confidence and, up to the end of the year, we hit four past Aberdeen without reply, beat Hibernian 4-3, lost away at Dundee United 1-0 and then beat Dunfermline 3-1, Kilmarnock 4-2, Hearts 4-1 and Raith Rovers 4-0. Then it was time to play Celtic at Ibrox again.

It was fairly even in the first half until we got a free-kick. Celtic lined up their defensive wall as Jorg Albertz ran up to take it. He smashed the ball, at eighty-something miles per hour and it flew past the wall, past the helpless hands of Stuart Kerr in the Celtic goal before nearly bursting the net. They managed to equalise and time was running out when Walter Smith brought on an unlikely substitute. Erik Bo Andersen's career at Ibrox was about to have its defining moment. A pass from Albertz allowed him to slide the ball into the net. 2-1 with just five minutes to go. "We are going to get an onslaught for these five minutes," said the guy beside me. Not to worry as, in a repeat of his first goal, Andersen scored again. Ibrox went crazy and we later saw in the television pictures just how much this meant to Walter Smith as he went as mental as everyone else.

Celtic were determined to stop us getting nine in a row – but we had beaten them three times out of three. How determined were they?

We went unbeaten until losing 2-0 at home to Dundee United at Ibrox on 12th March. Then there was a Sunday afternoon date with destiny at Parkhead. With Andy Goram injured, Walter Smith signed goalkeeper

Andy Dibble and thrust him into the red-hot atmosphere of a vital Glasgow derby. He also pulled off a master-stroke by bringing back Mark Hateley to rattle the Celtic defence. Interviewed at Glasgow Airport when he arrived, Hateley simply said, "I feel like I've come home."

In a very tight game, Brian Laudrup scored the only goal of the game, and Mark Hateley was sent off near the end – but he'd done what he was brought back to do. Four wins out of four. We had beaten Celtic in every league game. We were in the final stretch now.

Or so we thought. We lost the next game at home to Kilmarnock, but then beat Dunfermline 4-0 and Raith Rovers 6-0 to set up the title decider at home to Motherwell on the May holiday Monday. The crowds rolled up to Ibrox ready to party, but Motherwell had other ideas. They won 2-0 meaning that we only had two games left to clinch it. On the Wednesday night, we had to go to Tannadice but Dundee United had recently beaten us at Ibrox. We were without our inspirational captain, Richard Gough and Alan McLaren captained the team on that historic night.

We won 1-0 thanks to a great header from Brian Laudrup and Nine in a Row was ours. We had equalled Celtic's run of titles from 1965-74 and in the process had won more games and scored more goals. They had done it in the days of the old First Division when there were a lot of far easier games. We had done it in the Premier League which only included the top ten or twelve teams in the country and you played them four times each.

Fans congregated in George Square to greet the team back from Dundee. 'Gazza' hadn't even changed out of his kit. We lost to Hearts on the final Saturday but it didn't matter. We had equalled the record. Now, we needed to beat it.

There was more "tinkering" with Ibrox's capacity during the summer when the two spaces between the Govan, Copland and Broomloan Stands were filled in with seats and two giant Jumbotron screens were installed. Where we sat, in the back row of the Govan Front Stand, we were unable to see these screens. At the first game they were there, we all got a printed leaflet telling us about the screens and saying that the Club was looking at doing something of the rows that couldn't see them. In 2015, we are all still waiting!

The ground was officially renamed Ibrox Stadium after these renovations were completed in 1997, and Ibrox now had a capacity of just over 50,000.

That summer, our Boys' Brigade camp was to a farm near North Berwick. As well as the Officers and Boys from our own company, I extended the offer to another nearby company to come with us, meaning a few more Boys and staff. One of the Boys from the other Company turned out to be Stephen McDonald, the son of John McDonald, our player from the late 70s and early 80s. John brought him along to our church but I never got the chance to speak to him as I was so busy organising a hundred and one things.

During the summer, Walter Smith re-built the team with a cosmopolitan flare. He signed Stale Stensaas, Tony Vidmar, Jonas Thern, Jonatan Johansson, Antii Niemi and four Italians – Lorenzo Amoruso, Sergio Porrini, Marco Negri and Rino Gattuso. David Robertson left for Leeds United, Mark Hateley, Richard Gough and Andy Dibble were released once the season started, Trevor Steven and John Brown retired, and Erik Bo Andersen went back to Norway. Could this new team maintain the consistency that was needed?

One of them certainly could. Marco Negri just couldn't stop scoring goals. He scored in every one of the opening ten league games including five against Dundee United, four against Dunfermline and three against Kilmarnock. He was just sensational. He scored in Europe too as we beat GI Gotu 11-0 on aggregate in the first Champions' League qualifier. He wasn't the only scorer – Albertz, Laudrup, Gascoigne and some of the other new players all got goals.

We lost our next European tie to IFK Gothenburg, but thanks to a new rule, we 'parachuted' into the UEFA Cup instead.

We were looking unstoppable in the league, but events across the Channel were to have a significant effect on us. We were due to play Celtic at Parkhead on Sunday 31st August, with Negri having just scored five against Dundee United, but the game was postponed following the tragic death in Paris of Diana, Princess of Wales in the early hours of the Sunday morning.

Her funeral was to be the following Saturday and Scotland were due to play that day. SFA Secretary, Jim Farry said the game would still go ahead, but the Rangers players in the squad, led by Gordon Durie, said that there was no way they could concentrate on the match when the whole country was in such a state of mourning. Eventually, Farry gave way and that game was postponed as well.

The following week, we drew 3-3 against Aberdeen at Ibrox with Brian Laudrup scoring directly from a corner. Strasbourg knocked us out of the UEFA Cup with two 2-1 wins, but Marco Negri resumed his scoring and we won five of our next seven games. We beat Celtic at Ibrox thanks to a Richard Gough goal and, for the first time, Negri wasn't on the score-sheet. Dundee United came to Ibrox and knocked us out of the League Cup. We then drew three league games including the re-arranged game at Parkhead.

Instead of playing them when Negri was in top form, and scoring all the time, we played them when he'd gone off the boil a bit. He did still score but Paul Gascoigne was sent off for the most trivial of offences that hardly even warranted a yellow card. Celtic managed to equalise in the very last minute of stoppage time – which they had caused to be added on – so, instead of all three points, we only got one. Instead of none – they got one. That was to prove very crucial at the end of the season.

The area of Bearsden was proving to be a popular place to live for the Rangers players. Antii Niemi moved in just up the road from us, with his glamorous Finnish wife. He would have had no worries leaving her on her own when he was involved in away games as they had a very mean looking Doberman Pinscher dog that they used to walk past our house. It looked as if it would bite your leg off given the slightest encouragement.

Lorenzo Amoruso also moved in not far from us. The local children knew this and, on Hallowe'en, they were all at his door guising and wanting to meet him. The following year, he got wise to this and went out for dinner instead of staying at home.

Marco Negri and Rino Gattuso lived near Milngavie. On a Saturday evening after we'd been away at Dunfermline, I bumped into them at the local petrol station. Apparently, the arrangement was that Gattuso always had to go in and pay since his English was just slightly better than that of Negri. Sounds like a good excuse!

We won four of our next five games including a 5-2 win away at Hearts just before Christmas, but Celtic won the New Year game – their first win in this traditional fixture since 1988. We drew and lost too many games in the spring and slipped behind Celtic. Walter Smith had announced that he would leave the Club at the end of the season, and that may have had a tangible effect on the form of some of his players.

On 3rd March, 50,000 turned up to pay tribute to our 'Nine in a Row' manager, Walter Smith. We played Liverpool and beat them 1-0 thanks to a goal from – Ally McCoist – who else?

After a couple of replays, against Motherwell and Dundee, we got through to the Scottish Cup semi final against Celtic. Before that, we'd won three league games and it was beginning to appear that the league wouldn't be decided until the very end of the season. In the semi-final, a goal from Ally McCoist followed by a great, charging run and shot from Jorg Albertz saw us into the final. Celtic came to Ibrox on league business the following Sunday looking for revenge.

I went with Fraser Thomson, a fellow BB Officer, and I told him that I'd had a weird dream the night before. I dreamt that Jonas Thern would score a wonder goal from outside the area. Fraser just nodded. When Thern hit a screamer into the net, Fraser just turned to me with a look of utter disbelief on his face. "You should have had a bet on that!" Albertz also repeated his goal from the previous week and we won 2-0, putting us right back into the Championship race.

The next one of our 'Nine in a Row' heroes to have a testimonial match would be Ian Durrant. On 28th April, over 26,000 turned up to see us draw 2-2 with Sheffield Wednesday with goals from Durrant himself and Jorg Albertz

As Celtic dropped points, we beat Hearts but lost to Aberdeen away and Kilmarnock at home. We beat Dundee United at home on the last day but it just wasn't enough. Celtic won the league by two points. The earlier draw at Parkhead proved to be crucial although we should never have lost to Kilmarnock.

Walter Smith's last game in charge would be the Scottish Cup Final at Parkhead. It would also be the last game for most of our Nine in a Row heroes as well. I got the train to Parkhead, expectantly. Surely, they couldn't lose Walter's last game. We had, after all, thumped Hearts the last time we'd played them in the league, but we reckoned without the utterly appalling refereeing of Willie Young.

I sat down in the corner. What a terrible stadium! I couldn't see up the left wing when Laudrup was attacking. The view was pathetic. What a stupid design! I'd got loan of a mobile phone that afternoon (this was in the days before every single person had one) as Norma was close to giving birth again. I don't know quite what she would have expected me to do if she went into labour in the middle of the cup final! Our second daughter Victoria was born five days later.

Willie Young gave Hearts a penalty in the first half – for a foul outside the box. Amoruso made a defensive mistake and Hearts scored again in the second half. Ally McCoist got one back and then, at the very end, there was a foul inside their box. A penalty to us! That would get us back into the game. Young gave a free-kick outside the box. Hearts won 2-1 and the season had ended trophy-less for the first time in twelve seasons. The players trudged round the pitch at the end, completely devastated that they'd let themselves and Walter Smith down at the final hurdle.

Legendary 60s captain, Eric Caldow, was outside the ground afterwards and said he'd seen the replays on television. "Their one was never a penalty. Never!" Years later I head a story that Willie Young was given a hero's welcome when he attended a function at Hearts!

We traipsed slowly back to the station. We already knew that Walter Smith would be replaced by the great Dutch manager, Dick Advocaat, and I heard another depressed fan say that it would be back to business as usual once the new season started.

ELEVEN
Going Dutch

Advocaat was tasked with completely re-building the team. Ally McCoist, Andy Goram and Stuart McCall were released, while Richard Gough, Brian Laudrup, Ian Durrant, Alec Cleland, Peter van Vossen were given free transfers. Alan McLaren retired through injury and Joachim Bjorklund (£2.5 million to Valencia), Rino Gattuso (£4 million to Salernitana in Italy), Craig Moore (£0.8 million to Crystal Palace), Gordan Petric (£0.3 million to Crystal Palace) and Steven Boyack (£25,000 to Dundee) were all sold, bringing in a combined total of £7.625 million. That might have appeared to be a reasonable amount to bring in for what was an aging squad, but that was nothing compared to what Advocaat spent to bring in new players.

£35,950,000 was spent on Arthur Numan, Gabriel Amato, Giovanni van Bronkhorst, Andre Kanchelskis, Lionel Charbonnier, Daniel Prodan, Colin Hendry, Stephane Guivarc'h, Neil McCann, Stefan Klos, Claudio Reyna and Lee Feeney. Craig Moore was also bought back for £1 million. This was spending that was beyond our wildest imagination. Souness had already spent big at the time, and Walter Smith had spent on Duncan Ferguson, but some of us could easily remember when Willie Waddell refused to release any funds towards the signing of players. We watched the News each night as another top player was being linked with us and it seemed that money was no object. This had been a massive re-building job and we couldn't wait for the new season to start.

There was a World Cup in France that summer, so we got our first chance to see Arthur Numan in action, playing for The Netherlands. Scotland qualified and were to play in the opening game of the tournament against Brazil. The game was held in the afternoon and Whyte & Mackay decided that everyone could get away early and could go to the pub, go home or could watch the game with colleagues on the office television, and drinks would even be provided. I opted to head for home and was instructed to get some baby things from Boots in Sauchiehall Street on the way. I got these and caught the bus to Bearsden, listening to the first half on the radio, intending to be home for the second half. Most folk must have been watching it as the bus was deserted. As we approached Bearsden, Scotland got a penalty and I went up to the doors to tell the driver what was happening before I got off at my stop. Obviously distracted by the excitement and the goal that was scored, I jumped off ... leaving all the baby stuff on the bus!

The day of calamities wasn't over. I sat down to watch the next game in the group that evening, between Norway and Mexico, holding baby Victoria on my lap. Hilary was messing about with the telephone and I shouted to her to put the phone down. Less than half an hour later, the doorbell rang, and I went and answered it. There were two Police officers standing on the doorstep and they said they were answering the 999 call that had been placed from our number. The operator just heard a man's voice shouting "Put that phone down!" and she thought that some violent deed was being committed so she traced our number and called the Police. I was mortally embarrassed and explained what must have happened – but they weren't convinced. Norma had to come through from the kitchen to prove that she wasn't lying in a battered heap! Needless to say, Hilary has never been allowed to forget it!

Once the World Cup was over, we could turn our attention to the first match of the Advocaat era, a UEFA Cup qualifying tie away to Irish club, Shelbourne. To avoid the chance of trouble, the game was switched to Tranmere Rovers' ground near Liverpool. Despite fielding a team of multi-million pound international stars, we found ourselves 3-0 down at half time and in serious danger of getting knocked out. Fortunately, goals from Albertz (2), van Bronkhorst, and Amato (2) saw us win 5-3 and a serious embarrassment was prevented. 46,906 turned up for the second leg at Ibrox a week later and we won 2-0 with a double from Jonatan Johansson.

The league season got underway that weekend with a visit to Tynecastle. Hearts beat us 2-1 but the signs were there that the team was starting to gel together. Our goal was scored by Rod Wallace – a striker we had got on a free transfer. Despite all the millions spent on the rest of the team, Wallace would prove time and time again to be the best value signing that we had made. He went on to score in every league game in August and in our next UEFA game against PAOK Salonika. We won our league games against Motherwell, Kilmarnock and St Johnstone before drawing with Dundee United, Celtic and Aberdeen. We saw off PAOK and qualified for the next round of the UEFA Cup. The team was starting to play some really good quality football and, as well as all the new players, there was a distinct improvement in some of the players who were still there from Walter Smith's time.

We beat Beitar Jerusalem in the UEFA Cup (5-3 on aggregate), won three more league games and qualified for the League Cup Final without even conceding a goal. As we entered the UEFA Cup 'proper', we faced a tricky tie against Bayer Leverkusen. We beat them 2-1 away in the first leg, and the highlight was the midfield display by Barry Ferguson who, with a turn similar to something Graeme Souness would have done, sent four defenders the wrong way. It was sublime to watch. Advocaat's influence was beginning to tell in our European performances. The next round was to prove the most difficult – against Italians Parma who were favourites to win the competition. We drew 1-1 at Ibrox in the first leg but lost 3-1 in the away leg. However, it was our best European season since the epic 1992-93 run, and Parma went on to win the trophy.

In the league in October, we beat Dundee 1-0, Hearts 3-0 and Dundee United 2-1 but lost 1-0 away at Motherwell. We then beat St Johnstone 7-0 and Aberdeen 2-1 before a disastrous defeat at Parkhead (5-1) but we were then unbeaten until March, including 4-0 and 6-1 against Dundee and 5-0 against Kilmarnock.

At the end of November, goals from Guivarc'h and Albertz were enough to beat St Johnstone 2-1 in the League Cup Final at Parkhead, giving Advocaat his first trophy.

On a personal note, at the end of 1998, Whyte & Mackay had a re-structuring and decided that they no longer required my services, after almost 21 years. I decided that I should have a change of career but couldn't see anything of interest. Within a week of leaving Whyte & Mackay, I started work with United Distillers, who became Diageo.

At the beginning of March, the next player to receive a testimonial was central defender Alan McLaren – the team captain on the night we achieved Nine in a Row – whose career had been cut short by injury. Middlesbrough were the opponents, and the Rangers team had a few guests in it, including Rangers fan Robbie Fowler from Liverpool. He scored the first goal in a 4-4 draw. Our others came from Stephane Guivarc'h, Rod Wallace and a penalty taken by McLaren himself.

In the spring, Rangers continued picking up league points and progressed through the Scottish Cup without any difficulty, beating St Johnstone 4-0 in the semi-final. A 3-1 league win at home to against Aberdeen put us in the position of being able to clinch the league, the first new-style SPL, in our next game – away to Celtic on Sunday 2nd May. The new SPL had a deal with SKY TV that they would show SPL games on Sunday evenings at 6:05pm, and we had already played in a few of these televised fixtures. Everything was set for the visit to Parkhead. Could the "Little General" deliver the SPL at the first time of asking?

Not having SKY myself, Brian Martin, a neighbour had invited a few of us like-minded individuals round to watch the match – but first, we had a family visit down to Ayrshire on the Sunday afternoon to a school-friend of Norma's. Her husband was a Rangers fan and we spent the afternoon discussing what might happen later. He worked in the Traffic Police and let slip that his colleagues on the A77 would be changing shifts when I would be driving back home so there wouldn't be any speed traps lurking on the road. That was useful information as we hurried back to Bearsden so that I could go and watch the match.

We got home, I grabbed some refreshments, and I hurried up to Brian's. We sat and watched the drama unfold. Mayhem doesn't even come close. The tension was absolutely real. The last thing that they wanted was for us to clinch the league in their home and they were wound up beyond fever pitch as they tried to stop us. Neil McCann nipped in to score a fine opener, then all hell broke loose. Their full-back Stephane Mahe went berserk and was sent off, further reducing their chance of getting back into the match. The scenes that followed will never be forgotten by anyone who witnessed them. They had fans getting onto the pitch, throwing coins, and trying to attack Hugh Dallas, the referee. Giovanni van Bronkhorst was about to take a corner, despite objects being thrown at him, and then the camera cut to the referee. He was on his knees with blood running out of his head. He'd been struck by a coin so the game was stopped while he got treatment from the Celtic physio, Brian Scott. Minutes after the game re-started, he awarded Rangers a penalty. Bedlam erupted once again. Jorg Albertz strode up and scored. 2-0 and we had one hand on the trophy. In the second half, Neil McCann scored another and then Rod Wallace was sent off. Celtic's Vidar Riseth was next to go for an assault of a tackle on Claudio Reyna. It finished 3-0, Dick Advocaat was hugged by his assistant manager, Bert van Lingen and we'd won the first ever SPL in the most dramatic circumstances.

Brian's next door neighbour, Robert, was at the match but his wife Shona (future Director Ian Hart's daughter) told us that she knew the score from all our shouting and cheering!

The Rangers players had, by and large, kept their cool and played football when mayhem was breaking out all around them. Celtic completely lost the plot, yet the newspapers the next day were already calling it the "Old Firm Shame Game" – despite the fact that all the rioting, pitch invasions, coins being thrown, attacks on Hugh Dallas, and even the attempt at sky-diving off the front of the upper stand, had all been by Celtic fans.

Strathclyde Police took a very dim view of all the ensuing trouble and they decided that games, especially Old Firm games, should not be allowed to kick off as late as 6:05 pm because that had given the fans far too long to drink before the match, especially at a holiday weekend, so the lucrative TV deal with SKY had to be scrapped. They had been paying the SPL good money to show live games at that time but the Police put a stop to that. That meant that the SPL and all Scottish clubs lost out financially because the Celtic fans, once again, couldn't behave themselves.

It was less than a month until the Scottish Cup Final and the two clubs would meet again. This time, Celtic wanted to stop us winning another Treble and they promised revenge. Senior Police officers met with both clubs and warned them about their behaviour, as they didn't want a repeat of all the trouble.

The last stage of Hampden's renovation had begun in November 1997 and £59 million had been spent, funded by the National Lottery. The capacity was now 52,025 and the Cup Final would be the first match at the new stadium.

The game was relatively well-behaved and Rod Wallace nipped in to score the only goal in the second half. Dick Advocaat had spent big, rebuilt the team and won the Treble. The SFA were delighted with the stadium's new safety arrangements which were put to the test at the end of the game. Celtic fans proved that half the ground could be easily evacuated in less than 30 seconds!

I stood and watched Lorenzo Amoruso being presented with the cup, and the lap of honour which followed. I was looking forward to watching the highlights on Sportscene that evening, and we were due to fly out to Spain on holiday the next morning. That Saturday was the night of the Eurovision Song Contest and, as usual, it over-ran. The News followed and then ... a film. No Sportscene! What was BBC Scotland playing at? Where were the highlights of our great triumph? I checked the schedule. Because of Eurovision, Sportscene had been moved for one night only to BBC2 – and it had already finished! I'd missed the whole thing. At the airport the next morning, I bought some newspapers to read on the flight instead. Our record-breaking sixth Treble was in the bag, and we looked forward to another summer of big spending.

The 'revolving door' was in action again although not so much money changed hands. Jonas Thern and Theo Snelders retired and Stephane Guiarc'h was sold to AJ Auxerre for £3.4 million. Dutch striker, Michael Mols, arrived from FC Utrecht for £4 million and was an instant hit. The 'Smiling Assassin' scored nine goals in his first nine matches.

Ian Ferguson was the next player to receive a testimonial after twelve years loyal service to the Club. On 21st July, we played Sunderland, and won 3-1 with goals from Barry Ferguson, Giovanni van Bronkhorst and an own goal.

In the league, we got off to a great start, winning our opening eight games, including 4-0 against Hearts, 4-0 against Motherwell, 4-1 against Dundee United, and 3-0 against Aberdeen, although they got their revenge by beating us 1-0 at Pittodrie in the quarter-final of the League Cup – denying Advocaat a second Treble.

We also got off to a flying start in the second qualifying round of the Champions League, beating FC Haka 7-1 on aggregate but the smiles were temporarily wiped from our faces when we drew Parma in the next round. Although they weren't one of Italy's biggest clubs they were going through a period when they had money to spare. After winning the UEFA Cup, they had strengthened their team with a summer spending spree of £65 million. A Celtic fan at work thought this was hilarious. "You thought you'd get into the group stages but you've got no chance now you've drawn Parma!"

How wrong they were! On one of the greatest European nights ever at Ibrox, the Italian stars were out-played. When Tony Vidmar scored the opening goal, Ibrox erupted, and when Claudio Reyna hit the second, the noise was deafening. Advocaat's side were at their peak and played superbly but we had to be careful in the second leg a fortnight later. We defended well and limited them to 1-0 so we went into the group stage where we were drawn with Valencia, Bayern Munich and PSV Eindhoven. We couldn't have got a tougher draw.

We lost our opening match 2-0 away in Valencia but we completely outplayed Bayern Munich at Ibrox and were on course for a famous 1-0 win before they got a free kick right at the end which should never have been given. There was a real sense of disappointment when they scored from it and it finished 1-1. That was a measure of how we had played and how much we had improved in Europe that we were bitterly disappointed with a draw against such opposition. We then beat Advocaat's old team, PSV Eindhoven 1-0 away thanks to a Jorg Albertz shot, and 4-1 at Ibrox with Mols scoring two of them. We lost again to Valencia before going to Munich for our last game. The score was 1-0 to Bayern but the game will sadly be remembered for the injury to Michael Mols. Their goalkeeper, Oliver Kahn, came out of his area to tackle Mols who tried to hurdle over him. In doing so, he badly twisted his knee and put himself out of the game for months. He was never the same player again and we could only imagine what he could have gone on to do for us. We failed to qualify and dropped into the UEFA Cup where we would meet Borussia Dortmund.

We won the first leg fairly convincingly at Ibrox 2-0 scoring one of the greatest European goals ever. A fantastic passing move that started at the back was finished off by Rod Wallace and it was a great example of team-work. The second leg would be played in the afternoon and a few of us gathered round a radio in the office to listen. We were losing 1-0 and the commentator told us we were in the last minute. We thought that we were there, but the game kept going for about five minutes and Dortmund scored again to level it up. There were no goals in extra time and we lost 3-1 on penalties – a pretty poor display of penalty taking!

In the league, after an away draw 1-1 at Kilmarnock, we beat Aberdeen 5-1, Celtic 4-2 and Hibernian 2-0 before losing our first league game at home to Dundee at the end of November. Billy Dodds was signed from Dundee United for £1.3 million as a stop-gap replacement for Michael Mols.

We beat Kilmarnock 1-0 and Motherwell 5-1. Then on 22nd December, we celebrated the centenary of Ibrox Stadium which had opened on 31st December 1899, with a 1-0 win over Hearts thanks to a late Jorg Albertz goal. Coincidentally, we had beaten Hearts in the first game 100 years earlier. In the New Year game, Billy Dodds scored at Parkhead to earn a 1-1 draw – the only point Celtic would take from us that season. Turkish midfielder Tugay Kerimoglu joined us from Galatasaray, and we then beat Aberdeen 5-0 and Dundee United 4-0 before drawing away at Hibernian and St Johnstone.

We progressed through the Scottish Cup, beating St Johnstone, Morton and Hearts to reach the semi-final, which is more than Celtic did. In one of their most embarrassing results, they were knocked out by Inverness Caledonian Thistle prompting the headline *"Super Caley Go Ballistic Celtic Are Atrocious"* and the sacking of their manager John Barnes.

Our whole department at work had a "team-building" night away at the Crutherland Hotel in East Kilbride, and we discovered that the Celtic first team squad were all staying there as well, the night before some match. Kenny Dalglish had been appointed as their manager. Most of the time, they kept to themselves and looked bored stiff, loitering around the reception area. As a Rangers supporting colleague and I walked along the corridor, when we saw them coming towards us, we just had to ask each other, "Which conference room are we supposed to be in?" "The Inverness suite, I think!"

We thumped Dundee 7-1 before a midweek visit to Parkhead where we won with a Rod Wallace goal. We were virtually uncatchable but, in a post-match interview on television, Dalgish was asked if he conceded the league. "I didn't see any prizes being dished out tonight!" We were so far ahead, it was just a matter of time.

We beat Motherwell 6-2 and then easily beat Celtic 4-0 at Ibrox before drawing 1-1 at Aberdeen. We won our next eight games, but on the last day of the season we lost 2-0 to Motherwell – only our second league defeat of the season, and it was a meaningless game anyway. Advocaat had won the league again, by a massive 21 points.

Having simply beaten Ayr United 7-0 in the Scottish Cup semi-final, we met Aberdeen in the final. As a tribute to Advocaat, van Lingen and our Dutch players, it became the Orange Cup Final as thousands of fans wore Dutch shirts at Hampden.

As the number of substitutes in Scottish Cup matches was still limited, Aberdeen had chosen not to name a reserve goalkeeper and were forced into putting Robbie Winters in goal when Jim Leighton got injured in the first half and had to leave the game. The rule was changed the following year. We won comfortably 4-0 with goals from van Bronkhorst, Vidmar, Dodds and Albertz.

No repeat Treble – just a Double this time so, once again, Advocaat wielded the cheque-book during the summer. Peter Lovenkrands (1.3m), Kenny Miller (£2m), Bert Konterman (£4.3m), Fernando Ricksen (£3.6m) and Ronald de Boer (£4.5m) arrived to boost the team.

We defeated Zalgiris Kaunas 4-1 on aggregate in the Champions League qualifier before winning our first four league games against St Johnstone, Kilmarnock, St Mirren and Dunfermline. We beat Herfolge BK 3-0 at home and away to qualify for the group stage of the Champions League where we were drawn with Sturm Graz, AS Monaco and Galatasaray.

Our consistency from the previous seasons appeared to be continuing and our next game would be away to Celtic. They had appointed Martin O'Neil as their new manager and had invested a bit of money re-building their team. The game was to be shown live on "beam-back" at Ibrox and I sat in the main stand, unable to believe what I was seeing. Our new defenders, Ricksen and Konterman were both an absolute shambles, the referee gave them an off-side goal while disallowing a good one of ours, and they won 6-2. What a nightmare! Fans had gone to Ibrox, thinking that we would enjoy another good victory against our old rivals but we trudged out feeling as depressed as it is possible to be. I said at the time that, in Bert Konterman, we thought we were signing another Japp Stam (the solid Dutch central defender at Manchester United) – but we had ended up signing his granny! Ricksen looked like a rabbit caught in a car's headlights and he was removed from the game.

We did bounce back quickly by beating Aberdeen 4-2 in the League Cup, but then drew with Dundee in the league. Our next game was at Ibrox and we recorded our biggest ever Champions League victory by beating Austrian side Sturm Graz 5-0. We beat Hearts, AS Monaco 1-0 away, Motherwell and Dundee United but lost 3-2 away at Galatasaray with both our goals coming late on after they'd gone 3-0 up. We then lost three league games in a row, drew 0-0 at home to Galatasaray, and lost away to Sturm Graz although we eliminated Dundee United from the League Cup. There was just no consistency.

We beat St Mirren 7-1 at Ibrox with Kenny Miller scoring 5 times, but then we drew 2-2 at home to Monaco in our last group game We had been leading 2-1 but they scored late on to deny us the points that would have seen us through to the next round. Two wins and two draws would have been enough in other years to have qualified but not that year, so we dropped into the UEFA cup. We beat Aberdeen but drew with Dunfermline before Dick Advocaat broke the bank by signing Tore Andre Flo from Chelsea. In fact, he not so much broke it as smashed it to pieces. If we thought that £4 million was a lot to spend on Duncan Ferguson, Flo cost a record-smashing £12 million bringing our net spending that season to £26.7 million.

Flo's debut would be against Celtic at Ibrox and we got sweet revenge for the earlier defeat by hammering them 5-1 with goals from Ferguson, Flo, de Boer, Amoruso and Mols. This would be a result that obviously angered supporters from the other half of Glasgow – even the young ones. As my Dad and I drove along Govan Road on our way home towards the Clyde Tunnel, a group of youngsters stood at the side of the road throwing raw eggs at any cars that had Rangers fans in them. They must have seen my scarf because our car was targeted. No damage was done and we had to laugh as their ability to hit the target was as good as their heroes had been earlier. The car's passenger window was wide open and, had the egg got inside the car, it would have caused a real mess - but, it was thrown so accurately, it only hit the door.

The next mid-week, we could only manage to beat Kaiserslautern 1-0 at Ibrox. We then beat Hearts away thanks to an Albertz penalty before losing 3-0 away in Germany to go out of the UEFA Cup. Our league form was better as we won seven and drew one of our next eight games before losing a "double header" to Celtic in the League Cup semi-final and the league.

Our spring league form was very mixed as we won some, drew some and lost some, and Dundee United knocked us out of the Scottish Cup. We won our last three league games 4-1 against Hearts, 5-1 against Kilmarnock and 4-0 against Hibernian but it wasn't enough. We ended up losing the league by fifteen points and finished the season without winning any trophies.

That summer, the Club opened a new state-of-the-art training complex at Auchenhowie just outside Milngavie. It had been suggested, or even demanded, by Dick Advocaat when he arrived in 1998, and the total cost was around £14 million. The thirty-eight acre site has areas for the first team and the youths, a gym, a medical centre, dining facilities, stores, and a press area. There are six full-size pitches, and two half-sized ones. Some of the outdoor pitches have undersoil heating and there is also an indoor synthetic pitch. As well as being used by Rangers, several visiting clubs and national teams have used the facilities, and many Rangers players moved into Milngavie or Bearsden to be near it, so we got quite used to seeing a lot of the players around the area.

The next season didn't start very well as our inconsistency continued. Full-back Michael Ball signed from Everton for £6.5 million and that was our biggest purchase. Also joining us were Christian Nerlinger, Claudio Caniggia and Russell Latapy, and Shota Arveladze would sign in mid-season.

On the way out were Jorg Albertz, Sergio Porrini, Rod Wallace, Lionel Charbonnier, Giovanni van Bronkhorst, Tugay Kerimoglu, Claudio Reyna and Kenny Miller. Instead of our spending exceeding our outgoings, this was reversed. Perhaps Mr Murray was beginning to realise that he didn't actually have such deep pockets as he thought.

The last of our Nine in a Row legends to receive a testimonial was 'Bomber', John Brown. On 21st July, we played Belgian side Anderlecht. We lost 2-1, and our goal was scored by Claudio Caniggia.

Christian Nerlinger would go on to achieve some kind of unique distinction for us as he managed to score in the first game he played for us in the SPL, the Scottish Cup, the CIS Insurance League Cup and the Champions League – both in the qualifiers and the group stage proper. He wasn't a recognised goal-scorer as such, but it was quite special.

With the expansion of the UEFA tournaments as more new countries were created around Europe, the qualifying rounds took place so early that they were now the first competitive fixtures being played. Due to Scotland's lowly standing, some clubs even had to play these matches as early as July, during the Glasgow Fair. That season, two Scottish clubs got the chance to qualify for the Champions League although, as SPL runners-up, we had to play more qualifying ties.

Our opening match was in Slovenia against NK Maribor and we won it 3-0. On the following Saturday, we repeated this score against Aberdeen at Pittodrie before completing the job against Maribor at Ibrox with a 3-1 win. We then drew our first league game at Ibrox, 0-0 against Livingston, and that score was repeated in the Ibrox leg of our next Champions League tie against Fenerbache. We then beat Dunfermline away but drew at home against Hibernian, before Fenerbache beat us 2-1 to knock us out of the Champions League and into the UEFA Cup.

We ended August with a 2-0 home win against Dundee, and then we drew 2-2 at Tynecastle. We beat Motherwell 3-0 and Dundee United 6-1 which included a Tore Andre Flo hat-trick.

This was followed by an unusual UEFA Cup round 1 tie. We had been drawn against Anzi Makhachkala from the Russian region of Dagestan. The Foreign Office said that the British nationals should not travel there because it was a war zone so Rangers told UEFA that they couldn't play the match for obvious safety reasons. There was much arguing as Anzi said it was perfectly safe and Rangers threatened to withdraw from the competition. With time running out, UEFA decided that there would be a one-off match at a neutral venue instead of the usual two legs. Rangers traveled to Warsaw and won 1-0 thanks to a Bert Konterman goal.

The following weekend, we lost 2-0 to Celtic at Ibrox. We had failed to win four of our opening nine games but we went on a good run in October and November as we beat Kilmarnock, St Johnstone, Livingston, Aberdeen, Dunfermline Athletic and won both legs of the UEFA Cup Round 2 against our old foes, Moscow Dynamo (3-1 at Ibrox and 4-1 in Moscow).

We had two 0-0 draws with Paris Saint-Germain but managed to win on penalties to ensure European football after Christmas for the first time in nine years, but we then lost 2-1 at Parkhead. By December, we were trailing Celtic in the league because of our inconsistent form. There were stories that Advocaat had "lost the dressing room" and even of a Dutch clique. Dick Advocaat announced his resignation, moving to the new post of Director of Football, and recommended Hibernian manager Alex McLeish as his successor.

I can remember discussing his appointment with a colleague and feeling rather non-plussed, saying that McLeish had no European experience and wasn't really a Rangers man. We had grown accustomed to a European tactician, and had seen some great football being played. What were we going to see now?

TWELVE
Man Management From McLeish

We saw Rangers league form improve greatly. We went unbeaten right through to mid-April, only losing one more league game that season, and it was put down to McLeish's style of man management, getting a lot more out of the players than Advocaat had been able to.

We saw good wins against Hearts, Dundee United, Hibernian, Livingston and Dunfermline, and in the Scottish Cup, we knocked out Berwick Rangers and Hibernian. The first big test came at Hampden at the beginning of February in the League Cup semi-final against Celtic.

By that time, I was working down in Ayrshire, commuting from Bearsden every day, so I went straight from work to the game. I parked the car off Cathcart Road, got a fish supper for my dinner which I ate in the car, and then went along to Hampden.

It was a tight game. Peter Lovenkrands scored for us and it was 1-1 after 90 minutes. The game moved into extra time and McLeish brought on Bert Konterman, to the loud ridiculing jeers from the Celtic end – but that was to be the night that defined his Ibrox career. A ball came out to him, and I was standing right in line with him as he hit a ferocious shot right past Rob Douglas and into the net. The Rangers end erupted as the other players jumped all over him. Konterman looked absolutely calm and relaxed as we all went mental. Celtic had no reply and McLeish had scored the first 'point' against them.

We met Ayr United in the final on St Patrick's Day and got a comfortable 4-0 win with goals from Caniggia (2), Flo and Barry Ferguson gave Alex McLeish his first trophy.

In the UEFA Cup, we drew 1-1 with Feyenoord at Ibrox but lost the second leg 3-2 with ex-Celt, Pierre van Hooijdonk scoring two replica free-kicks from just outside our box. They went on to win the trophy.

The earlier gap opened up by Celtic meant that, despite the good run in the league, we could only finish second, but we thumped Forfar Athletic 6-0 and then Partick Thistle 3-0 to reach the Scottish Cup Final against Celtic in what was to become known as "The Lovenkrands Final".

I went to the game myself and parked the car off Cathcart Road in my usual place in Dixon Avenue. As I parked, I noticed that there were quite a few Celtic fans walking along from the Victoria Road direction. As with all big matches, the Police had issued strict guidelines about how each team's fans should make their way to the game and where they should be parking. In other words, that area should have been for

Rangers fans only. I waited in the car for a few minutes until they had passed and then I walked round to the main road.

There were some of them hanging about there, who looked as if they'd been drinking heavily, and they were shouting and causing a nuisance. As a car of Rangers fans passed by, shouting at them, one of them threw a beer bottle at the car. It missed but smashed on the road.

I had my Rangers top on, under an open denim jacket, and was carrying my rolled up scarf and I was aware that there were no other Rangers fans anywhere near me, so I nipped into one of the shops to take my time buying some sweets or chocolate. After hesitating for a few minutes, I stepped out of the shop. They were still there and were looking for trouble. They saw my shirt, but I just walked as quickly as I could towards Crosshill Station where I hoped there would be more Rangers fans.

I was subjected to a torrent of vile abuse and then one of them decided that he would start punching my head. He did so several times but I just kept walking quickly, hoping that they wouldn't hit me with a bottle or break my spectacles. They were right round me, shouting obscenities and punching. I got to the station and they then crossed the road to head in the correct direction. At last I saw a Policeman and told him what had just happened. He could see I was shaken and asked if I was alright. I could still see the culprits and I pointed them out. The Police went after them and, within seconds, a minibus of Policemen came charging along towards us. I didn't wait to see what happened but I could see the Police dealing with them.

From then on, I avoided Dixon Avenue and made sure that I always parked a couple of streets nearer the ground where there would be more Rangers fans about.

I got into the Rangers end and found my seat. The game turned out to be a classic. In the first half, they took the lead but Peter Lovenkrands equalised. At half-time, I met my neighbour Brian's father-in-law whom I knew. He could see that I'd been roughed up a bit and I told him what had happened on the way to the game. In the second half, they scored again, but we continued to press towards our end. You could just sense that we would score as our play got better and better, but Barry Ferguson cracked a shot off the post. Then, Celtic's Bobo Balde clattered into Lorenzo Amoruso just outside their box, giving us a direct free kick. They lined up their defensive wall but Barry Ferguson curled a delightful kick over the wall and into the net. 2-2 and there wasn't much time left.

With seconds remaining and extra time looking likely, Neil McCann broke on the left. He hit a perfect cross into the Celtic area and it was met by the head of Peter Lovenkrands. As it bounced down and over Rob

Douglas, time seemed to run in slow-motion as we all held our breath. It hit the net and we went crazy as Lovenkrands ran round behind the goal to celebrate. There was hardly time to re-start the match before the final whistle was blown. McLeish had done it again. In the two big games, he had shown how to beat Celtic. He seemed to know how to get the best out of the players in the league and the cups. Surely next season would bring more success.

When I got home, I had to explain the cut on my forehead and my broken glasses. That didn't go down well!

During the summer, McLeish let Sebastian Rozenthal, Scott Wilson, Tony Vidmar and Andrei Kanchelskis leave the Club as their contracts expired. Tore Andre Flo was sold to Sunderland for £6.75 million – just over half what we had paid for him. The money was used to bring in Spanish midfielder Mikel Arteta from Barcelona and Australian defender Kevin Muscat from Wolves.

We crashed out of Europe at the first hurdle, losing to the unknown Czech team Victoria Zizkov on away goals but, in the SPL, things went very well. After drawing with Kilmarnock in our opening game, we then won our next eight games, scoring 25 goals and conceding just 2. Our next game was at Parkhead and, that season, the Glasgow derby games were to be televised nationally on the BBC.

It was a great match, which finished 3-3 and, in the studio, presenter Gary Lineker said, "If that's an example of what we're going to see, I can't wait for the next three games."

* * * * *

One thing that we have grown accustomed to at Rangers is that, when the team is doing well, we can expect certain "journalists" in the media to have a go at us for something else. It might be the fans' behaviour, or it might be some minor misdemeanor, but those who have no love for Rangers whatsoever always seem to raise the old chestnut subject of "sectarianism", and play the old worn-out record by complaining that Rangers didn't sign Catholics, or the fans were heard singing offensive songs. We can always rely on BBC Scotland to display a picture of Rangers fans on screen whenever they mention the subject – whether their story has anything to do with Rangers or not.

Since our founding, Rangers have been the most successful team in the country, and have won more honours than any other team. To do so, we must have consistently had the best players in our teams over the decades, so for someone to criticise us and say we only sign certain players seems to be a futile accusation. Do they think that we might have been even more successful if we had signed different players?

It doesn't need me to point out that Rangers are seen as the Protestant, Unionist team, wearing the colours of the Union flag, while Celtic are seen as the Catholic, Irish republican team, and football fans in the West of Scotland identify with one side or the other almost as soon as they are born. There may, of course, be fans whose personal allegiance does not follow the doctrine of their own side of the community – but they must be in a very small minority indeed.

When the subject raised its head in the early 1980s, one Sunday newspaper decided to ask several Scottish players, who happened to be Catholics, if they would ever sign for Rangers if they were asked. Every one of them said that they wouldn't, mainly because their families would be totally against it. It did seem to us then, that if Rangers were ever to sign a Catholic player, he would come from somewhere else in Europe or, even, South America. Rangers had, in fact, signed Catholic players – but the media always tried to make out that they had been signed by accident or through ignorance when they had kept their backgrounds secret. There was an allegation that Rangers scouts always asked a player's name, or what school he went to, before deciding whether or not to follow up their interest, and that some Protestant players had been missed out on because of that.

In Scottish society as a whole, there have been religious differences, in all walks of life, for centuries. It can't be denied that certain employers only hire personnel from their own side, and for decades, it was known that Catholics were never employed in the Police. Hiring managers who may have close personal connections with the Freemasons or Orange Order in their own private time are hardly likely to choose a Catholic employee over a Protestant one if that is the option. Certain private clubs such as golf clubs didn't admit Catholic members, and Protestant teachers know that they will not get a job or any chance of promotion in a Catholic school. That is just a fact of life.

Rangers, from the start, were run by Glasgow businessmen who were from a Protestant background, while the families who ran Celtic were from the other side of the divide. They were each allowed to get on with running their own clubs the way they chose. The fans were attracted to one side or the other, they wound each other up with their chants and songs, they tended to live in their own areas, they mixed with their own kind, and it just seemed to be accepted.

When Jock Stein became manager of Celtic, he added a new factor to the equation. If there were two players, a Protestant and a Catholic, that were attracting the interest of Glasgow's big two, he knew that he should concentrate on the Protestant player since Rangers would not sign the Catholic one. He could prevent Rangers from signing either of them, and could then have his pick of both.

As the 1960s progressed into the 1970s, society in general became less reliant on people blindly following what their parents and grandparents had done before them. Statistics show that church attendance has fallen steadily across the country, and those who may claim to be Protestants or Catholics probably never actually see the inside of a church except for weddings or funerals – and even then, these can be non-religious affairs nowadays. Yet fans of both sides still cling to those identities. The onset of "the Troubles" in Ireland gave both sides a focal point and caused a greater divide between the two fan bases. Once again, fans could cling to either side even though they may never have set foot in Ireland. It is a source of bafflement how Celtic supporters actually claim to be Irish when they may only have a tenuous link to Ireland, and they use that to take offence at everything Rangers do, saying it is anti-Irish and, therefore, racist. Yet, they are quite happy being anti-British, anti-Royalty, and anti-the armed forces.

Of course, in modern times, Rangers have signed scores of players from many different religious backgrounds. We have even had a Catholic captain and a Catholic manger. We are able to accept that – yet "for some reason", Maurice Johnston was hounded out of Scotland, being called "Judas" and receiving death threats because he played for Rangers – yet we are seen as the sectarian club.

For journalists to concoct accusations against us has become a way of life – so, in The Herald, on 9th October 2002, I wrote:

"How Rangers have fought against bigotry

I was disappointed to read the article by Graham Spiers in which he stated that "the Old Firm don't do enough to be rid of bigotry" and "Rangers certainly appear to do less than Celtic".

The only "evidence" he cites to "prove" this is the tannoyed playing of a song and the colour of a football jersey which is to be used as a second choice for one season out of the 130 that the club has been in existence. The fact that many prominent Rangers players are now Catholics and the club has an open recruitment policy, seem to have been forgotten.

I, along with many other Rangers supporters, could counter these allegations with instances, many of them recent, suggesting that Celtic (the club and its support) seem to do far less than Rangers to be rid of bigotry.

After Sunday's troubles, the police are again saying that games may have to be moved to an earlier time slot in the afternoon. The trouble seems to me to be worse when results do not go Celtic's way at Parkhead. Was there as much trouble after last season's CIS Cup Semi-final (7:45pm kick-off) when the crowd was split 50-50 or at any games at Ibrox last season? I don't think so.

I am a Rangers fan who goes to Ibrox, watches a game, and then goes home again. I strongly object to having matches at Ibrox moved forward to noon or 12:30pm on a Sunday instead of being played at the "normal" time because a minority of supporters cannot behave at Parkhead. If the police and the first minister want to stamp out these troubles, can I suggest that the first step should be to enforce strictly the part of the Criminal Justice (Scotland) Act which is intended to prevent admission to a football match while under the influence of drink? I have seen many instances where this is not being enforced. A further step might be to close all licensed premises within a set distance of the venue of an Old Firm match for an hour before and after the match."

Irresponsible drinking is a blight on Scottish society. Who wants to go to a game, and not enjoy it properly? Why can fans of other sports go along and enjoy a peaceful drink – but football fans think that they have to get 'tanked up' before a game? In all my years of going to football, I could count on one hand the number of times I have had a drink before a match, or after it. Personally, it doesn't bother me at all, but many fans see it as part of their day out, part of their routine – especially at away games or European ties, but they must miss parts of the game when they keep having to go in and out of their seats. As I have already said, I have seen the worst of what excess drink can do, and personally, it is something I can do without. When I stewarded at Hampden, I saw fans having to be helped up the stairs and into their seats because they were incapable of standing due to drink, and I had to wonder how they'd ever been let in the turnstile in the first place.

As for "sectarianism", it is something I'm aware of but it certainly doesn't affect my life. I don't have any affiliation to the Orange Order even though it seems that, to all Celtic fans - and their then future manager, that every single Rangers fan is a "dirty Orange bastard". Wrong on three counts! I might joke about a referee or linesman if they have a name which would suggest that they have a different background – but that's about as far as it goes, and Rangers and Celtic fans at work have a bit of fun on a Monday morning after a game but there is nothing malicious about it. As for the songs at matches – they are simply a way of winding up your opponents and there should be no harm in that. If folk get offended by them – there is a simple remedy. Don't go to the games, or turn the television sound down.

Over the years, we have had to become used to Rangers being accused of sectarianism at every turn. All the Government initiatives seem to be one-way as if anti-Catholicism or anti-Irishness, were the only types of discrimination that occur. "No-one likes us .." seems to be the order of the day when Celtic fans can get away with anything they like, claiming that it is "political" and therefore not as stigmatised somehow. They have anti-British banners, they are anti-monarchy, and they support a banned terrorist organisation – yet Rangers are always portrayed as the "villain" in this argument. We don't want favouritism – we just want fairness.

* * * * *

In the League Cup, we beat Hibernian away 3-2 and Dunfermline 1-0 away in the quarter-final. Our SPL form continued as we beat Motherwell, Kilmarnock, Dundee and Hibernian before drawing 2-2 away at Aberdeen. We then beat Dunfermline, Hearts and Livingston before Celtic visited Ibrox.

It was the usual noisy, tempestuous affair. We gave them a goal of a start when Chris Sutton stayed on his feet and bundled it in after just 19 seconds. Despite such an obvious set-back, we weren't put off, and Craig Moore equalised when he rose to head in a Ricksen corner. Ronald de Boer scored from a Neil McCann cross and Michael Mols scored our third with a low shot. We hadn't even played half an hour! Stefan Klos made a great save from an Alan Thompson shot before John Hartson scored a low shot after a poor clearance. Before the end, Lorenzo Amoruso cracked a 45-yard freekick off the post. It finished 3-2. Just another quiet Glasgow derby!

We then beat Dundee United and Partick Thistle before losing our first league game away to Motherwell on Boxing Day. When the transfer window opened, we released Billy Dodds and Russell Latapy, but bought Steven Thompson from Dundee United for just £200,000.

We kept on winning our league games and on a bitterly cold night at Hampden at the beginning of February we beat Hearts 1-0 thanks to a Ronald de Boer header to reach the League Cup Final. Our League run went on until 8th March when we lost 1-0 at Parkhead – a week before we would face them again, in the League Cup Final.

We beat them 2-1 with goals from Peter Lovenkrands and Claudio Caniggia, and they missed a penalty at the end which would have taken it into extra time. Once again, Alex McCleish had shown how to beat Celtic at Hampden.

In the Scottish Cup, we knocked out Arbroath, Ayr United and Dunfermline after a replay to reach the semi-final.

We had league wins against Motherwell, Partick Thistle and Dundee before we lost 2-1 at home to Celtic. The league was looking like it was going to be very close indeed and every point was now vital. At Dundee, we were awarded three penalties but missed two of them before Mikel Arteta took over penalty taking duty from Barry Ferguson who had failed with his efforts. The match finished 2-2 but there was a bitter feeling that Dundee manager, and Celtic fan, Jim Duffy had played his strongest team against us but fielded a much weakened side when they played Celtic who won 5-2.

At Hampden, we came from behind to beat Motherwell 4-3 in the Scottish Cup semi-final to set up a final against Dundee.

There were just three league games to go. On Easter Saturday, my dad had fallen outside the house and broken his hip in a couple of places. He required more than one operation and metal pins were put in. His mobility was greatly restricted and, for someone who played golf five or six times a week, this was a real nuisance. His visits to Ibrox were very limited so he let my daughter Hilary use his Concession ticket to start going to games. He did decide to make an effort to go to the third last league game, at home to Kilmarnock and we arranged to go over really early before the crowds built up. I dropped him at Mafeking Street, off Copland Road so he could walk slowly up to the stadium while I went and parked the car somewhere nearby.

We got into the ground really early and we met Lorenzo Amoruso who wasn't playing that day. I think he was on his way up to some hospitality or VIP area, again before the crowds came in. Coincidentally, he was on the front of the match programme that day and he very kindly signed it for me, as I chatted to him in my best Italian.

We won 4-0 and then beat Hearts 2-0 at Tynecastle. With just one game to go, we were neck and neck with Celtic with the same points and the same goal difference. For the first time in years, the title would be decided on the last day. We were at home to Dunfermline while Celtic were away to Kilmarnock. Both games would be shown live on TV and the league bosses would wait, somewhere on the A77, to deliver the trophy to either Ibrox or Rugby Park. If both results were the same, whoever scored more goals would win the league.

Hilary and I went to Ibrox where the tension was unbelievable. We'd chatted with friends on the way in, wondering if four goals would be enough. As the players warmed up, you could sense the pressure. They went through their usual routines but it was obvious that their minds were somewhere else. Everyone was watching our game but keeping tuned to events down at Kilmarnock as well. We took the lead after just two and a half minutes, but Dunfermline had the cheek to equalise through Jason Dair. Ibrox was temporarily silenced. We took the lead, but heard that Celtic were also winning at Rugby Park. We scored again. So did they. They were now in the lead at this point. Stefan Klos had to make a wonder save from Craig Brewster. We scored again. Celtic were 4-0 up and then they missed a penalty. We went 5-1 ahead. The goal difference was the same, and then we got a last minute penalty. Mikel Arteta took it – and scored. We all waited very nervously but their game finished 4-0, and ours finished 6-1 – giving us a goal difference of 73, just one ahead of Celtic but we had also scored an extra goal. We won the league in what we thought would be circumstances never to be repeated. How wrong would that prove to be?

We later found out that Celtic players had asked their former goalkeeper, Gordon Marshall, who was now playing for Kilmarnock, to let in plenty of goals so they could win the title - but he declined. Then Chris Sutton accused Dunfermline of lying down to us so that we would win. Gracious in defeat? Not a bit of it!

The third leg of the Treble was completed the following week when we beat Dundee 1-0 in the Scottish Cup Final with a goal from Lorenzo Amoruso who was playing his last match for the Club.

That summer, we were in Spain as usual and decided to take the girls to visit Gibraltar. We hired a taxi to take us on a tour of all the sights, and the driver asked us where we were from. When we told him that we were from Glasgow, he then asked if we were Rangers fans or Celtic fans. We quickly told him that we were Rangers fans and he was thrilled because he had watched the climactic last day of the season and was aware of all the drama and excitement, and when I said that Hilary and I had been at Ibrox on the last day, he was quite astounded. At the end of the tour, he got a good tip!

In his first full season, Alex McLeish had secured the Club's seventh Treble success and had matched the achievements of Bill Struth, Scot Symon, Walter Smith and Dick Advocaat. During the summer, we lost Arthur Numan, Claudio Caniggia, Bert Konterman and some fringe players whose contracts had ended, and we sold Lorenzo Amoruso and Barry Ferguson to Blackburn Rovers, Neil McCann to Southampton, and Kevin Muscat to Millwall. Arriving at the Club was a very cosmopolitan group – Zurab Khizanishvili, Paolo Vanoli, Henning Berg, Emerson, Egil Ostenstad, Hamed Namouchi and perhaps the warmest welcome of all went to Nuno Capucho who had helped FC Porto beat Celtic in the previous season's UEFA Cup final.

The season began well, with seven league victories in our opening seven games with some convincing scorelines – 4-0 against Kilmarnock, 3-2 away at Aberdeen, 5-2 against Hibernian, 3-1 against Dundee United, 4-0 against Dunfermline and Hearts away, and 3-1 against Dundee with some of the new players starting to score goals. In Europe, we beat FC Copenhagen 3-2 on aggregate, thanks to a late Shota Arveladze goal in Denmark, to qualify for the group stage of the Champions League.

In our first group game, we beat VfB Stuttgart 2-1 at Ibrox and then we managed a 1-1 draw away at Panathinaikos. Despite that promising start, we then lost our other four games including a 1-0 defeat at Ibrox by Manchester United, thanks to a Phillip Neville goal. There had been a lot of pre-match hype with McLeish, the apprentice, taking on Alex Ferguson, the master. United also won 3-0 in Manchester, and we lost in Stuttgart, before finishing the group with a 3-1 defeat at Ibrox by Panathinaikos. We finished bottom of the group.

We beat Forfar Athletic 6-0 in our opening League Cup game but then hit a league slump with a defeat at Ibrox by Celtic and draws against Motherwell and Livingston. Things improved with wins against Partick Thistle, Kilmarnock, Aberdeen and Hibernian followed by a League Cup quarter-final win against St Johnstone. Our league form was up and down as we beat Dundee United, Hearts, Dundee, Motherwell and Livingston but lost to Dunfermline and again to Celtic.

In January, Ronald de Boer's brother, Frank, came to join us from Galatasaray on a free transfer meaning that we still had two genuinely world class players in the team.

We knocked Hibernian out of the Scottish Cup and beat Partick Thistle in the league before facing Hibernian again, this time in the League Cup semi-final. The game finished 1-1 after extra time so it would be decided on penalties. Despite the poor international record of The Netherlands at taking penalties, we allowed both de Boer brothers to take kicks. Frank missed the decisive kick and we were out.

We knocked Kilmarnock out of the Scottish Cup and beat them in the league, then we drew 1-1 away at Aberdeen before getting some revenge on Hibernian by beating them 3-0 at Ibrox. We then lost away at Dundee United before Celtic knocked us out of the Scottish Cup.

After a 1-1 draw at Tynecastle, we beat Dundee 4-0 and Dunfermline 4-1 before losing yet another game against Celtic at Ibrox. We picked up 11 points in our next five games before losing to Celtic at Parkhead. This really was a most depressing run of results against them and, despite McLeish's early success against them, they now had the upper hand against us. We ended up 17 points off the top spot in the league and had another trophy-less season despite winning the Treble the year before. There had to be a massive improvement the following season.

During the summer, there was the now usual cost-cutting transfer moves. Christian Nerlinger, Emerson and Nuno Capucho had their contracts terminated, while Henning Berg, Michael Mols, Frank and Ronald de Boer left when their contracts expired. Mikel Arteta was sold to Real Sociedad and several of the youngsters left to pursue their careers elsewhere.

We brought in Dado Prso, Alex Rae, Marvin Andrews and Jean-Alain Boumsong on free transfers which went to show that we didn't have to spend big money to sign good players. Nacho Novo moved from Dundee for just £450,000 while £1.1 million was spent on Dragan Mladenovic, and Gregory Vignal joined for an undisclosed fee. Many of these 'bargain' players would go on to become huge favourites among the fans.

We started with a 0-0 draw away at Aberdeen before losing 2-1 away to CSKA Moscow. This was followed by two good wins against Livingston and Hibernian before we drew the second leg of the Champions League qualifier at Ibrox, knocking us out. Then we lost 1-0 at Parkhead and drew away at Hearts. We had only picked up eight points from our first five matches. Hardly an inspiring start - and we fell behind Celtic in the league.

We dropped into the UEFA Cup, and managed to qualify for the group stages following a tense penalty shoot-out against Portuguese team, Maritimo at Ibrox. We won that 4-2 with Gregory Vignal scoring the decisive kick, and that result seemed to kick-start our season.

Our league form improved and we weren't to lose another league game until the middle of April. In the new group stages of the UEFA Cup (each group had 5 teams so you played 4 matches – two at home and two away), we won our first two games - 5-0 away to Amica Wronki and 3-0 at home to Grazer AK but lost the other two – 1-0 to AZ Alkmaar and 2-0 to Auxerre, and that meant that we went no further. I had to work with a Dutch fan of AZ Alkmaar and he really rubbed it in, sending me a load of club merchandise, which managed to get conveniently misplaced somewhere. Once again, we had failed to achieve European football after Christmas.

In the league, our good run saw us beat Inverness Caledonian Thistle, Dundee, Kilmarnock and Motherwell – all without conceding a goal. We also beat Aberdeen 2-0 away in the League Cup. In the league, we drew with Dundee United and then beat Dunfermline, Aberdeen and Livingston before facing Celtic in the League Cup at Ibrox. It was a much awaited match after our recent poor run against them which we hoped we could start to put right. My dad couldn't go, and since it was a school night, the girls weren't allowed to, so I advertised on the internet that I had a spare ticket if anyone wanted to go with me. The anticipation and excitement to get tickets led me to meet a big Geordie fan called Rob who regularly travelled up from Durham to come to Ibrox. Sometimes, he stayed in a nearby hotel so he could enjoy some post-match refreshments and sometimes he drove home – not getting back until two or three in the morning.

We met outside the Club shop, introduced ourselves and went into the game. It was a very tense match and we went behind before Dado Prso equalised to put it into extra-time. Shota Arveladze scored and we won 2-1. We then played them in the league at Ibrox. We got a penalty when Nacho Novo was chopped down in a rash challenge. He took it and scored, and Dado Prso made it two when he rose to head in a Ricksen free-kick. Chris Sutton was booked for that foul. Alan Thompson head-butted Peter Lovenkrands and was sent off. Neil Lennon lost the plot and Chris Sutton was dismissed for a second yellow card when he handled the ball twice. The team we had out that day was not one made up of big money superstars but players who did their jobs and who worked for each other. I can't really imagine the likes of Alex Rae, Hahmed Namouchi, Marvin Andrews or Zurab Khizanishvili getting a game during Dick Advocaat's time in charge but they all did their bit. These two victories over Celtic led to the amusingly titled DVD, 'Remember, Remember, Two Wins in November' being released.

Someone else who occasionally came to games using my dad's ticket was a colleague Billy McIntyre. Billy was crazy but he loved Rangers. When European draws were made, work got ignored as he was straight onto the budget airlines or Eurotunnel to book his transport before the prices went up. One legendary story of Billy was about the evening that he went out to collect a Chinese take-away for him and his girlfriend. As he walked home, there was a supporters' bus meeting to head down to a game at Southampton. They shouted to Billy, "We've got a spare seat. Do you want to come?" So he did, all the way to Southampton, take-away in hand, before the days of mobile phones, and his girlfriend was sitting at home waiting for her dinner. He called her from somewhere to let her know where he was, and he returned home three days later – still with the take-away!

Another time, he was at a night-out in Kilmarnock and dossed down on somebody's floor. He got up on the Saturday and came straight to Ibrox. He was shattered and fell asleep in the seat. We went two up, and the crowd roared - but he was completely oblivious. At half time, he woke up and decided that he would just go home. He had no idea what the score was!

In the league, we had wins against Hearts, Dundee, Kilmarnock and Motherwell, plus a draw against Inverness Caley to see us up to Christmas. During the winter transfer window, we let Craig Moore and Paulo Vanoli leave on free transfers but the best bit of business was the sale to Newcastle of Jean-Alain Boumsong for £8 million. That funded the purchases of Thomas Buffel, Sotirios Kyrgiakos, goalkeeper Ronald Wattereus (since Stefan Klos was injured) and, on the last day of the transfer window, a homesick Barry Ferguson returned from Blackburn.

In January, Celtic knocked us out of the Scottish Cup, but we beat Dunfermline, Aberdeen and Livingston in the league. On 2nd February, we played Dundee United in the League Cup semi-final at Hampden 7-1. The loudest cheer was for Barry Ferguson coming on as a substitute in the second half.

It was a resounding result and we were into the final. I got home late, but had to be up very early to catch the dawn flight out to Amsterdam for an all-day meeting with some Dutch and American colleagues. As the afternoon wore on, I was getting rather tired but a late night out "celebrating" soon cured that.

We beat Hibernian 3-0 and then went to Celtic Park, hoping to end a poor run of results there. A shot from Gregory Vignal was misjudged by Rob Douglas, and then Nacho Novo lobbed the ball over him for a second and we won 2-0.

Wins over Kilmarnock, Hearts, Dundee and Motherwell plus a draw against Inverness meant that the league was neck-and-neck.

Unfortunately, our full-back Alan Hutton broke his leg in the Kilmarnock match and would be out of action for eight months.

Around this time, our good friends, Paul and Marianne Ferrier had bought a spacious bungalow just as few doors up the road from our house, but Paul got a chance of a job over in Miami. They decided to go and live there for six months to see how they got on. While they would be away, they would rent out their home. Sandy Jardine got in touch and it was agreed that Rangers would rent the bungalow from them, and could let any new signings live there until they got fixed up with permanent accommodation. First to move in was Sotirios Kyrgiakos and we often heard him standing in the garden, talking away in Greek on his phone. The US job became a success and the Ferriers settled in Miami. They continued renting their house to Rangers and there was a succession of players staying there over the next few years.

Other players moved into the area, since it was handy for the Auchenhowie training ground, and we often saw players at Asda

Bearsden or in the local area, such as Alec Rae, Hamed Namouchi, Daniel Cousin, Kyle Lafferty, and Steven Smith – who Victoria accidentally bumped into with a shopping trolley. No wonder he was out injured for so long! On a Sunday morning before an Old Firm game, Sergio Porrini and his Juventus friend Attilio Lombardo were casually wandering around Asda with their wives. Lombardo was at Crystal Palace at the time and must have been invited up as Porrini's guest for the game. He was approached by many of the staff for an autograph.

The 2005 League Cup Final was between Rangers and Motherwell and, since it was ten years since the tragic death of Davie Cooper, who obviously had starred for both teams, it was decided that the final would be The Davie Cooper Final and his image was printed on the tickets and there was a profile of him in the match programme. It wasn't a close match and Rangers won 5-1.

In April, we lost to Dundee United and scraped a 1-0 win against Dunfermline before the SPL split for the last five games. The SPL had decided that, as one of these would obviously be an Old Firm game which might decide the title, they wanted no repeat of the 1999 "shame game" so it would be the first match of the five. Celtic came to Ibrox and won 2-1. Rangers were now five points behind with just four games to go. Celtic fans already believed they were to be champions and two of them had held up a banner at Ibrox saying so. The Sun newspaper also declared them as champions in waiting.

As the old proverb goes, "Pride comes before a fall" and, in their next match, they lost to Hibernian. Alex McLeish rallied the troops and we won away at Aberdeen. Central defender Marvin Andrews, a man of great religious faith, defied all medical reasoning when he carried on playing despite a cruciate ligament injury that doctors said required an operation and a lengthy recuperation, and he encouraged us all to "Keep Believing". That became the motto to keep us going, and we won against Hearts and then beat Motherwell very easily 4-1 at Ibrox. The gap was now just two points but I really couldn't see Motherwell, who would be at home to Celtic on the last day, being able to mount any kind of challenge whatsoever if they played like that.

In the last game, we would have to beat Hibernian at Easter Road, and Celtic would have to draw with Motherwell. That would make us even on points, but we had the better goal difference. Setanta Sports who had the live television rights to the SPL would show one game on Setanta 1 and the other game on Setanta 2. To most Rangers fans, it looked a bit forlorn but big Marvin kept us going.

Saturday 21st May was Victoria's birthday and she had her party at Clydebank on the Sunday morning. One of the other girl's mums was trying to think confidently. "I think they'll do it. I know they will. Anything can happen."

After the party, back at home, we were having a late lunch, and Victoria and I were sitting in our conservatory, listening to the game on the radio. Celtic went one up and looked on course. Nacho Novo scored for us, but it did look like too little, too late. The SPL helicopter with the trophy was heading for Fir Park.

Time was ticking by and it wasn't looking good. Then a Motherwell cross went into the Celtic box and Scott MacDonald swung round and scored. The news came through immediately. That would put us ahead – but there was still time for it all to unravel. At Easter Road, the Rangers fans were going berserk and the players were unsure what was going on. Meanwhile at Motherwell, Scott MacDonald scored again. Easter Road erupted as video footage would later show. But how long was there to go? Not long enough – there was no more scoring. Rangers were champions and Celtic were devastated. Their expected party had disappeared in front of their very eyes. Incredibly, the helicopter had changed direction!

It wasn't just the fans at Easter Road who were going mad. Victoria and I were shouting loudly. Afterwards, we heard that neighbours two doors down had heard all the noise! Amid all the celebrations, it was announced on the radio that the team would arrive back at Ibrox at six o'clock. We just had to go. We had a quick early dinner, and Hilary, Victoria and I donned our scarves and headed over.

As we got nearer, it got busier and busier. The fans were thronging to Ibrox in their thousands. We got in, somewhere up near the back of the Govan Stand Upper. The party music was blasting out as Ibrox got fuller and fuller. Then came the first announcement – the bus had just turned off the motorway – and the volume of noise got louder. Then the second announcement – the bus is at the roundabout – and the cheers got even louder. When they said that the bus was at the front door, it was deafening. I couldn't remember a more spontaneous outpouring of celebration – not at Easter Road, Pittodrie or Parkhead. Perhaps against Aberdeen in 1991 – because we had seen the goals going in and we knew we'd be champions by the second half. Not in the last couple of minutes, in such dramatic fashion. It was unbelievable. Well, perhaps not to Marvin Andrews. Underneath his Rangers top, he wore a T-shirt that read "The things that are impossible for man are possible with God".

When the team came out onto the pitch with the trophy, Ibrox went wild, and we cheered and cheered. When it was all over and we went outside, it was obvious that the crowds had caught out the Police and stewards as there was no-one to direct the traffic, and it took us ages to get back home.

'Helicopter Sunday' was now part of the Rangers legend. The pictures and video clips that would emerge over the next few days and weeks would add to the story. There were "Keep Believing" T-shirts and a video of Dado Prso singing on the team bus. Celtic would always refer to it as 'Black Sunday' and their summer would be thoroughly miserable.

During the summer, when the girls were off school, we decided to take a wander down to Auchenhowie to see who we could see or meet. We didn't really know what the best time would be but we went down in the morning. It became clear that, for road safety reasons, the players were not allowed to stop their cars on the way in as they might block the road, but they were apparently told that they had to stop for fans waiting for them on the way out. We saw a few of the players arriving – big Marvin Andrews arrived with deafening reggae music blaring out of his car stereo - Barry Ferguson and Stefan Klos. We were going to give it a few more minutes, when Alan Hutton came out. He was still recovering from his leg break but could drive. He stopped and said hello to the girls and signed their autograph books. They were dead chuffed of course. I asked him about his recuperation and he told me he would be back soon.

There was another summer of cost-cutting and we let Shota Arveladze go at the end of his contract and Michel Ball, Dragan Mladenovic and Maurice Ross left on free transfers. Several of the youngsters left as usual and Allan McGregor was loaned to Dunfermline as was Charlie Adam to St Mirren, and Zhurab Khizanishvili to Blackburn Rovers. In came Ian Murray from Hibernian, Brahim Hemdani from Marseille, Jose-Karl Pierre-Fanfan from Paris Saint-Germain, Julien Rodriguez from Monaco, as well as Filippo Maniero, Olivier Bernard and 'the fox in the box', Francis Jeffers. Of these new arrivals, you could say that Hemdani was the only one to go on to make a name for himself. The others would turn out to be abject failures, and not anywhere like Rangers class.

The season started terribly and we only won six games out of the first seventeen. The team would go through one of the worst runs in their history – going ten games without a win. Hearts however, under new manager, George Burley, were the early pace-setters going on a tremendous run of form.

There was no hint of what was to come as we beat Livingston and Inverness Caley in our first two league games. We then beat Cypriots, Anorthosis Famagusta 3-0 in the home leg of our Champions League qualifier. We lost 3-2 away at Aberdeen but beat Celtic 3-1 at Ibrox before beating Famagusta 2-0 in the second leg to go into the group stage, but we then lost 3-0 to Hibernian at home.

Our up and down form continued into September as we beat Kilmarnock 3-0 but drew with Falkirk and lost to Hearts. We did win our first Champions League game 3-2 against Porto but lost the second to Inter Milan – a game played behind closed doors in the San Siro to punish Inter for some previous "misdemeanour". We opened our League Cup account with a 5-2 win over Clyde.

A 2-0 win over Motherwell was our only win in October as we drew with Dundee United, Livingston and Inverness Caley, and drew at home with minnows Artmedia Bratislava. There were no league wins in November – Celtic knocked us out of the League Cup at Parkhead and won there 3-0 in the league. We drew away with Artmedia but managed a creditable 1-1 draw away in Porto thanks to a well-taken Peter Lovenkrands goal.

Into December and our form picked up at last. We drew with Falkirk and Dunfermline, but beat Kilmarnock, Hearts and Dundee United. We also drew at Ibrox 1-1 with Inter Milan and, after hanging on to hear the other result in our section, that draw was enough to take us through to the knock-out stages – the last 16 - the first Scottish club to achieve this, and there would once again be European football after Christmas.

In the transfer window, we sold Steven Thompson to Cardiff and Zhurab Khizanishvili to Blackburn Rovers, and we spent the money to bring striker Kris Boyd from Kilmarnock. In his first game, he scored a hat-trick against Peterhead in the Scottish Cup so that appeared to be money well spent.

We beat Motherwell, Livingston and Inverness Caley in the league before crashing out of the Scottish Cup at home to Hibernian. On the following Saturday, we lost 2-0 at Aberdeen and Alex McLeish then announced that he would be leaving Rangers at the end of the season. We then lost at Parkhead but beat Hibernian at Ibrox.

Villareal of Spain were our Champions League last 16 opponents and we drew 2-2 with them at Ibrox and 1-1 away to be eliminated on the away goals rule.

Our league form improved and we would be unbeaten to the end of the season, but it wasn't enough. We finished third in the league behind Celtic and Hearts – who were at Ibrox on the last day. Match compere Andy Cameron announced to the Hearts fans, "We'll be back next season, but where will you be?"

Before that game, Graham Dott, a Rangers fan from Larkhall, paraded the World Snooker Championship Trophy which he'd won the previous weekend by beating Peter Ebdon 18-14 in the final.

Once again, there was an element of managerial hypocrisy from David Murray. When Graeme Souness had announced that he would leave the Club at the end of the 1990-91 season, Murray showed him the door immediately as he believed that his continued presence might disrupt the team – but when Walter Smith and Alex McLeish announced in mid-season that they intended to leave, they were both kept on until the trophy-less end of the seasons. To the fans, this seemed like a serious case of double standards but there might have been good reasons for it which we were not privy to.

With McLeish's imminent departure, there was debate on-line about how he would be treated when his reign came to an end. Would fans say 'good riddance' to the manager who presided over our worst series of results against Celtic and a dreadful run of games without a win, or would they instead choose to applaud him for the Lovenkrands cup final, the Konterman thunder-bolt, the dramatic title win against Dunfermline, the Treble, and Helicopter Sunday? In the end, he was warmly applauded and it was recognised that, for much of his time, he had been working with one hand tied behind his back as the Club constantly sought to cash in on players or ended their contracts early. Despite my own personal reservations around his appointment, he had done his best. He did manage to bring some great players to the Club and he did get us through to the knock-out phase of the Champions League – something that Dick Advocaat, with all the millions he'd spent, had never achieved.

During that summer, three additional rows of seats were built on to the front of the Govan Rear stand as part of the new 'Bar 72' facility and Ibrox's capacity was now increased to 50,987. In September, the Main Stand was renamed the Bill Struth Main Stand, to commemorate the 50th anniversary of the great man's death. That day, there was a special Matchday Programme, A4 sized with lots of picture and stories of Britain's most successful manager.

The new capacity of Ibrox still rankled many fans. Although Ibrox was state-of-the-art, modern and safe with a prestigious, listed red brick façade, it still holds fewer than Parkhead. After all its re-building in the 90s, with plain bricks, breeze-blocks and cheap materials, Parkhead now holds 60,355. That means it has 9,368 more seats than Ibrox despite all the additions that have been put in place. If the basic match price is, say, £20, that means a potential extra income for them of £187,360 per game. Over an 18 home-game season, that could mean an extra £3,372,480 from tickets alone. Extra people mean extra programmes and catering, and that means a much higher income, repeated every season. It might cost more for stewarding, policing, and staffing but extra pairs of eyes at games could also mean that stadium advertising can generate more revenue over a season.

Basically, they could probably afford to spend an extra £4 million on new players every single season. New plans for Ibrox, its surrounding area, and for money-generating schemes have come and gone. It would cost an absolute fortune for Ibrox to be demolished and re-built – keeping the façade, marble staircase and offices – but building a 21st century arena that looks something like the Olympic Stadium in Berlin, the Nou Camp in Barcelona, the Etihad or Old Trafford in Manchester, and where would that money come from? Some fans suggest removing the Jumbotron screens and replacing them with seats. That might be the answer, one day …

THIRTEEN
"Sacre Bleu!"

Despite the disappointing season, we were still able to look forward with a fair degree of optimism since, on 11th March 2006, David Murray announced that McLeish's replacement would be Frenchman, Paul Le Guen who had turned down Lazio, Benfica and Fenerbahce to come to Ibrox. This news stunned French football but it was greeted with great anticipation among the Rangers fans. Le Guen was well known as a successful manager – he was the so-called "new Arsene Wenger" – and had won three successive French titles with Lyon, and had taken them to the quarter-finals of the Champions League. David Murray announced him as a "massive moonbeam" heading for the Club.

Le Guen ticked all the right boxes. He was a strict disciplinarian and a fitness fanatic. We then heard that he would be competing in the 156 mile cross-Sahara 'Marathon des Sables' run before he came to Ibrox. This was looking even better, and the Rangers Supporters Trust even had a French-themed night at the Thistle Hotel in Glasgow during the summer.

Le Guen went about building his own team. Out went Sotirios Kyrgiakos, Peter Lovenkrands, Alex Rae, Ronald Wattereus, and a number of youngsters whose contacts had all ended. Marvin Andrews, Jose-Karl Pierre-Fanfan and Olivier Bernard all had their contracts terminated. It was very annoying to see Bernard being released and paid compensation only for him to sign a new deal with Newcastle within days. Why could he not have been transferred for a fee?

In came Dean Furman from Chelsea, Libor Sionko from Austria Wien and Lionel Letizi from Paris Saint-Germain on free transfers. Karl Svensson was bought from IFK Goteborg, Jeremy Clement followed Le Guen from Lyon, and Filip Sebo and Sasa Papac were bought from Austria Wien. In addition, we brought in two youngsters on loan from Manchester United – Phil Bardsley and Lee Martin.

Le Guen went on to prove his disciplinary status as Fernando Ricksen 'misbehaved' in a drink related incident on a trip to an away friendly. Ricksen would quickly depart – on loan and then be transferred - to Zenit St Petersburg.

The girls and I spent another morning at the Auchenhowie gates and Le Guen came out and signed autographs for them. Being a linguist, I was able to speak to him in French and I wished him good luck for the first league game, on the following Sunday away at Motherwell.

Le Guen's signings all came from respected European clubs but they just couldn't adapt to Scottish football. Despite an opening day win 2-1 at Motherwell, the team then drew its next two games against Dundee United and Dunfermline. We then beat Hearts 2-0 at Ibrox and it looked as if we had turned the corner but we then drew away at Kilmarnock. We lost away at Hibernian and Celtic. Points were being dropped far too frequently and the team was playing very badly. Svensson was a centre-back who seemed unable to defend or head the ball. Filip Sebo was a striker who couldn't score. Lionel Letizi was a poor goal-keeper who earned the nick-name "Lets-In-Easy". Bardsley was proving to be a hot-head and Jeremy Clement proved to be too soft and was easily knocked off the ball.

As early as October, we had fallen behind Celtic in the title race and, in November, we suffered the ignominy of being knocked out of the League Cup at Ibrox to a team from a lower division – 2-0 to St Johnstone – for the first time ever in our history. Le Guen's record in his first ten league games was the worst start to a season since John Greig's first season in charge. We did manage a 1-1 draw against Celtic at Ibrox thanks to a late Brahim Hemdani goal.

The only glint of success came in European competition where the players could escape the hurly-burly of the Scottish game, and had time to play football. In the first round of the UEFA Cup, we knocked out Norwegians, Molde, 2-0 on aggregate, and then were undefeated in our group section. We beat Livorno, Maccabi Haifa, and Partizan Belgrade, and drew 2-2 away to Auxerre. In the third round, we knocked out Hapoel Tel Aviv 5-2 on aggregate so there would be European football after Christmas once again.

By Christmas, we were 17 points behind Celtic in the league and, as the New Year started, Le Guen had a massive fall out with Club captain Barry Ferguson who was stripped of the captaincy and dropped for the following match, with Le Guen stating that Ferguson would never play for Rangers again while he was manager. We beat Motherwell 1-0 away and then, on 4th January, after 200 days and just 31 games, David Murray announced that Le Guen had left the Club by mutual consent, making him the Club's shortest-serving manager.

A lot has been written about why Le Guen failed so spectacularly. Was it the language barrier? Had he not done his homework? It was revealed that, prior to his appointment, Dick Advocaat watched videos of all Rangers games so that he would be familiar with the players and all the other teams. Le Guen had not done that, and had arrived in Glasgow with not much time left to prepare for the new season. Was he not given enough money to spend? Were the players he signed unable to gel as a team? Was Scottish football too rough for them? Did he have problems getting his tactics, methods of play and philosophy over to the Scottish players? Did he try to change too much too quickly?

He had no time for anybody who challenged his rules, and he expected a certain level of professionalism from his players. He tried to do away with the alcohol and junk food culture that existed and he even banned tackling in training. The frenetic style of Scottish football made it far too easy for other teams to stop Rangers playing. Le Guen became unwilling to change things when a new approach was needed and he claimed that Barry Ferguson was undermining him.

There was a split within the Club with some believing that he needed time to get things working his way, and others who had had enough, and saying that Le Guen had no idea what was really needed to succeed in the SPL.

FOURTEEN
Steadying the Ship and The Blue Tsunami

With Le Guen gone, Ian Durrant was appointed care-taker manager for the Club's third round Scottish Cup tie away at Dunfermline. We lost 3-2. We needed someone to "steady the ship" and quickly, and David Murray turned to the then Scotland manager, Walter Smith, who could not turn down the Rangers call. He brought with him his assistant Ally McCoist and appointed Kenny McDowall as first team coach, enticing him from Celtic reserves.

Smith had the January transfer window to sort things out, and he let Lee Martin and Phil Bardsley go back to Manchester United, released Julien Rodriguez, sold Jeremy Clement back to Paris Saint-Germain, and terminated the contract of Lionel Letizi. Realising that a poor defence was the main reason for Rangers' position, he signed defenders David Weir from Everton and Ugo Ehiogu from Middlesborough, Andy Webster from Wigan Athletic and defensive midfielder Kevin Thomson from Hibernian. These weren't huge stars – but they were well experienced professionals who had mostly been around the Scottish game for many years, and who wouldn't be intimidated by the opposition. Webster moved into the Ferrier's house up the road from us.

When Walter Smith was previously the manager, he didn't have to contend with the two transfer windows. If he had players injured and needed to sign someone, he just went out and did so. He could easily add to the squad at any time he wanted such as when he signed Dale Gordon, Gordon Durie or Alan McLaren. He also knew that he had the financial power of David Murray behind him and multi-million pound players could be lured to Ibrox. Things were different now with restrictions on when players could be signed, but more significantly was the fact that Rangers no longer had deep financial reserves and he would find that he might be forced to "cash in" on any sellable assets when the windows opened.

We needn't have worried as form immediately picked up and we went unbeaten for 13 games. Weir and Ehiogu were seen as 'stop-gap' signings but they showed their experience when we won at Parkhead in March with Ehiogu scoring a spectacular overhead kick goal. If there was one thing that Walter Smith knew well – it was how to beat Celtic.

We got knocked out of the UEFA Cup in March, 2-1 on aggregate to Spanish side Osasuna, but in May we beat Celtic 2-0 at Ibrox. Kris Boyd scored his first goal against Celtic when he beat the offside trap to hit in a low shot. It was his 100th SPL goal. The second goal came from a Charlie

Adam free kick. The Celtic defensive wall expected him to hit it over them towards the goal and they all jumped up as he took it. Anticipating that, he drilled the ball along the ground and under them into the goal.

We finished the season eight points behind Celtic but had managed two wins and a draw out of the four league games against them. Walter was back where he belonged and expectations were high for the new season. We could never have imagined what was going to happen ...

During that summer, Glasgow was to be in the News but for all the wrong reasons. On Sunday 1st July, we were to fly from Glasgow to Portugal, and a family from up the road were due to fly to Majorca. On the Saturday afternoon, I was standing outside chatting to that neighbour when Hilary came out and said there was a fire at Glasgow Airport. I just assumed she meant that one of the cafes' or restaurants' kitchens had caught fire and it would be put out quickly. I went back into the house and the TV was on. There was a scene of the front of the terminal building with a car ablaze, and the reporter said that terrorists had attacked the airport. What the hell was going on?

We all watched as the story emerged, and local hero, John Smeaton, the off-duty baggage handler, "set about" the burning terrorists, helped the Policeman, and thwarted the attack. They had tried to drive a burning jeep full of explosives right into the terminal building but had failed. It could have been so much worse as that was one of the busiest days of the year for the airport. After a lot of messing about, we did still manage to get away the next day, with a lengthy delay.

The last time I had seen John Smeaton was when he was a baby in a pram as his mother and father were friends of our family and his mother used to baby-sit my brother and me. When John was a baby, they brought him over to ours for a visit one Sunday.

In the weeks after the attack, he became a world-wide celebrity and made a variety of public appearances, including appearing on the pitch at Ibrox before our pre-season friendly against Chelsea where he was given a most rapturous welcome. Chelsea were a week behind us with their pre-season preparations so the sides were pretty evenly matched. Having been a bit of a laughing stock for his inability to score goals, Filip Sebo showed that he did actually know how to score when he unleashed a screamer into the Chelsea net. Nacho Novo scored another to seal an encouraging 2-0 win against our "Blues Brothers".

During the summer, Stefan Klos, Dado Prso and Gavin Rae all left when their contracts ended. Karl Svensson was sold to Caen and Libor Sionko was sold to Copenhagen. Filip Sebo was loaned to Valenciennes, and Ian Murray was given a free transfer to Norwich City.

Smith brought in several new players, many on free transfers and his biggest purchases only cost just over £2 million. We welcomed DaMarcus Beasley, Kirk Broadfoot, Roy Carroll, Jean-Claude Darcheville, Lee McCulloch, Steven Whittaker, Daniel Cousin, Steven Naismith, Alan Gow and Amdy Faye. Smith brought in Scottish players that he knew from his time as the International manager as well as some experienced professionals from around Europe.

In the course of a normal season, Rangers can expect to play 50-55 games, depending how well they perform in the cup competitions and in Europe. In season 1992-93 when the Treble was won and there was the run in the Champions League, the team played 64 games, but that was with a fairly large squad. In 2007-08, they surpassed that by playing an unprecedented 68 competitive matches and some of them went to extra time and penalties, so the squad's energy resources were stretched considerably.

That season, Carlos Cuellar played 65 competitive games, while Barry Ferguson and David Weir played in 61. For Weir especially, at his age, this was a remarkable achievement, remembering that he had really only been signed as a temporary measure. His experience and influence became very important on the defenders around him and there was no doubt that he helped Cuellar settle into the Scottish game with relative ease.

Our opening competitive match was against Montenegran side, FK Zeta in the Champions League qualifying round two and we won 2-0 at Ibrox, and then 1-0 away. In the SPL, we started well, beating Inverness Caledonian Thistle, St Mirren, Falkirk, Kilmarnock and Gretna. We also progressed to the Champions League group stages after a hard-fought qualifier against Red Star Belgrade. We won 1-0 at Ibrox and then held them to a 0-0 draw away.

After losing 4-2 away at Hearts, we beat Aberdeen 3-0 at Ibrox. In the Champions League, we were drawn in Group E with VfB Stuttgart, Lyon and Barcelona. We started off with two wins, against Stuttgart and Lyon but everyone was eagerly anticipating the games against Barcelona, one of the best teams in the world.

In the SPL, we drew away at Motherwell before losing to Hibernian at Ibrox, but as if to show that the players' minds were not on the following midweek's Barcelona match, we beat Celtic 3-0 at Ibrox.

There was the usual frantic start with both teams having chances. In the 27th minute Alan Hutton hit a low cross into the Celtic penalty area. Nacho Novo "the man for the Old Firm occasion" got in through three defenders to stoop and head the ball into the net. In the second half a shot was blocked and Barry Ferguson was fastest to react as he scooped the ball into the net. Alan McGregor made a couple of great saves and a Daniel Cousin cross was blocked in the penalty area with an arm, but no penalty was given, before Charlie Adam side-stepped his way into their box to be brought down by an Evander Sno lunge. He leapt to his feet desperately wanting to take the penalty he had just won but he was over-ruled. A limping Nacho Novo stepped up to score and make it 3-0 before being substituted. Near the end, Lee McCulloch pounced and hit the ball into the net. As he began his celebrations, it was disallowed for an offside decision that television pictures proved had been incorrect. So it was a fairly comfortable afternoon. Celtic completely lost the plot and amassed nine bookings. We expected them to be called up before the SFA Discplinary Panel to get a hefty fine for their behaviour, but we are still waiting for that. Recently, they managed to pick up seven bookings in a European tie and UEFA wasted no time in fining them. Once again, the SFA failed to deal with the matter properly and Celtic got off the hook. There's that bias happening again!

Barcelona came to Ibrox with a team boasting the likes of Messi, Henry, Xavi, Iniesta, Puyol and Ronaldinho. Instead of having a go at them and possibly suffering a substantial defeat in the process, Rangers simply "parked the bus" and stopped Barcelona playing. The game finished 0-0 and Messi accused Rangers of playing "anti-football". Nevertheless, in a very tough group, we had seven points from our first three games.

On our first competitive visit to the Nou Camp stadium in Barcelona since the famous night when we won the European Cup Winners' Cup, the "Barcelona Bears" squad from 1972 were the Club's special guests for the game. Unfortunately, their presence was not enough to inspire the current team, who lost 2-0. They then managed to lose 3-2 in Stuttgart before succumbing 3-0 to Lyon at Ibrox in a reverse of our earlier win in France, and we finished third in the group, meaning that we "parachuted" into the new UEFA Cup, into the knock-out rounds.

Putting Europe aside until after the New Year, the team went undefeated in the SPL until Christmas. We were due to go to Parkhead on the 2nd of January, and we were full of confidence. A long unbeaten run and the fact that Celtic had injuries and suspensions to worry about made us strong favourites for the game, but the tragic hand of fate would prevent the game from going ahead.

On Saturday 29th December, Motherwell were playing Dundee United. Just as he was about to be substituted, the Motherwell captain, Phil O'Donnell collapsed, and was treated by the clubs' doctors for several minutes before being taken by ambulance to the nearest hospital. He was pronounced dead, and the post-mortem revealed that he had died of heart failure, aged just thirty-five.

Celtic immediately asked for the game against us to be postponed as a mark of respect, stating that O'Donnell's death had had a profound effect on the staff and players at Parkhead. "As a former player, Phil was part of Celtic's extended football family."

The SPL granted their wish, and also postponed Motherwell's next game, and the one after that which was due to be against Celtic – but Dundee United, who had watched him collapse on the field beside them, were not granted a postponement. Celtic now had two big games re-arranged, giving the injured players plenty of time to recover, and the suspended players would have to miss less important fixtures instead.

The SPL allowed Celtic to play the 'victim card' but forced Dundee United to play their game. How unfair was that? It has to be remembered that Celtic never asked for postponements when far more popular former-players passed away, or when Tommy Burns their coach and former manager died. O'Donnell won just two medals in five years while at Parkhead, and left when he failed to agree terms on his new contract. He was not even a popular player at the time. But they got things their way and it would be a bigger help than they could have possibly imagined.

Meanwhile, the January transfer window opened and we let Roy Carroll and Ugu Ehiogu leave on free transfers but the biggest blow was the sale of Alan Hutton to Tottenham Hotpsur for £9 million. He had been one of our best players that season and we thought we could look forward to several years of seeing him develop as the best right-back in the country. His surging runs from the back led to a lot of goals and chances, and his marking and tackling were top notch – especially when playing Celtic. He didn't want to leave but it was now obvious that we were a Club who would cash in on any sellable assets especially if the rich English clubs came looking. We didn't realise it at the time but Hutton's presence might have made a huge difference with what was to happen in the spring. He might have earned us the couple of points that we would eventually need, and he could then have been sold in the summer window.

We brought in goal-keeper Neil Alexander from Ipswich in what turned out to be an inspired move. Alexander was just starting to appear in Scotland squads and would prove to be a more than capable back-up for Alan McGregor. We also brought in the experienced Christian Dailly from West Ham United and midfielder Steven Davis, a Rangers fan since childhood, on loan from Fulham. None of these cost us a penny in transfer fees.

We went through January and February with maximum SPL points, playing eight games and conceding only three goals but scoring twenty-one, and progressed to the semi-final of the League Cup where we beat Hearts 2-0. We also beat East Stirlingshire 6-0 in the Scottish Cup fourth round, and, in the next round, we could only manage a 0-0 draw at Easter Road which meant a replay – an extra fixture we could have done without. Fixtures were beginning to increase but we didn't realise how big a problem that would turn out to be.

We turned our attention to the UEFA Cup knock-out stages where we would face the Greek side Panathinaikos. In previous years, and even decades, the philosophy had always been to win your home leg and build up a good lead to take into the away leg, to give you a good chance of progressing. That began to change as Walter Smith realised that, to give yourself a chance, you had to avoid conceding anything at home, even to get a 0-0 draw, and when the opponents tried to score against you in the second leg, they would create gaps at the back which could be exploited on the break or from set-pieces. The Italians had perfected this tactic years ago and it was known as "Cattenacio". Our form was now referred to as "Wattenacio"!

In February, we drew 0-0 at Ibrox but drew 1-1 away to Panathinaikos to go through on the away goals rule, and we would meet the Germans of Werder Bremen in the Round of 16. Ibrox was packed for the first leg and we beat them 2-0 with a great, professional display. We completed the job by limiting them to a 1-0 win in Germany, due particularly to an amazing goal-keeping display by Alan McGregor including a wonder save that had to be seen to be believed, and we progressed to the quarter-finals where we were drawn against Sporting Lisbon – the same team we had beaten on our way to or last European success in 1972. A good omen?

We continued winning in the SPL beating Aberdeen, Hibernian and Celtic. We won 1-0 at Ibrox thanks to a Kevin Thomson goal right on half-time which put us in a great position in the league. We won our Scottish Cup replay against Hibernian but drew in the quarter final against Partick Thistle meaning yet another replay.

In the League Cup final, we met Dundee United who we had recently drawn 3-3 against in the SPL, and twice came from behind thanks to goals from Kris Boyd. The game finished 2-2 after extra time (yet more playing time) and we won 3-2 on penalties with Alan McGregor saving two of them and Boyd scoring the winning kick. There was no time for celebrations as the fixtures were piling up.

At this stage, we had a ten point lead over Celtic in the SPL but they had games in hand. April would prove to be a crucial month as we earned a 0-0 draw against Sporting Lisbon at Ibrox and won our Scottish Cup replay against Partick Thistle. We only played two SPL games that month and both were at Parkhead, due to postponements and our midweeks being tied up with European games or cup replays which got preference. We lost the first one 2-1 but, when the game was tied at 1-1, an injured Alan McGregor saved a penalty before limping off to be replaced by Neil Alexander. We then met St Johnstone in the Scottish Cup semi-final which finished 2-2 after extra time. We won 4-3 on penalties but yet more energy sapping minutes had been played. The next weekend, we were at Parkhead again and lost 3-2. In the two matches, Celtic had got away with a succession of disgraceful fouls, some of them being chest-high kung-fu style assaults. We were playing lots of high pressure minutes, and the fixtures were still mounting up - as was our casualty list.

In another disciplined display, we drew 0-0 with Sporting Lisbon at Ibrox before winning the away leg 2-0 to progress through to the semi-finals. The tactic of defending as well as possible and then hitting on the break worked perfectly. The second goal came after a long run from the half-way line from Steven Whittaker who had gone past three or four defenders before scoring. What a finish!

The month of May was going to be one of the most important in our long history with the team going for three trophies. Time was running out but there were still ten games to be played. The SPL looked at the possibility of extending the league season to give us a chance but Celtic put a gigantic spanner in the works. They announced that they were going to Japan as soon as the league finished to take part in a mini-tournament that they were contracted into playing. They refused to accept a delay to the last league games, and that meant that Rangers had to play too many games in too short a time. We couldn't afford to rest any of our players as every game was vital at that stage so we just had to keep going.

At the end of April, we drew 0-0 with Fiorentina in the UEFA Cup semi-final first leg at Ibrox. The same, proven tactic once again. All eyes were now on the Stadio Artemi Franchi in Florence on the 1st of May. I nervously watched the game on television at my parents' house. After 90 minutes of resolute defending, the score was still 0-0, so extra time was needed once again. Where on earth were the players getting the energy from? By that stage, they weren't even doing any training, just playing the games.

After 210 minutes of goalless football, a penalty shoot-out would decide who would go into the final. There had been chances and goal attempts but neither team could score. Daniel Cousin had been sent off for head-butting Fabio Liverani with just ten miutes to go. If we managed to get through, he would miss the final. Once again, we had the chance of European success but we would have to do it without a big bustling striker. The stadium was at fever pitch. In the back of our minds was the fact that the final that year would be just down the road at the City of Manchester Stadium, a mere four hours away by car or a short train ride away.

Leading the way, our captain, Barry Ferguson stepped up to take the first kick. We held our breath as he ran up … and it was saved. At that stage, I admit that I felt that we wouldn't win. We had done so well to get to the semi-final but we had reached "a bridge too far". Fiorentina scored their first kick. Steven Whittaker did what his captain couldn't do, but they scored their second. It was now 2-1 after two kicks each. Sasa Papac scored our third kick, and then Neil Alexander saved Fiorentina's next one. It was now level with just two kicks to go.

Brahim Hemdani scored our next kick putting us ahead. Fiorentina's top player on the night, Christian Vieri, stepped up to take the next kick … and he blasted it over the bar, meaning that, if Rangers scored their next kick, we would be in the final. We looked to see who was going to take it. It was our Mister Reliable, Nacho Novo. Could he do it? The tension was unbearable. We were on the edge of our seats.

ITV match commentator, Peter Drury uttered the immortal words, as Novo prepared, "Manchester, brace yourselves …" Novo ran forward and hit the most important kick of his career straight into the net. We were in the UEFA Cup Final. "Rangers are coming! The Scots are heading for Manchester and, you know what? Manchester may not be big enough! They won't need visas! They won't need passports. The battle for tickets starts now! They are on their way!"

The feeling of ecstasy was unbelievable. We watched for a short while longer and then I hurried home to get on-line to book my hotel, confidently expecting to get a ticket for the final as I'd had a season ticket since the early 80s and had been at every cup final since 1978. I had to get my accommodation sorted out quickly, but obviously I wasn't the only one with that idea. Rooms were filling up all over that part of the country. We browsed all the usual hotel-booking websites and checked all over a fairly wide area, and the best room I could get was at the Travelodge in Wigan. I wasn't too concerned with that – it would be easy to get to by car or train, and I could easily nip on a train from there to Manchester. When I went into work the next morning, I put in for the time off.

As in 1972, our opponents in the final would be from Russia. Was this yet another good omen? This time it would be Zenit St Petersburg, managed by our old friend, Dick Advocaat – the manager who had brought us such success at home and in Europe. Zenit were a team 'on the up' with big money behind them, but once again, Walter Smith had shown that you don't need a team of multi-million pound superstars to do well in Europe. Just as he had done in 1992-93, a tightly knit team of hard working professionals, and mainly Scots, could actually do better than a team with the likes of Laudrup, De Boer, Gascoigne or Souness in it.

The following Sunday, we could only manage a 0-0 draw at Hibernian, but on the Wednesday night, we beat Motherwell at Ibrox. By this time, tickets for the final on the 14th of May were already being issued to supporters. I was in the Continuous Credit Card Scheme (and had been for years) and I was constantly checking on-line to see if a payment had come off my card. The days were passing and there was still no news. Then our opponents returned a load of tickets since it must have been too difficult for their fans to travel, so another batch got released to Rangers. I kept checking and checking but still no payment had been taken.

I was still sure that I would get a ticket for this "Game of Games" but, as the days went by, there was still no news. I was on the internet all the time checking for news about new batches of tickets being available as the final got nearer. Travelodge phoned me 3 times to check that I definitely wanted the room.

I heard that the Diageo site at Shieldhall, Glasgow, was having to decide what to do that day, and how to keep operating, since such a huge number of the staff had asked for the time off. Word was already spreading that tens of thousands of fans were intending to travel to Manchester, although ticketless, just to be in the same city as the match. The messages from the host city were mixed to say the least. "Don't come if you've not got a ticket" or "There will be huge screens erected so fans can congregate in the city's squares to watch the game". More and more fans were saying that they were going to be there.

I heard that some guys who had been in the BB were heading down. "Are you going, too?" I was being asked. "Yes," I replied. "You'll recognise me. I'll be the one wearing a blue shirt with the word 'Carling' on the front, and wearing a Rangers scarf!"

Meanwhile we were still going for the SPL. On Saturday 10th May, we beat Dundee United 3-1 at Ibrox. We heard that the Russian football authorities had given Zenit a "weekend off" before the final so that they could rest and be prepared – yet here we were having to cram in vital games instead of being able to prepare properly. Not only that but the Russians were at an early stage of their season which, due to their climate, ran throughout the summer months. They would be fitter and fresher than we could ever hope to be.

The two ladies I sat beside at Ibrox told me that they already had their tickets. The daughter worked for Lloyds TSB and had got them from their main office in Sussex ... where my own brother works! I got straight on to him to ask if he had got a ticket. No, "It'll be over in the other building, but I'll check". He called back, "All gone!" I couldn't believe it!

The day before the final, I had to accept that there was no ticket with my name on it so I called Travelodge and released the room. I guess they re-sold it for many times what I had been going to pay.

I decided to go to Ibrox to watch the match on the big screens. I was to take both my daughters and one of their school-friends, so I had to cancel my time off at work. On the morning of the match, there was very little work done and I kept seeing updates on the internet of a "blue tsunami" heading down the motorway. Fans waved flags and hung huge banners from the motorway bridges to wish everyone 'good luck'.

I heard that a couple I knew were heading down the M6 with their teenage son. They had got tickets. At nine o'clock, they had to 'phone his school to let them know that he wouldn't be in that day. Sitting in a traffic jam on the motorway, they made the call and got put through to the school office. They explained that their son had a headache or sore stomach or something like that, and the lady on the other end of the phone noted that down. Just at that very moment, the traffic began to move a little and a minibus of supporters pulled alongside them. In their words, "The Sons of Larkhall Flute Band" let rip with some well-known anthem with the drums giving it full lick! The lady at the school laughed and said, "Oh! I see," but added cheerfully that she understood exactly what was going on.

A neighbour had even told me that he'd "arranged to attend a conference in Birmingham that week" so he got all his travel and hotel booked for him.

Leaving work in Ayrshire at lunch-time, I passed Ibrox on my way home. I stopped to buy a couple of match programmes which were on sale in the shop. People were queuing up already. I told the girls to eat their dinner as quickly as possible and we hurried over. The crowd was growing and more and more doors and stands were being opened. We got into the Copland rear with about an hour and a half to go.

The atmosphere was surreal. The sounds of women and children were everywhere. All the men must be down at the game, I imagined. The songs were rather high-pitched, flags were being waved everywhere, and there was a mile long queue for the ladies toilets! It was the oddest visit to Ibrox I had ever experienced. No actual game; hardly any men; kids and mums all over the place.

When the match coverage started, the picture on the screens was not actually that easy to see, due to the bright evening sunlight, but, once the sun went down, it became clearer.

Even though the players were running on empty, I was ever so proud of them. They tried to defend as usual, with the hope of getting a late chance on the break. Zenit scored but we pushed forward. They scored again. If only we had got a goal and got something to shout about. The noise in Manchester and Glasgow would have been like a sonic boom. It would have been the roar that was heard around the world.

The pictures showed that there were about 200,000 Rangers fans from all over the world in Manchester. It was the biggest ever crowd to travel to any sporting event. The aerial photographs and the stories from the motorway were sensational, as the 'blue tsunami' made their pilgrimage. Manchester and its surrounding areas were brought to a complete standstill.

Unfortunately, as we now know, Manchester was totally unprepared for that size of crowd – even though it was obvious in advance to everyone that vast numbers would be travelling. Large areas could have been set aside for fans with adequate space, catering and toilet facilities. Old Trafford could have been opened and the game screened there. That would have held sixty or seventy thousand fans – with proper facilities. The transport arrangements were chaotic. The city seemed perfectly happy to sell drink to the fans all day – but provide nothing else for them. Pubs and hotels must have made a fortune and many ran out of drinks. This was all a recipe for trouble, and when a big TV screen failed (or was turned off!) just before the match started, denying thousands the chance to watch, it was like lighting the blue touch-paper.

Obviously, I don't condone any kind of trouble, but Manchester must accept a lot of the blame for taking the fans' money but doing nothing for them. What should have been a well-organised carnival event was just chaotic. Some of the fans I knew, who were there, never saw anything of the scenes that the media were only too eager to show. Once again, our Club was tarnished with an un-deserved reputation caused by what was the tiniest of minorities.

Back at home, the fixtures kept coming. On the Saturday, we drew away at Motherwell and, on the following Monday (!), we beat St Mirren 3-0. The race for the SPL was going to the last match of the season. We were tied with Celtic on 86 points although they had a better goal difference of six. On the Thursday evening, we would be away at Aberdeen while they would be away at Dundee United. They had had plenty of time to rest and prepare while we were playing too many matches. It was too great a hurdle for us to overcome. Our aching tired legs just couldn't do it. We lost to Aberdeen 2-0 and they beat Dundee United 1-0 to win the title.

Reports even came through that Willo Flood of Dundee United actually joined in with the Celtic celebrations. How sad and pathetic!

There was, once again, no time to dwell on this as we had to play the Scottish Cup Final on the Saturday afternoon. Fortunately, or so we all thought, we didn't have to go up against an SPL side like Celtic, Aberdeen, Dundee United or Hearts. We were to play Queen of the South.

Despite the exhausted legs, we were two up by half-time with goals from Kris Boyd and DaMarcus Beasley, but Queen of the South somehow managed to score twice in the second half to equalise. Drawing on our last available gasps of energy, Kris Boyd managed to score the winner before we were faced with yet more extra time. The celebrations were rather muted as the team walked round the Hampden turf after the presentation.

In addition to the usual Cup Final songs and chants, there was a new one. It was strongly rumoured that Walter Smith was planning to re-sign Kenny Miller during the summer transfer window. He had played briefly for us during Dick Advocaat's management but had headed south to further his career. The Rangers fans now saw him as "damaged goods" since he had returned to Scotland, had signed for Celtic and had actually scored against us. Songs told Walter Smith exactly where he could stick Kenny Miller!

For fans, it had been a very expensive season with cup semi-finals, finals and so many European games to buy tickets for. It must have cost even more for the fans who also traveled to away games in Europe. I had to sell a chunk of my CD and DVD collection to help finance all the extra expense.

The season that had promised so much had ended in exhausted disappointment. The SPL had done nothing to help us. Instead, they placed insurmountable obstacles in our way. We had to play far too many games in too short a time. The players had gone the extra mile but it still wasn't enough, and Celtic had "turned the knife" to stop us. We are now seven years on and they still haven't gone on that tour of Japan that prevented the extension to the league which would have allowed us to play our games at reasonable intervals, and the re-arranged New Year game was fitted in at a time that suited them, when we were struggling with fixtures. The SPL allowed them to cheat their way to the title. We needed to get our revenge ...

FIFTEEN
Winning Ways Again

As I've mentioned, at Easter 2006, my dad fell in front of their house and broke his hip in a couple of places. His mobility was seriously impaired and he needed to get walking sticks and a Zimmer frame to be able to walk. When he finally got home again, he preferred to spend his days sitting in his favourite armchair watching the television. They got SKY Sports so that meant there was now somewhere to go and watch our away games. He contacted Ibrox to ask about disabled access but this was not really possible so, after managing to get to his last ever game, he let the girls use his season ticket, and they started going to all the games.

Later in the year, he fell in his room and banged his head on the corner of a chest of drawers. He was actually due to go into hospital for something else when his speech and memory began to be affected. The doctors discovered that he had a blood clot in his brain so he was rushed over to the Southern General Hospital Neurological unit and had to undergo an operation to remove it. For the next three years, he spent more time in hospital than at home, including two Christmases.

It was decided that we would transfer his season ticket officially to Victoria's name since she would count as a juvenile for three years more than Hilary would. At this time, Sasa Papac moved into a house up the road from us and his children went to the same school as Victoria who came back home one afternoon with his autograph on the back of her hand. He immediately became her favourite player. He and his wife Ivana often went to events at the school, or he collected his children from the school gates. The headmistress had to ask the pupils not to bother him when he was standing there.

As usual, during the summer, Walter Smith refreshed his squad. Out went Filip Sebo for £1 million, which was honestly a big surprise, Thomas Buffel on a free transfer, Carlos Cuellar to Aston Villa for £7.8 million and Daniel Cousin to Hull City for £3.5 million. Several youngsters and fringe players also left or were loaned out.

The money was spent on players who would form the nucleus of our first team for the next few years and who would bring success to the Club. In came Kenny Miller (Yes, he did sign), Kyle Lafferty, Madjid Bougherra, Steven Davis on a permanent deal, Maurice Edu as well as Pedro Mendez.

There would be a lot fewer games during the following season due in part to the Club's early elimination from European football. We drew with FBK Kaunas 0-0 at Ibrox but lost the away leg 2-1 when they scored in the 87th minute. Having got to a European final in May, we were out of Europe by the beginning of August – before the SPL had even started. There would be no "parachute" into the UEFA Cup and this meant a significant financial consequence for the Club as they would be denied the potential riches from the Champions League. The annual results would show a £3.9 million loss to the end of December 2008 and there was pressure on Walter Smith to reduce the playing squad, in the winter transfer window, to cut costs.

We started the season with wins over Falkirk and Hearts and a draw away at Aberdeen before our first visit of the season to Parkhead. It was a manic ninety minutes, as usual. Rangers scored first when Daniel Cousin powered his way past the trailing defender Mark Wilson before whacking a shot from a tight angle straight into the goal. They got an equaliser, and it was 1-1 at half-time. At the start of the second half, Kenny Miller scored a good volley, and celebrated as if his heart and head had always been at Ibrox, before Pedro Mendez scored his first goal for the Club – and what a goal. We got a corner at the far side and everyone jostled for position in the penalty area. Instead of crossing the ball, Steven Davis played it in front of Mendez, lurking unmarked outside the area. He hit a low, unstoppable shot right into the back of the goal! Kenny Miller then pounced when Celtic goal-keeper Artur Boruc fumbled an easy save and we were 4-1 up. Daniel Cousin picked up two yellow cards for challenging Stephen McManus with his elbows. He had given the Celtic defence a torrid afternoon. The numbers were level before too long as Celtic substitute, Jan Vennegoor of Hesselink was dismissed for an off the ball challenge on Kirk Broadfoot. They scored a late consolation goal but it didn't matter. What a way to assert our authority right at the start of the new season and to show that we were determined to get our own back for the events at the end of the previous one. The SKY commentator even said "Happy days are here again!"

We then defeated Kilmarnock, Motherwell and Hibernian as well as knocking Partick Thistle out of the League Cup - Mendez scored another beauty in that game, too – but we then lost away at St Mirren. After the International break in October, we returned to winning ways by beating Hamilton Academical in both the league and League Cup. We played seven games during November and recorded four wins, two draws – one of them was a 3-3 at home to Dundee United - and one defeat, away to Hearts.

Our form in December was erratic. We beat Hamilton Academical 7-1 at Ibrox, drew 2-2 away at Tannadice, beat Hibernian at Ibrox but lost the traditional seasonal game against Celtic, 1-0 at Ibrox. At the end of the month, we trailed Celtic by seven points in the league.

When the January transfer window opened, Walter Smith reduced his first team squad by letting Jean-Claude Darcheville go to Valenciennes and Chris Burke to Cardiff City on free transfers while Charlie Adam went down to Blackpool on loan, but the increased debt meant that the Club needed to find some more money. They tried to sell Kris Boyd to Birmingham City, even though he didn't want to leave, but it fell through because of his wage demands.

We were unbeaten in January, recording wins against Inverness Caledonian Thistle, St Johnstone in the Scottish Cup, Falkirk in the SPL and in the League Cup semi-final, and Dundee United, but drew away at Pittodrie.

At this time, an email arrived from the Club saying that they were inviting 50 young season ticket holders to be part of the guard of honour at the upcoming glamour friendly against AC Milan at Ibrox. Victoria agreed to be part of this and I had to take her over early to get kitted out with a blue sweatshirt and to have a practice. They were all to meet over in the Community Centre across the road from the front of Ibrox at about six o'clock. I dropped her off there, went along to the Kentucky Fried Chicken to get my dinner, and then went in to my seat. She was in the parade of junior flag-bearers who walked round the track before the game. The plan was that the Club's people who were in charge would bring them back to their seating areas as soon as the match kicked off and we could meet and collect them from the food concourse areas. I left my seat and went down to get her, and there were a few other adults waiting as well. A door along at the end opened up and a group of blue-shirted children appeared with the 'grown ups' but I couldn't see Victoria. All the children were met and the 'leaders' went to leave – but there was still another Dad and me, asking, "Where are they?" as our two were nowhere to be seen.

After some frantic radioing, and my name being Tannoyed over the loudspeakers, they were located and we were taken through the door to the back of the Copland Road stand where an anxious looking Victoria was standing with a steward. "I told them this was the wrong bit!" she said – even though they had a print-out of where each child belonged. "All these bits just look the same!" Then she just gave me a hug and started crying because the emotion of being "lost" just got to her. I gave the staff an "if looks could kill" stare and we were quickly led back to our seats. When we got there, a man and boy were sitting in them – even though Victoria's jacket was over the back of her seat! They were chased and we took our seats to watch us draw 2-2 with a good AC Milan side, and Sasa Papac even scored one of the goals.

What should have been an enjoyable experience for her turned out to be a bit of a shambles. No child should be at Ibrox feeling lost and vulnerable! Thing weren't over though. When we were on our way home, my phone rang and I told Victoria to answer it, expecting it to be Norma asking when we'd be home.

Victoria said, "It's for you. Someone at Rangers." So I pulled over to the side of the road to speak to them. I got a full apology for what had happened and was told that the person responsible was being quizzed about what went wrong. As a gesture, they invited Victoria to be the matchday mascot at the upcoming SPL game against Kilmarnock. I told her this and she took less than a second to accept!

We got a letter with the details and a permit for the Albion Car-park. We had to be at Ibrox by two o'clock where we would be met and taken for a tour. They'd give her a full kit to put on and she'd meet the players, match officials and Broxi before leading the team out. Back inside for a quick change and then be taken to guest seats. Two people could accompany her so Hilary and I would go as well. "What size kit does she need, and can we have a portrait photo for the match programme?" Victoria arranged for one of her friends and her dad to use our season tickets that day.

We went over and were met as arranged. The other boy who'd got "lost" was there too. We got the tour, and Victoria got changed. We could take photos at the side of the pitch as the crowd was beginning to fill up. Broxi came out to take them through some warm-up excercises in the tunnel as the players came out for their warm-ups on the pitch. The referee for the day, Brian Winter, came and introduced himself and explained what would happen. The boy could carry the match ball and Victoria could carry the coin for the toss. He also gave them each a souvenir yellow and red card.

When the players came off the pitch, they all stopped for photos against a wall with a Rangers crest. Every player stopped dutifully and Hilary was allowed to get her picture with her favourite player, Kyle Lafferty, as well. The one thing that was particularly noticeable was that the older, experienced players, David Weir and Christian Dailly, were the two who chatted most and made the mascots feel really welcome. The other players just stopped, stood for the photo and disappeared. Even our club captain never said a word. But these two were 'proper gentlemen' about it and I won't forget that.

Just before three o'clock, everyone lined up in the tunnel. "Victoria. Have you still got that coin?" shouted Brian Winter, and she held up her hand. We could see that the stadium was full and out they went. We watched from pitch-side as the coin was tossed, a picture was taken with the referee, captains and Broxi, and then the two of them ran off. Victoria even got to keep the pound coin!

They got changed quickly and we were led to our seats in the east enclosure. Kilmarnock scored first and I turned to Victoria and said, "You weren't much of a lucky mascot, were you?" Not to worry, as we scored three and took over top spot in the SPL. She was a lucky mascot after all. After the game, it took ages to get out of the Albion car-park. Later on, Victoria got a glimpse of herself running off the pitch at the beginning of the Sportscene highlights. She got sent a copy of the official photo and ordered a mug with the picture on it, which she still uses to this day.

Unfortunately, we didn't stay at the top for long – less than a fortnight actually – as we lost to Inverness Caledonian and drew with Hearts, both at Ibrox. In between those games, we lost the League Cup final to Celtic 2-0. We just didn't turn up on the day. It was a very poor performance, our first defeat in a final against Celtic since 1989. Kirk Broadfoot got sent off right at the end when he gave away a penalty by tripping Aiden McGeady.

Our Scottish Cup run continued with a 4-0 win at Forfar, and a 5-1 win at home to Hamilton Academical. In April, we won our four SPL games, and the cup semi-final 3-0 against St Mirren. When the SPL split came, we were one point behind Celtic.

We beat Hearts at Ibrox and then faced Celtic on a very wet afternoon. The rain was incessant, and Steven Davis slid in and scored the only goal which took us two points ahead of Celtic with just three games to go. We drew our next match 1-1 at Easter Road – but so did Celtic. Two ahead with one game to go. Our final game was at Tannadice, and a win by any score would give us the title. It was another last-day decider, and the players responded. Goals from Kyle Lafferty and Pedro Mendez put us two up at half time, and a goal in the second half by Kris Boyd sealed the win, and our first championship for four seasons.

The following Saturday, we met Falkirk in the Scottish Cup Final. It was a blistering hot afternoon with the temperature on the pitch reaching over 35 degrees Celsius. It was far too hot for Kris Boyd and he was replaced by Nacho Novo at half time. In the first minute of the second half, he got the ball at the touchline from a throw-in, spun and hit a shot which went straight into the goal. We won the cup and completed the double. What a great end to the season!

During the summer, twenty players left the club on transfers and loans – eleven of whom had played for the first team. Only one player was signed – Jerome Rothen on loan from Paris Saint-Germain.

Unfortunately, he lived up to his surname, and he would be sent back to PSG in the January transfer window.

Financial alarm bells were ringing - and ringing loudly! David Murray stepped down as Chairman to be replaced by Alastair Johnston, and he also looked to sell his shareholding in the Club. In October, Walter Smith would say that Lloyds Banking Group was "effectively running the Club", and in November, it would be revealed that we were £31 million in debt, up £10 million from the previous year.

Before the season started properly, we played and won a couple of friendlies in Germany, and we took part in a weekend tournament down at Arsenal. We beat Paris Saint-Germain 1-0 on the Saturday but a Jack Wilshere inspired Arsenal beat us 3-0 on the Sunday. On the Wednesday night, we beat Manchester City 3-2 at Ibrox, but lost 2-0 down at Portsmouth the weekend before the season started.

Our title defence didn't get off to a good start, as three wins were followed by three draws, and a victory over Queen of the South in the League Cup. We then beat Celtic 2-1 at Ibrox, with two Kenny Miller goals, but that was followed by a poor performance at St Johnstone. We won 2-1 but could only draw our next match at home to Hibernian. Wins at home against St Mirren and Kilmarnock were followed by our first league defeat - away at Aberdeen - but we then won every league game up to the end of the year, and we knocked Dundee out of the League Cup.

After years of illness, Dad passed away on Friday 6th November. I was just about to leave for work when Mum called me with the news. The staff at Drumchapel Hospital had gone in to his room to see how he was and had found that he had slipped away during the early hours of the morning. They had braced us for this when we'd been in to see him a couple of nights before.

He had still been going to Ibrox in his eighties and often moaned that, like his Golf Club, he should have got free life membership as he had been coming to Ibrox for over 60 years. He had started going when Bill Struth was the manager and had seen them through the decades of Scot Symon, Davie White, Willie Waddell, Jock Wallace, John Greig (who he played at golf a couple of times at Lenzie), Graeme Souness, Walter Smith, Dick Advocaat and Alex McLeish. We saw hundreds of matches together. Leagues being won, big European nights, Cup semis and finals, testimonials and friendlies. We saw big names come and go; great goals and great characters.

Over the decades, he had seen it all. He was a bit of a "glass half empty" kind of guy. No matter who we were playing, he would always say, "We'll be lucky to get a draw today". Fortunately, those predictions tended to be more wrong than right. Another one was, if we scored a very early goal in a game, "That'll be the only goal of the game!" predicting that we would have to sit through a completely uneventful eighty five minutes. Again, that usually proved to be wrong. It was probably a good thing that he never bet on the outcomes of games – he would have lost a fortune.

As his health had begun to deteriorate, it became too difficult for him to go to games, and he preferred to watch them on television as he was convinced that he saw more of the game that way. As his memory and abilities went downhill, he spent many years in hospital. But on a Saturday or Sunday evening, when we went to visit him, he would always smile when we told him that Rangers had won. There was a bigger smile if we also told him that Celtic had lost!

He couldn't even remember what he'd had for dinner an hour before but, if a player from way back was mentioned in conversation, perhaps if it had been reported that they had passed away, Dad could always remember them. He would recall a great save, a super goal, a classic match they had played in. "Now, he knew how to play." Or, "I played against him in the army." Or, "He was the best passer of a ball I've ever seen." But then, in his mind, players from the past could always play, dribble, score or save better than "these overpaid superstars nowadays!"

He never really said who his favourite player had been, but the following year when Sammy Baird, who played for Rangers between 1955 and 1960 – winning three league titles and one Scottish Cup – died, my Mum told me that he had been Dad's favourite. One of his former BB Boys told me that Dad used to take him to Ibrox and lift him over the gate to get in, and that was the first time I had ever heard that story.

Mum decided to keep going with the subscriptions to SKY and Setanta TV so I could still go to their house to watch our away matches without having to squabble over the television at home when there was a game on.

In November, we had an 'unusual' visitor to our church one Sunday – Ivana Papac. The church, and the primary school beside it, packed shoe boxes every year, for the Samaritan's Purse charity, to provide Christmas presents for children in various parts of the world who, for one reason or another, never got anything. The Papac's daughter must have heard about this at school and told her mum who went and spoke to the teacher, Mrs Henson. When Ivana had been a little girl in war-torn Bosnia, she had been the recipient of one such shoe box and it made a huge impression on her. She still had the knitted teddy bear that she'd been given and, when her family fled the country to start a new life, she took it with her. She spoke at the school and the church to give a personal testimony about how wonderful it had been to get a package of simple gifts like that, and said how she had never forgotten the feeling of receiving a gift at Christmas.

The final game of 2009 was at home to Dundee United – the most unpredictable of opponents. Kris Boyd needed four goals to become the SPL's all-time top scorer ahead of Henrik Larsson. On the night, he scored five as we won 7-1 but the best goal of the night came from Madjid Bougherra following a long run from deep in our own half. At the start of the year, we were top of the league, and we drew the New Year game against Celtic 1-1 to keep us there. Celtic scored first and thought they were on their way to a win, and they celebrated loudly. Television pictures showed Rod Stewart and his wife Penny Lancaster in the crowd. She stood up with a digital camcorder and began recording the celebrations. As she panned around, Rangers went up the other end and Lee McCulloch scored the equaliser. The Celtic fans were silenced as the Rangers fans went crazy. I wonder if Rod and Penny still look back at that video.

Our European challenge that season was basically non-existant. We were in a Champions League group against Seville, VfB Stuttgart and Romanians Unirea Urziceni. Despite being seeded in pot two, we could only manage two draws, away to Stuttgart and at home to Unirea. We lost every other game – including a terrible result, 4-1 away to Unirea, which was looked on as one of our worst ever European results - to finish bottom of the group so we were out of Europe by the beginning of December. The Club were fined 20,000 Euros by UEFA for "inappropriate conduct" by the fans in Romania, and we had to pay for repairs to their stadium.

In the January transfer window, the playing staff was again reduced. Jerome Rothen went back to Paris Saint-Germain at the end of his loan, and Pedro Mendez was sold to Sporting Lisbon. Six young players also left the Club.

About this time, the media began to look at the finances of several Scottish clubs. We will never be able to compete with the English Premiership which seems to be a license to print money. A team which suffers the pain of relegation from that league, gets a compensation payment of somewhere in the region of £40 million. The teams that do well can expect to earn tens of millions – yet some of their games can only attract crowds in the region of 25,000. Old Firm games, on the other hand, attract sell-out crowds of double that, and seem to get shown all over the world, but what do we get? A couple of million if we're lucky. Other Scottish teams play in small towns where there just aren't the numbers of fans who could go and see them. They have to rely on getting a draw against one of the big teams in a cup competition, and better still – a replay - or they have to sell their players to make ends meet.

I wrote in The Herald:
Sorry financial state of Scottish football
Several articles on February 3 describe the sorry financial state of many top Scottish football clubs and there was reference to the lack of crowds at Kilmarnock, Livingston, Dundee United and Aberdeen – especially at televised games.
I have a ticket for Thursday's CIS Cup semi-final at the National Stadium. It cost me £22 and the game is being shown live on Channel 5. I will probably have to park some distance from the stadium; it will possibly be raining; the game might be poor.
The other week, I went to the Odeon Cinema at Springfield Quay to see a multi-million-pound blockbuster. I parked very near the doors; I had a very comfortable seat; I was thoroughly entertained for over three hours. The cost of my ticket was £3.60.
It does not take a genius to work out why the crowds are so poor at football matches. If the clubs took a gamble and slashed the price of admission, they would get bigger crowds. Perhaps families could afford to go. A crowd of 20,000 each paying £5 would bring on the same revenue as a crowd of 5,000 paying £20. But the club would sell four times as many programmes, pies and Bovril or whatever, souvenirs and so on. They could even charge their advertisers more as their brand or message would be seen by four times as many people. And there would be a far better atmosphere inside the stadium to cheer on the teams.

We drew 3-3 with Hamilton Accies away in the Scottish Cup but won the replay 2-0. Our unbeaten league run continued through January and February, and we progressed to the League Cup Final by beating St Johnstone 2-0 in the semi-final. By this stage, we were ten points ahead in the league. During a three week spell at the end of February and beginning of March, we were to experience two of the most ecstatic wins ever in the league and League Cup.

On 28th February, we met Celtic at Ibrox and, as usual, it was a tense affair. Falklands War hero Simon Weston was a special guest and got a very warm reception from the Rangers fans. Celtic fans, on the other hand, acted appallingly by waving Argentinian flags. We nearly scored when Kris Boyd rounded Arthur Boruc but hit the side net with his shot. Then Lee McCulloch got injured, and had to go off. Maurice Edu came on as a substitute and scored almost immediately but it was disallowed as the ball had struck Kenny Miller on the hand a moment before. The game ebbed and flowed and it looked like finishing as a draw which would keep us seven points clear. Then the Assistant Referee held up the board to indicate that there would be an additional three minutes. Two minutes passed with Celtic having more of the possession. Nobody had left the stadium. Rangers got a corner at the Copland Road end when Boruc saved a shot from Sasa Papac. Kevin Thomson took it and the ball fell to Madjid Bougherra who shot at goal. Boruc saved it and the ball bounced around in front of him. Kris Boyd tried to score, but it was blocked and then the ball fell in front of Maurice Edu who stuck out a foot and hit it into the goal. Ibrox erupted and the celebrations were just mental. "A giant leap towards the title!" Ten points ahead and the title virtually secured. The party started.

Following wins against St Mirren and Kilmarnock in the SPL, and a replayed win against the same St Mirren in the Scottish Cup, we went to Hampden for the League Cup Final, and it turned out to be one of the most dramatic afternoons ever. With the score still at 0-0, Kevin Thomson tackled Steven Thomson, and Craig Thomson – never one to hesitate in showing a red card to a Rangers player – sent him off. As the time ticked on, young defender Danny Wilson pulled back Craig Dargo before he could shoot, and he got sent off as well. We were down to nine men with eighteen minutes left. St Mirren must have thought it was their day. Surely, they could beat nine men, and if it went to extra time, we would be exhausted. They reckoned without the Rangers spirit and, particularly our captain, David Weir. He marshalled the defence brilliantly, belying his age, and with just six minutes left, he played the ball to Steven Naismith with a perfect pass. Naismith ran forward, and looking up, saw Kenny Miller charging towards the St Mirren area. Naismith sent over an inch-perfect cross and Miller rose to send a header right into the goal. The Rangers crowd went absolutely mad. St Mirren couldn't believe what had just happened.

Craig Thomson blew his whistle and nine man Rangers had won the cup. What an amazing feeling to go from rock bottom to the summit in just a few minutes!

We needed a replay in the next round of the Scottish Cup as well, after conceding a daft late goal at Ibrox to draw 3-3 with Dundee United. We lost the replay 1-0 at Tannadice. United went on to win the cup that year.

Despite a defeat and a draw in the league, we clinched the title with an away win at Easter Road at the end of April. Kyle Lafferty scored the winner. Why did he always leave his best form until the end of every season? Two in a row and Championship number 53 was in the bag.

With the financial problems continuing, there was the annual summer transfer exodus with Nacho Novo, DaMarcus Beasley, Steven Smith,

Kris Boyd, Kevin Thomson, Danny Wilson, Andrius Velicka and eight youngsters departing for pastures new. £4 million pounds were brought in and this was used to bring Croatian striker Nikica Jelavic to the Club just before the transfer window closed. We also brought in young Vladimir Weiss on loan from Manchester City, and the two of them were to have a big impact on our season. In addition, we brought in James Beattie as well as Ricky Foster, on loan from Aberdeen.

After a pre-season tournament in Australia, Victoria and I watched us beat Newcastle at Ibrox before things began in earnest. We started well with eight wins out of eight, including 3-0 way at Hibernian, 4-0 at home to Dundee United, and 4-1 at home to Motherwell. We also won away at Pittodrie and Tynecastle. Kenny Miller was on fantastic form and was hitting goals in every game. We seemed to have a strange habit of letting our opponents score first before we took control of the game and went on to win. At Pittodrie, we even went two down before we got into the game. In the game at Tynecastle, a terrible tackle from Ian Black put Nikica Jelavic out for over four months.

Celtic had started in the same fashion, so when we met them at Parkhead in the ninth game, something had to give. It was Walter Smith's 50th Old Firm game as manager, and it started explosively. In the first minute, Anthony Stokes commited a terrible late foul on Sasa Papac. It should have been a straight red card but, for some reason ("You can usually get away with these types of fouls early on" !?), he only got a yellow. Gary Hooper scored just before half time with a close shot, but from a free kick at the start of the second half, Kyle Lafferty hit the ball towards the goal and it was helped in by two Celtic defenders. Celtic goalkeeper, Fraser Forster made a hash of a clearance that went straight to Steven Naismith. He quickly passed it forward to Kenny Miller who had time to look before hitting it into the net. A foul on Kirk Broadfoot gave us a penalty which Kenny Miller scored to give us a 3-1 win. It looked as if we would take early control of the league race – but we drew our next game at home to Inverness Caledonian, then beat St Mirren but lost the next one at home to Hibernian. In the League Cup, we knocked out Dunfermline Athletic 7-2, and Kilmarnock 2-0 away in the quarter-final.

The team was playing with power and speed, especially from Miller, Naismith, Davis, Lafferty and Weiss. Chances were coming from all angles, and some of the goals were quite spectacular.

In Europe, we went straight into the group stage of the Champions League where we drew Valencia, Bursaspor of Turkey and Manchester United. Our opening game was at Old Trafford and, with a great defensive display, we drew 0-0. We were the only team that whole season to play there and not concede a goal. We beat Bursaspor at Ibrox and drew 1-1 at home to Valencia with Maurice Edu scoring at both ends, and full back Ricky Foster missing a great chance to win it right at the end, to leave us undefeated after three games. We then lost 3-0 in Spain before meeting Manchester United at Ibrox. We nearly managed another draw but conceded a very soft, late penalty which Wayne Rooney scored. Bursaspor hadn't picked up a single point but we drew 1-1 in Turkey so we finished in third place and qualified for the UEFA Europa League.

At the end of October, former player Tom Forsyth's autobiography, "Jaws – The Tom Forsyth Story" was published and it was announced that he'd be signing copies in WH Smith's book department in Argyle Street on a Friday afternoon. Tom was my absolute hero in his playing days and I decided that, since I got all Friday afternoons off, I would rush my lunch and head into town to join what I expected to be a lengthy queue waiting to meet 'Big Tam'. When I got to the shop, I have to say that I was heartbroken. There he was, sitting at a table, pen in hand, beside a stack of the books – but there was nobody else there. There was a poster in the window advertising the event but the place was empty. How could this be? We were talking about a real legend – the man who scored the famous cup final winner against Celtic, the iron man who stopped Mick Channon scoring for England with the greatest tackle ever seen in a Home International match. The upside was that I therefore had more time to speak with him, and I told him that I'd been going to Ibrox since before he signed and had obviously followed his career closely. He signed the book for me and I wished him all the best with it, but I left feeling utterly forlorn. He had already done signings at Waterstones and, I think, at the Megastore, so perhaps the fans had already queued there instead.

Meanwhile, in the SPL, we beat Aberdeen and Kilmarnock, drew with Inverness Caledonian and ended the year with a 4-1 away win at Motherwell on Boxing Day.

When the January transfer window opened, we said farewell to Kenny Miller, James Beattie, Andy Webster, Ross Perry and a couple of the youths, but we brought in lifelong Rangers fan David Healy, Kyle Bartley on loan from Arsenal and the controversial El Hadji Diouf on loan from Blackburn Rovers.

We started the New Year losing 2-0 to Celtic at Ibrox before beating Kilmarnock in the Scottish Cup fourth round. The game against Celtic marked the 40th anniversary of the Ibrox Disaster and it's no excuse but it seemed that the players' minds were elsewhere. Both teams wore black armbands and were led onto the pitch by John Greig and Billy McNeil who had been captains in 1971. A one-minute silence was observed before the game kicked off.

The following morning, a somber crowd gathered at Ibrox, down in the corner closest to where Stairway 13 had been, and were led in remembrance by the Rev. Stuart McQuarrie. All the families were represented and players from the present day and from 1971 were there as were representatives of Celtic. Hymns were sung, prayers were said and all the names were read out as relatives and players on their behalf placed memorial flowers on a stand. I was there with my Ibrox neighbour, who was too young to have remembered the actual day, and his family, and the whole service was shown live on BBC Scotland. It was extremely poignant especially for those who had been there in 1971 or who had lost a friend or relative.

Back on the pitch, we beat Hamilton Accies and Inverness Caledonian before losing away to Hearts in the SPL, but we then beat Hibernian at home before winning the League Cup semi-final 2-1 against Motherwell which was Hilary's first ever visit to Hampden. Season 2010-11 was to be the season with an abundance of Old Firm games. As well as the four in the SPL, we would meet them in the League Cup Final and in the Scottish Cup fifth round.

We were drawn at home and got off to a great start. Young Jamie Ness scored a wonder goal but it finished 2-2 so there would be a replay at Parkhead. In a match that was remembered for all the wrong reasons – we had three players sent off and there was a touchline spat between Ally McCoist and Neil Lennon - we lost 1-0. Representatives from both clubs, the SFA and the Police all attended a meeting to discuss ways of improving behaviour at such volatile fixtures.

We thumped Motherwell 6-0 at home but lost the next league game against Celtic 3-0 at Parkhead. We did make progress in the Europa League by knocking out Sporting Lisbon on the away goals rule – having drawn 1-1 at Ibrox but drawing 2-2 in Portugal. We finished February by beating St Johnstone 4-0 at home.

Around that time, the tensions between the two clubs overflowed out of the football world. Neil Lennon was sent bullets and parcel bombs in the post and he had to have 24-hour security. Two Celtic players – Paddy McCourt and Niall McGinn – were targeted as were two well known Celtic fans, Paul McBride QC and former MSP Trish Godman who had made the mistake of wearing a Celtic top to the Scottish Parliament. All these incidents reflected very badly on our Club and the media made sure that they hyped them up, always looking to lay the blame firmly on Rangers' doorstep.

The cold spell had led to a number of postponed matches and for a while, we were behind Celtic in the league - but had games in hand. They lost at Motherwell and we regained top spot briefly until we lost at home to Dundee United. PSV knocked us out of the Europa League by winning 1-0 in Eindhoven after a 0-0 draw at Ibrox. Next up was the League Cup final and Celtic were favourites since they had won the Scottish Cup game and had beaten us in the last two league games.

I had a ticket for the final as usual but I chanced my arm at the Ticket Office by asking if I could swap that for two together if I paid the difference. Amazingly, there were tickets available so Hilary was heading for her first cup final, and an Old Firm one at that. We sat in the south west corner of Hampden, the traditional Rangers end. When I say "sat", that's not strictly correct as we all stood the whole time. We could see everything but there were two young boys in the row in front who, we guessed, could hardly see a thing!

Our goals were scored at the far end and there's always a moment for the reaction to kick in. The first was scored by Steven Davis when he hit a shot just inside the post, but they equalised from a close header shortly afterwards. It was 1-1 after 90 minutes so we were into extra time. We got a free kick which Vladimir Weiss took quickly, passing straight to Nikica Jelavic and he ran on and scored what would be the winner. Near the end, Celtic were reduced to ten men when Izaguirre charged into Weiss as he broke forward with no attempt to play the ball. Celtic favourites? Once again, the form book was thrown out of the window and Hilary saw the cup being presented and the on-field celebrations for the first time.

That season, the song "Penny Arcade" with its "Step Up and Play" chorus had caught on with the fans, and it began to be played before the start of every game. Sammy King who had written it many years ago was tracked down and told of the song's popularity at Ibrox. He was persuaded to re-release it with proceeds going to Erskine Hospital for ex-servicemen and women, and the fans tried to get it to Number 1 in the chart. It was decided that a flyer telling anyone who didn't know about the song, the plan, or how to download it, would be printed and handed to everyone going to the home game against St Mirren. Hilary and I went to the Wee Rangers Club, along Edmiston Drive, to get a bundle of these flyers, and we were asked to hand them out on the pavement at the Broomloan Road entrance. Hilary had never seen anything like the inside of the Club before a game. We could hardly make our way through the great throng of fans. We got our leaflets and started giving them out, encouraging everyone to support Erskine. We even gave a few to the St Mirren fans on their way in! The song didn't quite reach Number 1 but it raised a lot of money for the hospital, and it continues to be played at Ibrox to this day.

Over the plast few years, Rangers have fully supported our Armed Forces, and the Saturday nearest Remembrance Sunday has become Poppy Day at Ibrox with huge card dispays, troops invited to the game and being allowed to parade on the pitch at half-time to great applause, the players all wearing shirts with the poppy emblem sewn in, commandos abseiling down from the Govan Stand roof with the match ball, and a loud field gun being fired to mark the start and end of a minute's silence before the game. It has now grown into a great tradition which the service personnel really appreciate – as if we needed an excuse to wave Union Flags and to sing "Rule Britannia"!

With the league race being neck and neck, it was widely believed that the League Cup victory was the boost that carried us to the finishing line in the Championship. The title was in Celtic's hands with just four games to go but, as we have learned over the years, "it ain't over 'til it's over". We beat Motherwell 5-0 away and Celtic lost to Inverness Caledonian (a big thank you to our former captain, Terry Butcher who was their manager!) and that gave us a one point advantage with only three games left.

We beat Hearts 4-0 and Dundee United 2-0 at Ibrox, and our final fixture would be at Kilmarnock. A win would give us the title. We exploded right out of the traps and, in an incredible opening eight minutes, we scored three – Kyle Lafferty doing his usual end of the season scoring routine. It was all over by half time but we finished 5-1 winners to clinch our 54th league championship.

Walter Smith had announced that he would retire at the end of the season, but unlike the previous time that he left, we had finished the season with not just the League Championship but we had defeated our oldest rivals at Hampden. During his two spells in charge, Walter had won twenty-one trophies, a quite remarkable haul.

SIXTEEN
It All Came Tumbling Down

The day before the Hearts game, something momentous happened that was to have the most serious repercussions for the next four years of our glorious history although we didn't know it at the time. It was announced that, after twenty-two years in charge, and following six months of negotiations, David Murray had sold his majority control of the Club to businessman Craig Whyte for just £1. Well, not just £1 – Whyte took on all the debt as well. After being mobbed outside the stadium by exuberant fans, he took his place in the Directors' Box for the game.

Although we didn't really know who Whyte was or what was his background, he said all the right things and we thought that we could move forward from the years of selling players to keep our heads above water and to reduce the debt. A signing budget of £10 million pounds was promised so everything seemed to be in order.

He praised David Murray's achievements during his time in charge, and he acknowledged the outstanding contribution of Walter Smith to the Club's success. He said that he was proud to follow in the footsteps of William Wilton, Bill Struth and Willie Waddell, and he fully realised that Ibrox was overflowing with history. He spoke warmly of being brought to Ibrox as a youngster and seeing John Greig, Davie Cooper, Graeme Souness, Ally McCoist, Terry Butcher, Chris Woods and Graham Roberts as well as Brian Laudrup and Paul Gascoigne. He was delighted to win the league only days after his arrival, and was thrilled to be able to get a chance to take part in the Champions' League with all the huge financial benefits that could bring.

Stories began to emerge about Whyte's background. Although he lived in London, he had been brought up in Glasgow where he attended Kelvinside Academy. It was while there that he started trading in stocks and shares. He allegedly made a profit of £20,000 before he left school to go and work for his father's plant hire firm. Over the years, he built up his empire in financial services, commodities trading, and property with businesses in Britain and abroad. When it became known that he was negotiating to buy Rangers, the media began to take an interest in him and his businesses, but nothing untoward was discovered.

He admitted that "celebrity status" was something completely alien to him. He said that he thought he could just park his car at Ibrox and walk in the door, but he was besieged by fans wanting autographs. Being recognised wherever he went was something he would have to get used to.

With the huge debts run up by David Murray, and the looming 'Big Tax Case', Whyte's takeover put fans' minds at rest. He immediately wiped out all the Club's debts of £22 million, and promised significant investment over the following five years. Although we can't compete with the money available in England, he wanted to be able to attract the best players to Ibrox.

The gist of what he said was, "There will be investment but the Club has to pay its way. There is no way we will be making big losses here. We have to run this as a business and we need a long-term business plan. Expectations are huge but I don't think anyone is expecting us to run this business in any other way than as a commercial operation. People don't want to see a return to the difficulties in the past when Rangers overspent. I have an obligation to leave the Club in a good shape." He spoke of expanding the Rangers brand name abroad, seeking out commercial opportunities, making a profit from participation in the Champions League, and finding a way to bring more successful youngsters through the youth system.

In his short time in charge, he had said and done all the right things. Fans felt that the Club was in good hands and we could go forward from a position of strength.

Other potential buyers had been deterred by a spectre that was hanging over the Club. HM Revenue & Customs were investigating the method by which some players had been paid during Murray's tenure. He had used an Employee Benefit Trust (EBT) to pay part of the players' salaries and bonuses into an offshore account and that allowed these players to defer these payments and not pay Income Tax on them. At the time when the Club started using this scheme, it was perfectly legal, but the rules had changed and HMRC were now pursuing tax on these payments. The Club could face back payments and fines totalling nearly £100 million and this became known as "The Big Tax Case".

Suddenly, all our opponents and enemies became World class experts on the subject and every media pundit had a field day claiming that we would go bankrupt if we had to pay this, and that the Club had gained an unfair advantage on the field by attracting top international players and should have trophies won during that time expunged from our record as the world's most successful club. Radio phone-ins were awash with Celtic fans claiming that these trophies should rightly be added retrospectively to their record despite the fact that the investigation was ongoing and Rangers vowed to defend it robustly, and other clubs and not just Celtic had been trophy runners-up at the time. Besides, what would they do for games that we had lost despite apparently having an unfair advantage? The whole thing was a complete nonsense, but that didn't stop everyone having an opinion on it.

As the summer progressed, the transfer funds promised to Ally McCoist failed to materialise. Instead of having £10 million to spend, he only got £4.31 million. Some of his transfers fell through and we began to have doubts about Whyte's finances, but we did manage to secure the purchases of Lee Wallace from Hearts, Dorin Goian, Alejandro Bedoya, Carlos Bocanegra and Matt McKay, and the loan of Kyle Bartley from Arsenal was extended. First team regulars Allan McGregor, Steven Whittaker, Steven Davis and Gregg Wylde all had their contracts extended, some by as much as five or six years, and this gave the impression of the finances actually being in order.

These were countered, however, with the departures of Vladimir Weiss, Richard Foster, El Hadj Diouf, Madjid Bougherra, James Beattie and, as usual, a number of youngsters.

Our first league match was at home to Hearts and Whyte unveiled the league flag before we scraped a draw despite Hearts pressurising for most of the match. On the Tuesday night, we lost our Champions League qualifier at home to Malmo. Then Ally got the first win of his management career when we beat St Johnstone. We then drew 1-1 in Malmo to be eliminated from the Champions League – and had Steven Whittaker and Madjid Bougherra sent off in an ill-tempered match - and once again lost out on much needed (and, it would appear, much anticipated) revenue.

We racked up SPL wins against Inverness, Motherwell and Aberdeen but were knocked out of the Europa League by Maribor to end our European interest before the end of August. The team put together a good run in the league and we were unbeaten until the end of November, including a 4-2 win over Celtic at Ibrox in Ally's first game in charge against them. Steven Naismith scored after a poor clearance, but Gary Hooper equalised with a low shot. They got a free kick just before half-time and Alan McGregor let it squirm underneath him and into the goal. When the second half started, Steven Davis hit the bar and Kyle Lafferty had a goal disallowed for offside and, yet again, the television pictures proved that the goal should have been given. Another decision in their favour! From a Davis corner, Nikica Jelavic made it 2-2, and then Lafferty scored from a great Gregg Wylde cross that wasn't cleared properly. Celtic's Charlie Mulgrew was sent off for a second yellow card and, in the last minute, Naismith scored a fourth when he ran in unmarked to convert a low cross.

The problem seemed to be in cup matches. After coming back from two down against Falkirk in the League Cup, goalkeeper Neil Alexander made a mistake right at the end and Falkirk scored the winner to knock us out in our first match.

However in the league, we found ourselves ten points clear of Celtic by early October. By bonfire night, we were twelve ahead of Motherwell, who were in second place, and fifteen ahead of Celtic. Our cup form might have been poor but our league form was looking really good, until we drew with St Johnstone, and lost to Kilmarnock, St Mirren and Celtic at the end of the year.

In December, David Weir brought out "Extra Time – My Autobiography" and it was advertised that he would be signing copies in Waterstones in Braehead, round the corner from where I worked, so I went round and joined the queue. This time, there was a queue! There wasn't much time for chat but, while he was signing my copy, he told me that it had taken him about a year to write it. In the winter transfer window that followed, he left the Club as a way of easing the wage bill, and he headed back down to Merseyside to join his family. For someone who had initially been signed as a temporary experienced head, he went on to play such a significant part in or successes over the next few seasons, defying the supposed age-barrier in the process. Everyone rightly considered him to be a perfect ambassador for our Club, epitomising everything that it means to be a true Ranger.

Around this time, Victoria was told to prepare a school project on a famous person. She had to do a short 'Powerpoint' presentation on the person's life and fame. She chose David Weir as he was such an inspirational player, and she got pictures of him at various stages of his career. She finished with a picture of him and her, taken on the day she was mascot, and said something like, "He has met so many people over the years – even me!" She did well but was rather deflated when the teacher had to admit that she didn't even know who David Weir was!

2012 started well with wins against Motherwell, St Johnstone, Hibernian and Dunfermline and a draw with Aberdeen, from whom we signed speedy midfielder Sone Aluko for just £150,000. In the Scottish Cup, we beat Arbroath 4-0 before drawing Dundee United at Ibrox. The cup hoodoo struck again and we lost 2-0.

Once again, to ease our financial position, players were sold. Nikica Jelavic was sold to Everton for £5.5 million, and nineteen other players left the Club including David Weir whose contract was terminated to allow him to leave to save the Club money.

On 14th February, Craig Whyte stood at the front door of Ibrox, surrounded by security men, and announced that Rangers had officially gone into administration. It transpired that £9 million of PAYE and VAT was owed to HM Revenue & Customs – probably the amount that we would have earned if we had qualified for the Champions League. Rangers, or to be quite specific, Whyte, had been deducting PAYE from the players' wages but not paying the tax man. We were deducted ten points by the SPL (the standard "fine" for a club entering administration) and, with a period of on-field uncertainty, we lost to Hearts and Dundee United thus ending our league challenge. Celtic, meanwhile had gone on a long unbeaten run and could clinch the SPL if they won the next game, at Ibrox.

The media and the Celtic fans were, of course, having a field day. They were looking forward to rubbing our noses in it by winning the SPL at Ibrox, but having lost the previous two SPL games, the players rolled up their sleeves and played like they should. We won 3-2 and prevented them winning the league, temporarily at least.

London-based financial advisers, Duff & Phelps were appointed as administrators, but failure to submit annual accounts meant that we were not allowed to play in any European competition the following season, thereby removing a potentially lucrative income source. In April, it was revealed that our debts could be as much as £134 million.

We all went to Ibrox on the last day of the season, to watch us beat St Johnstone 4-0 but not knowing what would happen next. Would there be further punishments? Would we even be liquidated? The storm clouds hovered above Ibrox and the future looked very bleak indeed. It was also discovered that Craig Whyte was not the millionaire businessman he made out to be. He had borrowed millions from a football financing company, Ticketus, to be paid back from the money from season ticket sales for the next three years – despite not actually owning the Club at the time – to give the impression to David Murray that he had plenty of money to finance the Club. If it was as easy as that, any one of us could have done the same. What a way to operate.

It seemed that, every day, a new prospective owner announced their interest in buying the Club and investing millions. American trucker Bill Miller, Sale Sharks rugby owner Brian Kennedy, and a Singaporean businessman Bill Ng all entered the equation, all promising great deals.

The SFA and SPL seemed to be making up the rules as they went along, threatening to punish us with sanctions which included massive points deductions or seizing huge chunks of our income for several seasons. Outspoken directors of other SPL clubs wanted us hit with all manner of punishments. At the end of April, a fans' protest march to Hampden was arranged but the Police tried to stop it happening. At the last minute, they agreed to let the march go ahead, and, on Saturday 28th April, thousands of concerned fans met in Queen's Park and we marched peacefully along Cathcart Road, up Prospecthill Road, and round the eastern end of Hampden before gathering outside the main doors.

Former legendary player, Sandy Jardine, had become a spokesman for the fans and the Rangers Fans Fighting Fund, and he addressed the crowd and vowed that we would take whatever actions necessary to challenge anything that our Club was hit with. It was already proposed that we boycott any organisation that supported the SFA, such as bookmakers William Hill, and would boycott any away games the following season to deprive these other SPL clubs of any revenue that they might expect from a Rangers visit.

We had to wait to see what the SPL and SFA would do so that we could deal with any sanctions in an appropriate manner. Jardine said that we would wait to see which clubs had acted against us in a detrimental way and would then decide how to deal with them. It was estimated that these clubs stood to benefit to the amount of £250,000 per season from home matches against Rangers, and in the present financial climate, how could they afford to vote against that?

The event passed peacefully and a letter, appealing against the sanctions was handed in to the SFA. Jardine said that, "The supporters want to demonstrate a united front over disgraceful decisions against our club. There is a feeling in the supporters' group that they have been kicked that much, that if we have to we will go to the Third Division."

The SFA countered by saying that they had received the letter and, "We appreciate the frustrations of the Rangers support during this period of uncertainty and today's march showed the depth of feeling towards the club. The Scottish FA exists to govern with the best interests of the game at all times and will continue to do so throughout this challenging time for the Scottish game."

That would prove to be a false promise. When Portsmouth FC ran into financial difficulties, the English FA helped them out; when a Spanish club was in the same position, their FA helped them out. When it was us, the SFA hit us with sanction after sanction.

One disgraceful thing that Whyte did during his time of ownership was to sell shares that Rangers held in Arsenal Football Club. He was obviously trying to get funds to deal with the mounting debts but these shares were worth more than just money. These went back to the time of the great friendship between managers Bill Struth and Herbert Chapman. They represented something more than money. They reflected the historical respect between the two great clubs that stretched back over decades. They were part of our history and tradition and Whyte simply got rid of them.

On 13th May, Whyte sold his interest in The Rangers Football Club PLC for just £2 to a consortium led by Yorkshire businessman Charles Green. The desperate irony of 'Green and Whyte' was not lost on us. Green put a proposal to the creditors, offering them a percentage of their debt – better to get a percentage of something rather than 100% of nothing – called a company voluntary agreement (a CVA) so that the Club could exit from administration and could get on with operations, but HMRC said that they would not accept this. This formal rejection of the CVA resulted in Rangers Football Club going into liquidation, cancelling all debts. All the Clubs' assets (the name Rangers FC, Ibrox and Murray Park) were sold to a nominated company called Sevco 5088 Ltd, a consortium led by Green, for £5.5 million. The company was renamed The Rangers Football Club Ltd in July.

I had held one single share in the Club so that I could attend AGMs, see the Annual Reports, and feel in a very small way that I was officially as well as unofficially (as a supporter) a part of the fabric of the Club. When the company was liquidated and re-named, it became instantly worthless.

The liquidation prompted discussions about what sanctions could be imposed on an insolvent club. We had been immediately docked 10 points in the league and the other SPL clubs agreed to change the penalty for going into administration to either twenty-five points or one third of the club's total in the previous season.

A deal was offered to the players so that they could transfer their contracts from the old company to the new. It is known in employment circles as a TUPE agreement, but two of the players spoke out against this offer. Steven Naismith and Steven Whittaker held a press conference and said that they wouldn't transfer their contracts to the new company, making them free agents.

Other players did likewise and so became out of contract and free to leave for nothing. Kyle Bartley returned to Arsenal, Sasa Papac retired due to injury but David Healy, Salim Kerkar, and ten other players ended their contracts and left, while Naismith, Whittaker, Sone Aluko, Kyle Lafferty, Allan McGregor, Rhys McCabe, Steven Davis and John Fleck all refused to sign for the new company. The only one of these first team regulars to raise money for the Club was Steven Davis. He signed for Southampton and we got £800,000. Virtually our whole first team had left. Only Lee McCulloch, Lee Wallace, Neil Alexander and Andy Little decided to stay.

On 22nd June, I finally got to the City of Manchester Stadium, now known at the Etihad Stadium – but not to see football. I travelled down to see Bruce Springsteen in concert on his 'Wrecking Ball Tour'. The

Etihad is a fantastic stadium – the height of luxury – and I stood on the pitch, as the rain fell, and enjoyed a superb concert.

Back at Ibrox, something else deemed to be an asset was our membership of the SPL, but this could not be transferred to the new company without the approval of the other SPL clubs. Rangers' application for transfer was rejected by a 10–1 majority. Only Kilmarnock abstained. So Rangers were kicked out of the SPL, and the runners up from the First Division, Dundee, were promoted into our place.

The Club then had to apply to join the Scottish Football League, and some thought that we would join the First Division (the second level) so that we could get back up to the SPL as quickly as possible. The other clubs had obviously failed to realise that having Rangers in the SPL meant money. Two visits per season, as well as sponsorship and broadcasting revenue – but, under pressure from their own fans who delighted in having the power to punish Rangers, the clubs voted us right down. At this stage, all we had actually done was go into administration (and been duly punished for that) and not paid our PAYE and VAT. We hadn't been found guilty of anything else as we still awaited the verdict on the Big Tax Case. The power now swung to the SFL Clubs who were delighted to grant Rangers associate membership of the league but in the lowest division, the third, and across the country, chairmen and treasurers of clubs at that level must have gone to sleep with pound signs in front of their eyes.

But, it wasn't as simple as that. It wouldn't be. As part of the agreement allowing us to join the SFL, we were hit with a twelve month transfer ban, meaning that we couldn't register any new players over the age of eighteen. We challenged this as it wasn't even in the SFA rules but they made it clear that it was either that or no membership of the league. So, we had hardly any first team players and couldn't register any new ones, and we were hit with a £160,000 fine.

SEVENTEEN
Starting At The Bottom

When the players returned, from their summer break, for pre-season training, only four first team players actually turned up. Having gone through the summer not knowing what league, if any, we would be playing in, we now didn't know who was going to play for us. Others did return, and it was agreed that the twelve month signing ban wouldn't actually start until 1st September, allowing us a short period to bring in some players to supplement our team.

The transfer embargo would run from 1st September 2012 until 31st August 2013. That meant that we couldn't register anyone that winter but, when season 2013-14 started, we could play a limited number of "trialists" in July and August and we could pre-sign players, but they couldn't be registered until 1st September 2013. Fortunately the summer window would still, just, be open on that date. We could start that season in a slightly stronger place and, once September started, we could then be at our full strength.

On free transfers, we signed Ian Black and Kevin Kyle from Hearts, Dean Shiels from Kilmarnock, Francisco Sandaza from St Johnstone, Emilson Cribari from Brazilian club Cruzeiro, Sebastian Faure from Lyon, and Anestis Argyriou from AEK Athens. David Templeton signed from Hearts for £700,000. These were some experienced players but, for the next two transfer windows, we wouldn't be able to sign anyone else. The squad would be a mixture of youth and experience and, throughout the season, many of the Murray Park youngsters would get their chances in the first team.

The team which took to the field for our first fixture away to Brechin City in the League Challenge Cup was hardly recognisable from the one that had ended the previous season. Led by new captain, Carlos Bocanegra, we managed a 2-1 win, backed by a large travelling support.

The crowds turned out for our first home game the following midweek, when we comfortably beat East Fife in the League Cup 4-0.

Despite some confident fans predicting that we would simply cruise through the Third Division, we only just managed to scrape a 2-2 draw at Peterhead in our first league game with Andy Little scoring a very late equaliser. We then beat East Stirlingshire 5-1 in our first league game at Ibrox but we drew away at Berwick Rangers the following week. A pattern began to emerge. We won our games at Ibrox quite comfortably – but we kept drawing our away games. Yes, they were on tight little pitches, often with the crowd close to the pitch, and often not the best of surfaces, but these were not viable excuses.

Before the transfer window closed, Alejandro Bedoya was transferred top Helsingborgs in Sweden and Maurice Edu was sold to Stoke City. Dorin Goian was loaned to Spezia in Italy, Carlos Bocanegra was loaned to Racing Santander, and Kirk Broadfoot left for Blackpool after his contract was terminated.

In the League Cup, we beat Falkirk at Ibrox before putting on our best performance of the season when we beat Motherwell 2-0 in Round Three. From start to finish, the players battled for each other and never gave Motherwell any time to settle. We all felt that we could still compete at SPL level, despite our lowly status, and all the personnel changes – but were brought back to Earth with a bump when Inverness Caledonian beat us 3-0 at Ibrox in the quarter-final.

Competing in the League Challenge Cup for the first time, we saw off Falkirk 1-0 away in Round 2 before we fell to Queen of the South in the quarter-final at Ibrox. Leading 2-1, with minutes to go, they broke up the right, fouled Lee Wallace and scored what looked like an offside equaliser to put it into extra time. There was no more scoring and they won 4-3 on penalties to knock us out of that cup as well.

In the league, we lost 1-0 away to Stirling Albion but bounced back with wins against Queen's Park, Clyde (our first away win), Peterhead and East Stirling. The wins continued in December against Stirling Albion, Montrose, Annan Athletic, Elgin City and Clyde. On 29th December, we set a record for the biggest ever away crowd in the third division when we went to Hampden to play Queen's Park. The match was billed as 'the original Glasgow derby' since the two clubs used to play each other in the 1870s and 1880s before another Glasgow team came along. It was an instantly forgettable match which was only won in the closing minutes with a goal from young Canadian, Fraser Aird.

Due to our lowly status, we started our Scottish Cup campaign a lot earlier than we were used to in our SPL days. In September, we beat Forres Mechanics 1-0 away, and in November, we beat Alloa Athletic 7-0 at Ibrox. In December, we beat Elgin City 3-0 at home but were drawn against Dundee United away once the SPL teams would enter the competition. They proved to be too difficult a hurdle and they won 3-0 to end all our cup participation for the season.

In the winter transfer window, we terminated four contracts and let five youth players leave on loans. The SPL instigated an investigation into our transfer dealings between 2001 and 2011, after allegations of dual contracts (the aforementioned EBTs). The investigation was headed by Lord Nimmo Smith and, in February, he concluded that we failed to disclose to the SFA all the payments that were made to players and staff - but this didn't affect players' eligibility. Instead of punishing us by taking away titles and cups, we were fined £250,000 – or rather the former, liquidated company was fined.

In March, the company was floated on the stock exchange and over £22 million was raised, a lot of it from investment companies, but the off-field drama continued. Spanish striker Franciso Sandaza was sacked for trying to arrange his transfer away from the Club, there were allegations that Craig Whyte was somehow still involved with the Club, and Charles Green resigned after an internal investigation into racist remarks that he had allegedly made.

We maintained our form in the league though. In January and February, we won six and drew three games. After that, our form began to dip and it looked as if we would stumble over the finishing line rather than charge over it.

In March, we beat East Stirling and Elgin, lost at home to Annan Athletic and drew 0-0 with both Stirling Albion and Montrose. The latter result was enough to clinch the title as second placed Queen's Park lost their game that day. We beat them 4-1 at Hampden the following week to emphasise it. We were now promoted to Division Two. The first part of our return to the top was complete.

Teams in the lower division had all benefited substantially from Rangers presence in their league. Instead of their home crowds being in the hundreds, they sold out when Rangers came to town. There was a knock-on effect in the local area as well as lots of extra fans have to be fed and watered, and local pubs all did a roaring trade twice that season. The only moan I heard was from the Treasurer of Albion Rovers who had the misfortune of being relegated from the third level to the fourth as Rangers moved up the other way, so they missed out on two bumper pay-days. Fortunately for them, coincidentally, Rangers would be drawn against them in two of the following season's cup competitions so they were able to enjoy the benefits after all.

At the beginning of May, a Rangers Legends team beat Manchester United Legends 4-1 at Ibrox with the proceeds going to charity. After a season of youths and older players who were not of the standard we were used to in the past, it was great to see the famous stars of yesterday take to the Ibrox turf again.

As the summer progressed, Ally McCoist set about lining up some SPL standard players to boost his team – even though they couldn't formally sign until the 1st of September. Goalkeeper Cammy Bell was pre-signed from Kilmarnock, Nicky Law came from Motherwell, former Dundee United captain Jon Daly was next, followed by Nicky Clark, the son of our former striker Sandy Clark, from Queen of the South. At the beginning of June, we pre-signed Honduran midfielder Arnold Peralta, followed by the return of our former left back, Steven Smith, while Richard Foster, who had played in the SPL for us on loan, was acquired from Aberdeen. Bilel Mohsni arrived from Southend to complete the jigsaw. This did seem like taking a sledgehammer to crack a nut – signing SPL standard players to win Scottish League One, the old level three.

At the end of June, the first team reported for pre-season training, and on the same day, the Club opened a new store at Glasgow Airport, a week after opening one in Belfast. It looked as if we were starting to make the right kind of commercial progress – especially with the shop at the airport since huge numbers were expected to pass through for the Commonwealth Games being held in Glasgow in summer 2014.

On 29th June, our central defenders, Carlos Bocanegra and Dorin Goian were allowed to leave the Club as their contracts were mutually terminated, and, at the beginning of July, former player Gordon Durie was appointed as manager of the Under 20s team, and the Club announced that they had installed free wi-fi at Ibrox.

In season 2013-14, the team achieved something they hadn't done since 1899. They went through the entire league season without losing a single league game. Back then, the season was only eighteen games long, and it was against the sides in the top division. This time, it was against a lower standard of opposition, but it was over thirty-six games, and was still a remarkable achievement even if the football played at times was not the most exciting to watch.

July saw the deaths of two men from Rangers' history. Former manager, Davie White died at the age of eighty, and despite not achieving success at Rangers, he made his mark by being the manager of the Dundee side that beat Celtic to win the League Cup. Jack Gillespie, the motor dealer from Lenzie had been on the Rangers Board for nearly two decades back in the 70s and 80s, and he passed away aged 87.

The competitive season started with cup games once again. At the end of July, we beat Albion Rovers away 4-0 in the League Challenge Cup, but the following midweek, Forfar Athletic, inspired by our former heroic defender Marvin Andrews, (who had still never had that cruciate knee ligament operation) eliminated us from the League Cup in the first round, winning 2-1 in poor conditions at Station Park.

There was further sad news that week as we heard that our former player, Colin McAdam – "Beastie"- had died at the age of 61. It was also announced that Walter Smith, who had been a Non-Executive Director, had resigned from the Club.

We started our league campaign with a 4-1 win over Brechin City at Ibrox, and then won 3-0 at Stranraer and 6-0 at Airdrie. We beat East Fife 5-0 at Ibrox, and these were without our full squad to select from. Once September started, everyone was properly registered and we beat Arbroath 5-1. We were beginning to entertain thoughts of this super-squad winning every game easily, and winning this league in the fastest ever time. There was a slight blip the following week when we could only beat Forfar Athletic 1-0 but we then thrashed Stenhousemuir 8-0 to bring September to an end.

We had also progressed through the League Challenge Cup by beating Berwick Rangers and Queen of the South to reach the semi-final but, off the field, things were not running so smoothly. Midfielder Ian Black was served with an immediate three game ban, a suspended ban of seven games, and a fine of £7,500 after he admitted to breaching SFA rules on football gambling. He had placed bets, which did not actually affect Rangers matches, yet we would be hit with his suspension.

Worse still, with a much more serious effect on the Club, was the appointment of Greenock businessman Sandy Easdale to the Board. We would have to become accustomed to all manner of characters joining and leaving our Board as the Club desperately sought to bring in substantial revenue, and supporters had to become acquainted with business terminology such as Nominated Adviser (NOMAD), Broker and Consultant, as well as trying to keep up with who was an Executive or Non-Executive Director.

Improvements to the fabric were made as we opened the new Ibrox Bar, which could be used by fans after games, and installed a new artificial pitch at Murray Park to replicate the playing surfaces at several of our opponents' grounds and which seemed to cause us some degree of difficulty whenever we played on them.

At the beginning of October, our annual accounts were published, Ally McCoist won the League One Manager of the Month award, and – rather strangely for a team at our level – we decided to request the postponement of a match against Dunfermline Athletic since we had players selected for international duty - something more akin to a team in the SPL. It wasn't just due to Scottish players either since we had Northern Irish and Honduran internationalists in our squad who'd been called up.

In mid-October, we heard some more bad news. Our former goalkeeper, Norrie Martin, had died at the age of 74, and our former captain, Fernando Ricksen revealed in an interview on Dutch television that he had been diagnosed with the terminal condition, Motor Neurone Disease, a particularly devastating condition that our Boys' Brigade

Company had raised money for back in the 90s. I had tried to explain to the Boys all about the condition, it's symptoms and progress, only for one of the Boys to realise that this was what was wrong with his own father. His parents had decided to keep this from their children, and I had unwittingly gone and told him what was going to happen. The mother came and spoke to me the next week and I felt really awful.

At the end of the month, we scraped past Stenhousemuir 1-0 to reach the final of the League Challenge Cup for the first time in our history. Of course, we were only taking part in it for the second time ever, since it is only a competition for teams outwith the SPL. We would face Raith Rovers in the final, and we waited to hear where it would take place since Hampden would be out of commission due to work going on there for the Commonwealth Games. Surely, the League would let it be played at Ibrox since we would obviously make up the vast bulk of the crowd. They decided to hold it at Easter Road instead, so we would play our first ever domestic cup final outside Glasgow in April.

The Boardroom shenanigans continued with one Non-Executive Director resigning, the Chief Executive Officer leaving his position, and the Annual General Meeting being postponed after a group of shareholders won a court decision demanding changes in the Board.

Around this time, it was announced that Ibrox would host both the Scottish Cup semi-finals in April as Hampden was going to be unavailable.

In November, we appointed David Somers as Chairman, Graham Wallace as Chief Executive Officer, and Norman Crighton as a Non-executive Director. Yet more changes to our unsettled Board.

On the field, in the league, we kept on winning and, at the start of December, we broke the Club's post-war record for consecutive wins in competitive games when we thumped Forfar Athletic 6-1 at Ibrox. We were beginning to wonder if we could actually go through the entire season with a 100% record, and some fans were even starting to look at the odds being offered by bookmakers for that.

Very high winds and flooding caused our game at Stenhousemuir in the middle of December to be postponed. Not only that, but a burger van was blown against the Ochilview stand causing some structural damage.

The Annual General Meeting took place in December and the current board was re-elected, despite several shareholders' attempt to remove them. They did not secure sufficient votes to succeed with their attempt to remove the Directors who relied on institutional votes to remain in place.

After wins of 6-1 against Forfar Athletic and 3-0 against Ayr United, the long 100% run came to an end on Boxing Day when Stranraer drew, scoring their equaliser in injury time, but we responded with a 4-0 win against Dunfermline to finish the year. Our wins continued throughout January but they were less convincing than they had previously been.

In January, came the tragic news that our former player, Ian Redford, who had scored that great League Cup winner in 1981, and who had only recently published his autobiography, had been found dead in woods near his home. He had taken his own life at the age of just fifty-three.

During the following week, manager Ally McCoist accepted a 50% pay reduction as a cost-cutting measure, and it was put to the first team squad that they all take a cut of 15% until the end of the season as a way to prevent any of them having to be sold, but they unanimously rejected the proposal.

The comings and goings continued with Philip Nash being employed as a consultant, while Financial Director, Brian Stockbridge resigned from the Club. Meanwhile, the Board had managed to arrange short term credit facilities for up to £1.5 million.

With a place in the League Challenge Cup Final secured, and the league being only a matter of time, we turned our attention to the Scottish Cup, and progressed past Airdrie, Falkirk and Dunfermline to reach the quarter-final. We beat Albion Rovers after a replay, having drawn the first match at Ibrox, to reach the semi-finals. The last four in the competition were Aberdeen, Dundee United, St Johnstone and Rangers – Celtic having already been knocked out - and with the matches due to be played at Ibrox, we began to think that we could overcome the cup hoodoo and reach the final. We were drawn against Dundee United who had knocked us out the previous year, but we had significantly strengthened our squad this season so we should have been able to match them better.

Still unbeaten at the end of February, having won all but one game that year – a 3-3 draw at home to Stenhousemuir – we clinched the league on 12th March by beating Airdrie 3-0 at Ibrox thanks to a Lee McCulloch hat-trick. Now we could turn our attention to the cups as well as remaining undefeated in the league.

At the Club's Hall of Fame evening, a special award was made to Sandy Jardine to recognise his service to the Club as a great player and for his unstinting presence as a spokesman for the Club during the past two extremely difficult years. He wasn't able to be there to accept it, so Ally McCoist received it on his behalf.

At the beginning of April, we headed through to Easter Road for the Challenge Cup Final, full of expectation. The stadium was packed with Rangers fans waiting to see the cup being won, but we were all to be badly disappointed as the team chose that afternoon to produce their worst performance of the season. With hardly a shot at goal, we struggled to get into the game, and it finished 0-0. Our dreadful display continued during extra time and when it looked as if penalties were going to be needed to settle the contest, Raith Rovers scored a goal in the last minute to win the cup. We trudged out of the stadium unable to believe what we had just witnessed. What a thoroughly abject performance!

McCoist would have to lift the team for the following weekend for the Scottish Cup semi-final. The ground was split 50/50 with United getting the Broomloan Road and Govan Stands while we occupied the Copland Road and Main Stands. My ticket was for the back of the West Enclosure. We did put up a better show, and Arnold Peralta gave one of his best performances, but silly mistakes gave away goals at crucial times. We lost 3-1 and were out of another cup. To make matters worse, St Johnstone had progressed from the other semi-final and went on to win the cup. Surely, we could have beaten them in the final …

We were getting too used to hearing bad news but the announcement of the death of Club legend Sandy Jardine on 24th April, from throat and liver cancer, aged just sixty-five, was a real hammer blow. As a player, he was one of the best right backs ever to don the blue shirts of Rangers and Scotland. He had enjoyed a very long, honour-laden career at Ibrox before moving to Hearts where he helped them come within a whisker of a league and cup double. His Scotland performances on the way to, and in, the 1974 World Cup were immense, and I can remember him saying in an interview after the team returned unbeaten, but knocked out on goal difference, that he had enjoyed the experience so much that he would have taken part for nothing! He was a true gentleman and the best tribute that I can give him is to call him an embodiment of what it means to be a true Ranger.

At the start of May, we completed our league programme with a draw against Dunfermline to be the first Rangers team in 115 years to be unbeaten in an entire league season. At least there was something to celebrate that season.

During the summer, it was announced that Walter Smith had been appointed as Non-executive Chairman of the PLC Board, but there was bad news to follow. In July, Jame Easdale, the brother of Sandy was appointed onto the Board as a Non-Exectve Director., and Craig Mather was appointed as Chief Executive Officer.

Fed up with all the Boardroom goings on and their ability to get into contracts that did nothing for the Club, as well as the fact that they seemed completely unable to generate substantial funds and had to keep borrowing money just to keep going, the fans' organisations had had enough. When it came time for season ticket renewals, fans were encouraged to say "Not A Penny More". Proposals were put forward that suggested a way of fans being able to renew their season ticket but with their payments going to a controlled fund, and being drip fed to the Club to pay on a game by game basis. That way, fans could retain their seats but not provide substantial funds to the Board as we were worried what they might do with the money.

By renewal deadline, it was announced that only 7,500 fans had renewed, instead of the usual 30,000. Fans groups gave interviews and released statements demanding Boardroom changes with proper Rangers fans on the Board and people who could bring money to the Club. The Directors failed to budge, and the summer wore on.

I decided not to renew my tickets until I saw what was going to happen. Victoria was now coming to fewer and fewer games as her schoolwork was taking over at weekends, and she was losing interest in not seeing big games against teams and players that she knew. I was finding that I was going on my own more often, and I often arranged with my seat neighbour that he could bring one of his children to sit beside him if my second ticket was available. There was also the issue of Victoria's age as she had turned sixteen. That meant she was now an adult – even though she is still at school and, instead of her ticket costing less than a hundred pounds, it was now going to cost more than three times that.

My Dad had got his name put onto the back of his seat and I felt, although he was no longer with us, that it was still "his seat" but I would now have to decide what to do with it. Would I move along one seat or would I let it be sold to a complete stranger? Either way, it appeared that nobody was actually buying season tickets so it was 'safe' for the moment.

In June, it was annouced that Tommy Craig who had been the Club's Physiotherapist for years, including in Barcelona in 1972, and who had served the Club with great distinction, had passed away. In the old days when injuries were treated on the pitch by an old man with just a 'magic sponge', he seemed to me to be the first 'proper' physiotherapist who knew what he was doing when he ran on to treat someone.

In July it was also announced that HM Revenue & Customs had lost its appeal over Rangers use of EBTs and so there was no Big Tax Case to be answered. The threat of that punishment had put off potential buyers and had led to the Club being liquidated when it turned out that there was nothing wrong or illegal about what we had done. This was small comfort after all that had happened over the past three years but it proved that we had been right all along.

During the summer, Glasgow was invaded. The 2014 Commonwealth Games were taking place but, for some reason, the opening ceremony would be at Parkhead instead of the National Stadium at Hampden. No actual events were taking place at Celtic's ground but, bearing in mind that most of Glasgow's City Councillors are regular attenders at Parkhead, the opening ceremony would take place there – this in a stadium that doesn't fly a Union flag, that has nothing at all to do with the Queen, Britain or the Commonwealth – ensuring that they would benefit financially from the ceremony. The best part of the evening was watching the Red Arrows display team flying overhead and pouring red, white and blue smoke over Parkhead!

Ibrox got the Rugby Sevens tournament and the stadium was packed for the two days of the event. It was a great success – even if the pitch did get rather churned up – and Hilary was on duty as a volunteer. She was also at Hampden for the athletics and she had to be there at six o'clock in the morning those days. It was all very well her getting free travel vouchers – but there was actually nothing running that early enough to get her there, so I had to get up early and drive her over before going to work!

EIGHTEEN
A New Dawn At Last

As the start of the new season approached, I was in a dilemma. Should I renew my season ticket or should I join the boycott? The first game would be at home to Hearts. They had dropped down to the Championship as they had been docked points for financial irregularities. Hibernian, too, had been relegated, having lost out in the play-off against Hamilton Accies, so it began to look as if the Championship would be really competitive. I hesitate to describe it as "the place to be" since, of course, we would all rather be in the SPL, but it looked like the Championship was going to be a very tough division where all the interest would be. It was also announced that, before the opening league game, the Govan Stand was to be renamed The Sandy Jardine Stand in honour of the great man's memory. It was therefore appropriate that Hearts would be our opponents on that day.

Eventually, and with just a few days left, I decided to relent and I went over to renew my season ticket – only to find that someone else had already bought my seat, as well as the one that had been my Dad's for over twenty-five years. As I've said, he even had his name on the back of his seat – he had paid extra through the "Ready For the Future" scheme years ago – but I would no longer be able to sit there. Looking at the on-screen map at the Ticket Office of bought seats, it was obvious that a lot more than 7,500 had renewed or bought new ones … or they had all bought them for the front of The Sandy Jardine Stand. After 27 years of sitting in "my seat", I had to move. I got a new ticket for the next section along and one row forward. The guys beside me are all really friendly, and I soon settled in to my new location.

During the summer, Andrew Little, Chris Hegarty, Ross Perry and Emilson Cribari all left the Club, but we re-signed Kenny Miller for his third spell at the Club, and Kris Boyd for his second. We also brought in Darren McGregor from St Mirren and free agents Marius Zaliukas and goalkeeper Lee Robinson, who had also had a previous spell in the youths or reserves.

We got past Hibernian 2-1 in the first round of the Petrofac Training Cup, as the Challenge Cup was now known, but it was a less than convincing victory. Hearts beat us very easily on that opening day and then went on a determined crusade to get back up to the SPL as quickly as possible, leaving the rest of us trailing in their wake.

It appeared as if that opening day defeat had just been a blip as we went on to beat Falkirk 2-0 and then Clyde 8-1 in the Petrofac Training

Cup. We beat Dumbarton 4-1 before knocking Queen's Park out of the League Cup. We then defeated Queen of the South 4-2 at Ibrox. Before Rangers, Hearts and Hibernian had found themselves in the Championship, Falkirk and Queen of the South were the strongest teams in that division, and we had just beaten them both.

As we moved into September, we beat Raith Rovers 4-0 away before we got the chance to test ourselves against SPL opposition in the League Cup. In a tight game at Ibrox, we eliminated Inverness Caledonian 1-0. We drew away at Alloa before knocking Falkirk out of the League Cup and, just as things looked to be heading in right direction, Hibernian came to Ibrox and beat us 3-1.

Off the field, the current Board continued to be unable to generate sufficient funds to run the Club. Anyone turning up at Ibrox could see that the old ground was in need of more than a simple coat of paint, and it emerged that substantial emergency funding was going to be required. A deal was struck with Newcastle United and Sports Direct owner Mike Ashley – a man with very deep pockets – and Sports Direct took control of the Club's megastore and merchandising. There was even a worry that Ibrox could have to be renamed The Sports Direct Stadium. It became obvious that the Board was out of its depth and fans began to step up the boycott to try to oust them. Our opening game against Hearts had attracted 43,683 but we were now averaging under 30,000. Our cup games at Ibrox that were not included on the season tickets got very poor crowds indeed, and only 11,422 turned up for our Scottish Cup tie with Raith Rovers. Several wealthy fans began to make moves to try to take over the Club although there was a very understandable reluctance to put money into the Easdales' pockets to buy them out.

In October, we beat Livingston away and then Raith Rovers 6-1 at home before our next Petrofac Cup win against East Fife. Dumbarton were beaten 3-0 before another SPL encounter in the League Cup. Once again, the players managed to put on a professional performance as St Johnstone were knocked out in the quarter-final. Our Scottish Cup campaign started early once again, and we beat Dumbarton at the start of November.

Stories kept emerging that there wasn't enough money to pay the players' wages, and it was then revealed that the Sports Direct deal was only giving the Club 50p out of every £10 spent on our merchandise. Mike Ashley acquired more shares taking his holding up to just below 10% and he loaned the Club more money in exchange for getting two of his men, Derek Llambias and Barry Leach onto the Rangers Board. Despite owning less than 10% of the Club's shares, he had got himself in complete control. In addition, David Somers became Executive

Chairman on a temporary basis. Shortly afterwards, Llambias was appointed as a non-executive Director.

We recorded 3-0 and 4-0 wins against Cowdenbeath and Falkirk in the Championship before another draw with Alloa Athletic and a defeat at Tynecastle. There was another SPL club up next as we beat Kilmarnock 3-0 in the next round of the Scottish Cup. Three SPL sides had been beaten – but we couldn't beat Alloa, and Hearts were beginning to open up a sizeable gap in the Championship. The manager's job was proving to be too much for Ally McCoist and some of the games were becoming a tedious chore to go and watch.

December would turn out to be a critical month. We started with the Petrofac Cup semi-final away at Alloa which was to be shown live on BBC Alba television. We were two up, and looking as if we'd finally found a way to beat them at last, when three crazy defensive mistakes let them score three almost identical goals to knock us out. It was a terrible result, but we managed to beat Cowdenbeath 1-0 at Ibrox before going to Palmerston on the 12th of December for a Friday night game against Queen of the South. We were out for dinner that evening, since it was Norma's birthday, but both she and Hilary were getting Tweets on their phones saying that Ally McCoist had resigned. When we finished our meal and went out to the car, I put the radio on to listen to the match commentary. We were losing 1-0 but Ally McCoist was in the Technical Area so I assumed that the messages were incorrect. I got home in time to watch the last thirty minutes or so, and the true story emerged. Ally had resigned but had only handed in his notice and would see out the remainder of his contract – 12 months. We ended up losing 2-0 after yet another dismal performance.

In the run up to the Annual General Meeting, Norman Crighton left his role as non-executive director, but Derek Llambias was appointed as Chief Executive Officer and David Somers was re-appointed as non-executive Chairman.

On the Saturday before Christmas, we beat Livingston 2-0 at Ibrox but the quality of the football was becoming more and more tedious by the week. Crowds were dwindling and the Board was now the most unpopular in Rangers long history. On 21st December, on the eve of the A.G.M., Ally McCoist left the Club and a statement issued by the Club said that he would serve out the rest of his contract on "gardening leave".

His assistant, Kenny McDowall took over as caretaker manger, with Gordon Durie promoted as his assistant and club captain, Lee McCulloch, became first team player/coach. Ian Durrant was moved to take up the position as Reserve and Under 20s manager. In McDowall's first match in charge, the team gave another dreadful, clueless performance, losing 4-0 at Easter Road.

Once again, we were forced to cash in on a playing asset and young Lewis McLeod, our best midfield prospect, who had recently been called into the Scotland squad, was sold to Brentford FC as soon as the transfer window opened. Yet again, a player was sold down to the cash-rich English league and yet again, we got nothing like Lewis's true value. However, on the same day, we recalled several of our younger players who had been out on loan to other clubs.

We began 2015 with a 3-1 win at home to Dumbarton and then the team managed to do something they had failed to do all season – they beat Alloa Athletic, 1-0 away.

On 5th January, Mike Ashley's other "implant", Barry Leach was appointed as Finance Director. Ashley was clearly strengthening his stranglehold on the Club and it emerged that he already actually held the re-naming rights to Ibrox Stadium. We could find our historic home renamed as the Sports Direct Stadium or something awful like that. The fans made a legal move to prevent him from being allowed to have Ibrox as security on any further loans he was to make.

On Friday 16th January, we were to play Hearts at Ibrox in a BT Sport televised game and, as usual, I was preparing to make my way over to the game. Around five pm, it started to snow and it got heavier and heavier. Within a very short time, the gardens and the roads were getting very white as it was lying without clearing. The plan was that I would go to the game, and the family would go out for their dinner, but as it got even heavier, Norma decided that they weren't going anywhere – which led to a problem. There wasn't actually anything in the house for their dinner – so Norma and Hilary decided to walk up the road to the local Indian buffet restaurant. Victoria and I would eke out what I had planned to have for my dinner and split it in two. Norma then phoned from the restaurant to say that the main road was jammed with unmoving cars, and to tell me that, if I thought I was going to Ibrox, I was daft. The game obviously wouldn't be on.

We switched on the television and Reporting Scotland announced that there was to be a pitch inspection at 7 pm. That wouldn't give me enough time to get there with the weather being as bad as it was, so I made a very difficult decision. I would stay at home and watch the game, if it went ahead, on BT Sport. In all my forty five years of going to games, I had never not gone because of the weather. I had never sat at home watching Rangers play a home game that I should have been at. I'd been at games in blizzards, thick fog and torrential rain – but I'd always been there. My Dad and I once got to the stadium in the pouring rain for a match against Aberdeen, got a couple of coffees, and took our seats to watch the players going through their warming-up routine, only for the game to be abandoned before kick-off. Another time, we had driven through torrential rain to a Reserve game, and there had been a deep puddle at the dip in the Clyde Tunnel. When we were in our seats, we heard on the radio that the Tunnel had actually been closed due to the flooding.

I'd been at a League Cup semi-final at Hampden, a few years ago, when there was heavy snow and I could hardly find anywhere to park the car. After that game, I'd struggled to get home as my car was refusing to drive up the hill on the main road to our house – but I'd always got to the game.

This was now a first – to sit at home and watch a game. When I saw the picture showing the state of the pitch, I seriously wondered how it could go ahead, and how would fans – especially those coming from Edinburgh – actually get to the game. Of course, it was abandoned so I had made the right decision after all. That night, we spoke to a family up the road who had taken over three hours to drive the few miles home from the Erskine Bridge, and another neighbour had taken two hours to drive home half a mile, due to all the abandoned vehicles on the road.

But – didn't Ibrox have undersoil heating? Shouldn't it have cleared the pitch to let the game go ahead? Did the Board leave it switched off to save the cost of putting it on? Were they secretly pleased not to see the game go ahead to prevent another defeat from Hearts? Rumours were flying about, and there were no definite answers.

On the following Monday, Kenny McDowall handed in his resignation as caretaker manager, for personal reasons – but like McCoist, he would have to serve his twelve months' notice before being allowed to leave. Two days later, Honduran internationalist, Arnold Peralta's contract was ended by mutual consent.

The next Saturday afternoon, we were due to play away at Cowdenbeath, but many parts of Scotland were still in winter's grip. Following a morning pitch inspection, the game was postponed because the pitch was frozen. For the second successive week, the players had no game which was hardly ideal preparation for what was coming next – the League Cup semi-final against Celtic at Hampden.

But, before that, on Sunday 25th January, we got a distraction from the usual depressing league performances. Heading to Ibrox, there were a lot more cars on the road and it almost began to feel like "the old days". 41,349 turned up to see a Rangers Select take on Fernando's All Stars in a specially arranged benefit match for our former captain, Fernando Ricksen, who is trying to battle against the ravages of Motor Neurone

Disease. Former stars from not so long ago, such as Stefan Klos, Arthur Numan, Jorg Albertz, Ronald De Boer, Gordon Durie, Peter Lovenkrands, Marco Negri, Rino Gattuso, Andy Goram, Michael Mols, Nacho Novo, Barry Ferguson, Thomas Buffel and Bert Konterman, turned out for their Dutch friend, and the years rolled back as they showed that they can still play a bit. They were up against the likes of Teddy Sheringham, Darren Anderton, Ronald Wattereus, Mark Falco, Dave Beasant, James Beattie and Paul Bosvelt. The match finished 7-4 for the All Stars as they showed simply that their finishing skills are a lot better than those of the Rangers Select. Both teams had the same number of chances but the All Stars scored theirs. Marco Negri, who once couldn't stop scoring, found that he now couldn't start scoring as he missed a lot of these chances. Rangers' goals came from Durie, Lovenkrands, Buffel and Novo. 48 year old Teddy Sheringham impressed everyone as he defied his age and scored a great chip, and another goal as well as assisting with two others. Of course, we all wished that we didn't need to attend such a match in the first place!

Now, our attention could turn to the League Cup semi-final. The game was a sell-out as both sides looked forward to locking horns with each other once again. Celtic, being the SPL leaders, were firm favourites and were expecting to run up a cricket score. The one thing that you can say about these games is that they are completely unpredictable, and the form-book always goes out the window. Rangers this season had kept their best performances for games against SPL teams, and Celtic haven't always had the best of records against sides from lower divisions that they were expected to beat easily. Remember Morton and Clyde, as well as Ross County, Inverness Caledonian, Raith Rovers, Falkirk or, even, Partick Thistle?

I tried to park in my usual place near Crosshill Station. It was packed but I found a space on the next road. I walked down to Cathcart Road and headed towards Hampden. On the other side of the road, at the entrance to Cathkin Park, I saw a Police van and an ambulance. I learned later that a Rangers fan had been attacked there, in front of his son. Clearly, the situation that I found myself in thirteen years earlier had happened again – but worse. The Police's plans for keeping Celtic fans to their proper areas were, once again, being ignored. A few yards further along Cathcart Road, Celtic fans attacked a Rangers supporters' bus and had thrown a bottle in the face of a young boy. These instances are utterly deplorable of course, and any right thinking person should be appalled by them. We are only members of the public going to see a football match.

Inside the stadium, the fans were in full voice of course. After going to so many games with smaller crowds, it was good to be at a "big" match once again. Both sides taunted each other with songs and banners old and new. The game though was a disappointment. Not only was the playing surface hopeless – so was our defending. Our two central defenders allowed one of the smallest players on the pitch to jump up between them and score an easy header, and then a poor clearance went straight to a Celtic player who scored their second. We did rally a bit in the second half, but never put them under any pressure. They didn't get the huge victory they thought they were going to get, and our cup hoodoo had hit us once again.

Prior to Christmas, it was rumoured that Mike Ashley was going to loan us three Newcastle players to let them get games – a defender, a midfielder and a striker. It turned out on Monday 2nd February that he was to send five fringe players up to Glasgow until the end of the season.

Three of them were injured (it was later discovered that the five hadn't even had medicals before they moved up!) but two of them, Haris Vuckic and Remie Street started the Scottish Cup game against Raith Rovers at Ibrox the next weekend. Street only lasted until just before half time but Vuckic scored a good goal. It wasn't enough to prevent a 2-1 defeat and the end of our cup action for yet another season.

Off the park, positive things were, at last, beginning to happen. Former Director Dave King, the Glasgow born, South African based businessman, had acquired a chunk of shares from some of the institutional investors who were obviously fed up with the way things were being run at Ibrox. Other wealthy supporters did the same, and fan groups clubbed together to buy as many shares as they could. King called for an Extraordinary General Meeting to be held with a vote to be taken to remove the Board and install himself, former Director Paul Murray and John Gilligan as Directors. By Stock Exchange rules, such a meeting had to be held within 30 days and the date was set for the 4th of March.

Both sides declared that they were confident of winning, and fans were eagerly trying to predict who would vote for who. The Board then announced that the meeting would take place at a London hotel – a preposterous and expensive decision which would obviously prevent a great many shareholders from being able to attend. When it became apparent that fans were going to go no matter where it was, the hotel realised that their venue was far too small and they cancelled the booking. A larger hotel was then arranged but they cancelled as well. Finally, a degree of common sense prevailed and the meeting would take place at Ibrox on the new date of Friday 6th March.

The Board, the fans, the shareholders and the media went into overdrive. King announced that he was sure that he had more than the necessary 50% and he called on the Board to go, to save the cost of holding the meeting, but they refused to budge. Fans groups managed to buy more and more shares as they all hoped that the end appeared to be in sight.

On the pitch, in February, we lost 2-0 at home to Hibernian, but beat Raith Rovers 2-1 and drew 1-1 with Falkirk away.

On the 25th of February, James Easdale resigned as a director, blaming pressure from the supporters whose backing he realised he didn't have. Could he not have realised that months before? On the 2nd of March, David Somers resigned as Chairman. Two down and two to go! King again called on Sandy Easdale and Barry Leach to go, too.

On the morning of Friday 6th March at 11 am, the E.G.M. began. King didn't get 50% - he got 85% of the votes. He became Non-Executive Chairman, Paul Murray became Interim Chairman and John Gilligan became a Non-Exective Director with immediate effect. Derek Llambias and Barry Leach were voted off the board. Later that day, bus tycoon Douglas Park was also appointed as a Non-Executive Director. Sandy Easdale then resigned with immediate effect. After three years of appalling leadership, inability to raise money without loans, squandering of that money, improper running and living from hand to mouth, Rangers was in the hands of genuine Rangers men.

Under SFA regulations, King still had to be established as "a fit and proper person" before he could formally be appointed as Chairman – a procedure which, had it been as carefully examined in the recent past, could have prevented most of what happened in the past four years.

All the new Board's immediate statements said the right things. They would need to examine everything – every contract, all the books, all the papers. It would take time to re-build but re-build they would. They would raise investment and get a manager who had experience of building a team from scratch. They would get rid of players who weren't up to the job and replace them with players who could get us back into the SPL, challenging for the title and playing in Europe as soon as possible.

As soon as the new Board was in place, there was a rush to start getting much-needed revenue back into the Club, and the most obvious way to do that was to buy match tickets. After months of low crowds, an optimistic feeling took over, and fans bought individual match tickets as well as season tickets to cover the remainder of the season. The first match after the EGM was away at Cowdenbeath and, in deplorable weather conditions, the team could only manage a 0-0 draw – but there were to be three consecutive home fixtures so that would see an upturn in attendance and money starting to flow back into the Club.

On Tuesday 10th March, despite the increasing expectations, we could only draw 1-1 with Queen of the South in a particularly poor encounter. One on-line comment hit the nail firmly on the head by saying that Dave King would add 20,000 to the crowd – but Kenny McDowall would take 10,000 off it again. The Board acted, and on 12th March, ex-player Stuart McCall was appointed as manger on a short term contract until the end of the season. Another ex-player, Kenny Black was appointed as his assistant. On the same day, Kenny McDowall left the Club with the Board's gratitude for stepping in.

McCall described the lack of confidence that was surrounding the team as if they were all playing with lead boots on. He only had two days to work with the players before his first match in charge, and with the usual, now predictable, lack of invention, creation and everything else needed to win games, we could only draw 1-1 with Livingston. The following Tuesday, we looked a bit better but could still only manage a 2-2 draw against Alloa Athletic who once again proved to be a thorn in our sides.

Saturday 21st March was the forty-fifth anniversary of my first ever visit to Ibrox, and once again, we were found ourselves at the start of a new era. On Sunday 22nd, we were away to Hibernian, and having had more time to work with the players, McCall changed the formation of the team, and there was a return to form. We won 2-0 against one of the teams who had caused us problems all season, and the result meant that Hearts were mathematically un-catchable and they secured automatic promotion to the SPL. Who would join them via the play-offs still remained to be seen, but going by all the positive comments on-line on that Sunday night, Stuart McCall seemed to be the manager who could take us there. What a difference it was to go into work on the Monday morning with a good win behind us.

The following week, we were to play Cowdenbeath at Ibrox. I said to my neighbour that we should surely see a home win after all the good result at Easter Road. We had loads of possesion but were up against a yellow wall of defenders. 0-0 at half-time, and it wasn't looking too promising. Then, Nicky Clark got a goal to put us ahead and we looked for a second just to be sure. Bilel Mohsni made a mess of a pass to Lee Wallace, and it was intercepted by Cowdenbeath's Kudus Oyenuga who ran in to score. Instead of the heads going down as we had seen all season, we kept pushing forward. Darren McGregor capped off his Man-of-the-Match performance with a hard-hit, low shot that flew into the net and, in the last couple of minutes, Haris Vukic scored twice. Second placed Hibernian lost, so we drew level with them, with a game in hand.

In March, the financial results for the half year to 31st December 2014 were announced. It was no surprise when interim chairman, Paul Murray, revealed that the Club had incurred a disappointing loss of £2.9 million considering the number of empty seats at every home game before the ousting of the old Board. In addition, there have been no European games since 2011. Since the EGM, there has been a marked increase in the crowds, and the demand for tickets at home games, so one would expect a significant improvement in the second half of the financial year.

In his statement, Murray also addressed various other concerns. The main priority is obviously a return to the top league, and although this seen as a difficult task, Murray believed that Stuart McCall could do it. The task is to focus on the next seven years, and the target is to be back at the top by 2022. That is, of course, a significant year as it will be the 150th anniversary of the Club being founded, and the 50th anniversary of our European success in Barcelona. There is a lot of work to be done on the whole infrastructure of the Club from top to bottom, and the new Board is only too well aware of that. Finance has to be put in place, and players need to be signed to ensure that Rangers can be back competing and winning, as well as playing in Europe again.

Since Stuart McCall had taken over as manager, the team had remained unbeaten, and they secured good wins against Cowdenbeath and Hibernian. The feel-good factor was returning at last after years of gloom and depression. At last, we have a Board who are able to provide financing themselves, as well as being able to source other forms of investment. Murray's tone was positive, but he had to make mention of the previous board – some of whose business decisions he described as "simply staggering". Anyone who is a Director of Rangers holds an esteemed position and has a great responsibility to maintain. Murray pulled no punches as he described how the new Directors have already started to repair the damage caused by recent years of neglect and disrespect for the Club, its history and its people. He added, "No-one felt secure and the life was being sucked out of Ibrox and Murray Park."

How good it felt to hear someone who is now in a position of power come out and say things like that. We have waited a long time to hear common sense emanating from the boardroom. Those were early days, but the feeling of optimism was sweeping through the Club both on and off the park.

In Thursday 2nd April, the Club unveiled a bronze bust of Sandy Jardine which was to be put on display on the marble staircase just below the Hall of Fame board that Sandy had helped to create. His former playing colleagues, Willie Johnston, Alex Miller, Colin Stein, and his old friend Alex MacDonald were at Ibrox to pay tribute to their old friend.

On the following Sunday, the team rose to the occasion and beat Hearts 2-1 despite Captain Lee McCulloch being sent off. It was becoming more than apparent that McCulloch was past his best. He was being played in the centre of defence every game, even when off form, despite not being a true central defender. We were all too aware that he would automatically walk straight back into the team after serving his suspension, and that was basically where a lot of our recent problems had come from. Ally McCoist and then Kenny MacDowall consistently stood by the same players week in and week out – even when their form did not begin to justify their selection.

During the week, we lost 3-0 at Queen of the South, (McCall's first defeat) but bounced back to beat Raith Rovers 4-0 at Ibrox. A draw at Livingston was followed by a 3-1 win at Dumbarton to get us into second place in the division, but two successive 2-2 draws against Falkirk and Hearts meant that we finished in third place – presenting us with a difficult road if we were to get back into the Premiership.

The format for the play-offs was that the third team in the Championship (Rangers) had to play the fourth team (Queen of the South) over two legs and the winner of that would then play the second placed team (Hibernian) over two legs. The winner of that would then play the 11th placed team from the Premiership (Motherwell), again over two legs to decide who would remain or reach the top league. That meant that Rangers could face six tricky games against teams that we could not guarantee beating.

We started with an away win at Queen of the South and then drew at Ibrox so that got us through to play Hibernian. We won 2-0 at Ibrox but lost 1-0 at Easter Road when they scored in injury time.

The games were coming thick and fast (perhaps too thick and fast) as we looked slow and tired in the first leg at Ibrox against Motherwell. They led 3-0 but Darren McGregor threw us a potential life-line when he managed to score to make it 3-1.

On Sunday 31st May, we travelled to Fir Park, but despite a good start, we found ourselves two down before conceding a late penalty. Motherwell scored it and won 6-1 on aggregate. Despite some of the players' best efforts (but not enough of them), we had failed to get back up to the Premiership. The match ended with a punch-up between Bilel Mohsni and two Motherwell players who all got red cards. What a disgraceful way to end a disappointing season

Next season, we will be up against the likes of Hibernian, Falkirk and St Mirren. We'll need a squad of players who are able to compete, and win, at that level. We had had a squad of players who could win the SPL, but they walked out, and we received nothing in the way of transfer fees for them. We need to get back to that level as soon as possible, obviously without falling back into debt.

By the following Tuesday, the media were reporting that the Board had informed eleven out of contract players that they were no longer required. We released Steve Simondsen, Lee Robinson, Lee McCulloch, Bilel Mohsni, Steven Smith, Jon Daly, Ian Black, Richard Foster, Kyle Hutton and Sebastian Faure some of whom had appeared more than others, and David Templeton was told to find a new club.

We have to draw a curtain on what has been a most disappointing season. Three different managers; failure to achieve promotion; a shocking result in the Challenge Cup semi-final, and failure in the Scottish and League Cups – but we can, and should, take encouragement from the development of, and performances by, the latest group of youngsters to break into the first team. Andy Murdoch, Tom Walsh and Ryan Guthrie can all benefit from another season in The Championship, while we should expect to see more from Robbie Crawford, Fraser Aird and some of the others who already have considerable first team experience. We did also manage to achieve good results against Premiership teams – Inverness Caledonian Thistle, St Johnstone and Kilmarnock. With the new Board in place, we can look forward to substantial investment in the team, a scouting network, youth development as well as some repairs to Ibrox itself. What a difference it will be to see Rangers on the back pages of newspapers instead of the front pages.

Once we get our financial affairs back into proper order, we can look forward to being back in a position to start winning trophies again, and playing in European competitions. With our 150th anniversary on the horizon, we should be able to say, "The future's bright. The future's blue!"

EPILOGUE

Looking back over the decades, I've been able to go and see top teams such as Juventus, Ajax, Barcelona, Manchester United, Arsenal, Liverpool, Chelsea, AC Milan, Internazionale, Bayern Munich, Dynamo Kiev, Valencia, Porto, PSV, Feyenoord and many, many others playing at Ibrox and I have to hope that it won't be too long until we can again experience that great sensation of pride when these European giants walk out onto the pitch, especially when the Champions League music is playing. It was always a special thrill to be able to watch the likes of Cruyff, Best, Messi, Kempes or Cantona, as well as Souness, Gascoigne, Laudrup and many other top class players stepping onto the Ibrox turf.

Over 45 years, football has changed beyond all recognition. The stadia, the money, the coverage and even the pressure. Far more women and girls now go to the games, and obviously smoking and drinking are both banned inside the stadium – although some people are proposing that drink should, once again, be allowed. In fact, it is even suggested that it could be a major source of revenue for the clubs to be able to sell it to fans. Surely, that has to be a backward step which could cause a lot of trouble.

Looking back at videos of games from the 1970s, I am amazed that the players could actually play on what was a mud-bath. Games during the winter months seemed to be played on a pitch that was brown instead of green. Nowadays, the surface is like a bowling green by comparison.

Players back then had numbers 1 to 11 on their backs, with number 12 for the single substitute. Now, with a selection of three substitutions allowed, the bench has a goalkeeper and a plethora of available substitutes to cover defence, midfield and strikers. The players now have a squad number, and it is not unusual to see players on the pitch wearing numbers in the 30s, 40s or even 50s.

The kit and boots have also changed almost beyond recognition. New kits are brought out every season, as well as away kits and third kits. They have sponsors names on them – something that was unheard of in the 1970s when even stadium advertising was limited. Hibernian were the first Scottish team to have a sponsor's name on their shirts, and that almost led to a blackout by the television companies who were reluctant to broadcast their matches. Now it seems that there are adverts all over every available surface. Players hardly ever wear black football boots any more since they can choose boots that are blue, orange, yellow, red or white. They don't seem to make them play any better though!

Linesmen are now Assistant Referees, byes are now goal-kicks and shies are called throw-ins. Centre forwards are now strikers, half backs are now the midfield and the centre half has become two central defenders. Dug-outs are now "Technical Areas", while injury time is now "time added on". Every single game is recorded and televised and every goal or incident can be scrutinised from every direction. "Every other Saturday" at 3pm can be any time and any day of the week now. We first had games on a Sunday as something out of the ordinary in the 1980s but we can now have them on any evening of the week. When Friday night games were first suggested years ago, Bill McMurray, then Captain of the 5th Glasgow Boys' Brigade called in to a radio phone-in to express his deep disappointment at that, because Friday is considered to be the traditional BB night, and since both Rangers and the Brigade draw from the same demographic background, he was concerned at falling BB attendances.

The biggest changes are to do with money. At the end of the 1960s, Colin Stein's move to Rangers was the first £100,000 transfer between Scottish clubs, and Trevor Francis's move from Birmingham City to Nottingham Forest was the first £1 million pound deal. These seem almost insignificant now. We are now in an era where transfers can be done for tens of millions of pounds or Euros. Player's salaries are now in the superstar realms when, in the 60s, Rangers first-team stars like John Greig, Sandy Jardine, Jimmy Miller and Ralph Brand used to take the train to Queen Street from Edinburgh, and then stood and waited for a bus to take them to Ibrox for training. That is quite unimaginable now when players earn thousands of pounds per week.

Another huge change has been the number of foreign players who have played for us. In the 1950s, there were Don Kichenbrand and Johnny Hubbard from South Africa, and in the 1960s, we had some Scandinavian players. In the early 1980s, we had Swede Robert Prytz and David Mitchell from Australia but they were the exceptions. By and large, the team were all Scots although there were some from Northern Ireland. When Graeme Souness swept into Ibrox in 1986, we got used to seeing players from England, and in the years since, we have had players from Russia and Eastern Europe, North and South America, Africa, Australia and from all over the European Union. Some of them might never have heard of Rangers before they signed but nearly all of them have agreed that Rangers is a special club that gets into your system. Most of them love coming back to the Club just to visit, to renew old acquaintances or to play in benefit matches.

Until the late 1980s, post-match arguments and discussions only took place in the pub, on the supporters' buses or at work on the Monday morning, but now we have phone-ins, internet chat-rooms and newspaper comments sections to express our various opinions. Newspapers used to have just a couple of pages of football before they started printing multi-page colour sports sections. The vast number of internet sites with chatrooms gives fans the opportunity to discuss or argue about virtually anything. The expression "fans with laptops" was coined to describe the modern supporters.

I sometimes wonder what it would have been like to have been born a few years earlier so that I could have appreciated, and been thrilled by, the great team of the early 60s and could have seen Jim Baxter in his pomp. I might have been able – and allowed - to go to the 1970 League Cup Final; I could have appreciated the games on the road to Barcelona, and could have been at the semi-final against Bayern Munich. I could have been crammed in at Hampden for the 1973 Scottish Cup Final. On the other hand, I would also have been more aware of the Berwick calamity and Celtic's awful run of Championships and, even worse, I might even have been at Ibrox on that dreadful day in January 1971. So perhaps it was better to really get to know Rangers as we laid the foundations of the 1970s team that won two trebles, and to see all the things that I have seen since.

I've gone to many games with my daughters, but I don't quite think they get the same buzz as I do going in the turnstile, up the stairs to our seats, and setting eyes on the Ibrox pitch. I wonder if they can really appreciate just exactly what it means – the sense of history and tradition. The ghosts of old players and managers looking down and watching everything that's going on. Perhaps the girls will look back in the years to come at their first games, and remember those days as fondly as I remember my first and second visits. Perhaps they will understand what it is to have blue blood flowing through their veins, and what it means to Follow Follow the most successful team in the world as I have done for over forty-five years.

BIBLIOGRAPHY

BIG JOCK – THE REAL JOCK WALLACE
David Leggat
Black and White Publishing

COOP – THE LIFE OF DAVIE COOPER – SCOTTISH FOOTBALL HERO
Neil Drysdale
Black and White Publishing

FOLLOW WE WILL: THE FALL AND RISE OF RANGERS
Colin Armstrong, Iain Duff & 10 Others
Luath Press Ltd

GROWING WITH GLORY
Ian Peebles
Peebles Publications (Scotland) Ltd.

RANGERS THE COMPLETE RECORD
Bob Ferrier and Robert McElroy
Breedon Books

THEATRE OF DREAMS – THE CHANGING FACE OF IBROX
Iain Duff
DB Publishing

THE OFFICAL BIOGRAPHY OF RANGERS
Ronnie Esplin & Graham Walker
Hachette Scotland

UNPROVABLE

Gordon Cubie

In his debut novel, Scottish writer, Gordon Cubie, tells the story of Alan Gray a man for whom everything is going wrong.

His wife's left him. He's heavily in debt. Someone he hates is about to become his boss and make his life an absolute misery.

Then Alan comes up with a plan for a murder. A clever plan. The Police can catch him easily. They have fingerprints, DNA and witnesses. They know he did it – but they can't prove it.

The trial approaches. Has Alan Gray managed to commit the perfect crime?

SCOUTING FOR VENGEANCE
Gordon Cubie

Four men are linked by a terrible secret from their past.

In the summer of 2010, three of them die suddenly in seemingly tragic accidents. The fourth man in certain that the deaths were all deliberate and that someone is murdering them one by one.

He knows that he will be the next to be killed. He can't go to the Police without revealing the awful truth and exposing their sinister secret

Scouting For Vengeance is the second novel by Gordon Cubie

Printed in Great Britain
by Amazon